BY NASDIJJ

*The Blood Runs Like a River
Through My Dreams*

The Boy and the Dog Are Sleeping

Geronimo's Bones

Geronimo's Bones

A MEMOIR OF MY
BROTHER AND ME

Nasdijj

BALLANTINE BOOKS

NEW YORK

A Ballantine Book
Published by The Random House Publishing Group
Copyright © 2004 by Nasdijj

www.ballantinebooks.com

Library of Congress Cataloging-in-Publication Data
Nasdijj.
Geronimo's bones: a memoir of my brother and me / Nasdijj.—1st ed.
p.   cm.
ISBN 0-345-45391-3
1. Nasdijj. 2. Tso. 3. Navajo Indians—Biography. 4. Navajo Indians—
Social conditions. 5. Geronimo, 1829–1909. I. Title.
E99.N3N263 2004
979.1004'9726'0092—dc22
[B]   2003055686

Manufactured in the United States of America

First Edition: April 2004

1   3   5   7   9   10   8   6   4   2

For Navajo

May your horizons always be the kind you can run on;
may you always come home. To me.

Contents

‿‿‿‿‿‿

1   AND A TIN CAN OF WORMS   *1*
    Nasdijj introduces Tso, his younger brother by a year.

2   *THIS* IS THE STORY I HAVE TO TELL   *21*
    Nasdijj describes his father.

3   I AM IN BLOOD   *43*
    Nasdijj describes the transient migrant life,
    and picking cherries with the Chippewa.

4   THE FREAK SHOW WAS A SERIOUS BUSINESS TO ME   *50*
    The life of a carnival.

5   TO *WALK* IN BEAUTY WHEN IT CAME TO THE COWBOY
    WHO WAS MY DAD WAS AN ENORMOUS CONTRADICTION   *65*
    The Cowboy could not make his living as a cowboy.

6   IN THE SUMMER OF 1963, MY YOUNGER BROTHER AND I
    STOLE A CORVETTE   *86*
    The brothers go west.

7 THE FIRST CAR I EVER STOLE   *114*
In which Nasdijj explains why borrowing a car is not stealing a car.

8 WE WERE THERE   *121*
The brothers do not attend school but work as pickers in migrant camps.

9 I HAD GROWN SCATTERED LIKE A SCARECROW   *135*
The brothers meet Ronnie Spectacular.

10 THERE WERE NO ROADS ON THE WAY TO SA'S HOGAN   *148*
*Nasdijj introduces his Navajo grandmother, who raises sheep
on the side of an extinct volcano.*

11 TRAVELING WEST IS LIKE FOLLOWING THE SUN   *181*
The three car thieves drive the Corvette to California.

12 IT WAS A PILGRIMAGE   *197*
Visit to Geronimo's grave at Fort Sill, Oklahoma.

13 A DUST STORM BLEW THROUGH TEXAS   *202*
The police in a small Texas town release the car thieves.

14 THE COSMIC MICROWAVE BACKGROUND (CMB) IS A
PERVERSE RADIO EMISSION APPEARING TO HAVE A
TRULY DIFFUSE ORIGIN   *211*
Camping in Chaco, Ronnie Spectacular changes her name to Dancer.

15 WE TOOK DANCER TO THE GRAVEL PITS   *221*
Grandma Sa has died.

16 IN 1963, THE DESERT BLACKTOP TO LOS ANGELES UNFOLDED
LIKE A QUIVERING, SILVER APPARITION   *230*
Three car thieves meet Carmella, Queen of the Desert.

17 IN THE BEGINNING IT WAS NOT AT ALL WHAT I EXPECTED   *235*
The brothers sell pumpkins in Half-Moon Bay.

18 WE RODE STICKS AND BROOMS FOR HORSES   *239*
Nasdijj works three jobs so he can support his brother, who is still in school.

19   I SHOULD HAVE KNOWN   *246*
Nasdijj confronts the image of his abusive father.

20   WE HAD ALWAYS KNOWN OUR FATHER WAS A COYOTE   *253*
The Coyote teaches forgiveness if you can learn the lesson.

21   THAT NIGHT YOU AND DADDY BURIED THAT DEAD BABY
IN THE SUGARCANE   *262*
Remembering smuggling the Mexicans across the Rio Grande.

22   GERONIMO'S MOON LIT THE DESERT   *286*
Survival in Glen Canyon.

23   I HAD BEEN SHOT   *295*
Nasdijj's children move him to the woods.

Geronimo's Bones

~~~~~~

And a Tin Can of Worms

In the beginning we were two scruffy boys who owned nothing more than a couple of cane poles, some fishing line, two hooks, two bobbers, two sinkers, and a tin can of worms.

My brother is the real fisherman.

His *formal* name is Shawnee, but we hardly ever call him that. We call him by his Indian nickname, Tso. Mama said if Anglos can have nicknames, then Indians can have them, too. She would then proceed to suck on her bottle of whiskey, joking with the men, slapping her knees that outrageous way she carried on when she told stories, and she'd laugh her big hyena laugh. You could hear Mama laughing up and down the extinct volcano she grew up on with her goats and sheep. I loved that part of her. The part of her that demanded there be some music in her life.

She would sit in her rocker and she would squeeze my brother on her lap like she would never let him go although in time she would allow all of us to go, and, in fact, Mama was the one who left us. Worn to a shadow, she disappeared into a lost vortex of existence, and there was no one and nothing that could save her. There are some people who can fit perfectly into the quiet, eternal life of the sheep camp. Mama was not one of these people. She wanted more. She did not know what *more* meant, but she was willing to find out what the rest of the world looked like. So she took off with the man who was our father, and the two of them saw that world they sought, as migrant workers who lived in a state of perpetual move-ment. That hard life took its toll on Mama and on Daddy even if he was one tough, mad, cold son-of-a-bitch, and that life just about turned my brother into a lunatic who would have to live in institutions the rest of his life. But no.

It was up to me, Mama, to turn things around, and I did that, Mama, I did that. Every cold-breath morning when my winter's bones were in my beloved New Mexico, I would turn my eyes to gaze back at the volcano that was always there. Always waiting with its sheep camps, and quiet, dignified people. The people who walk the surface of the earth. There are no other people quite like them, the Navajo. The volcano waits, and the volcano watches. The minutiae and the vast-ness of our individual existences, our inconsolable sorrows, and the deep canyons with their rivers of memory running as they do into the sea.

I have forgiven her for that. Her leaving us. *Mama, I forgive you. Mama, I understand. I know what it was you wanted.* She would hold me in her lap like she had held my brother, and squeeze me like a rock as well. You had to value the part of her that would compress just about any situation to see if she could put her hands around it, and drip the humor out. As if we boys were her morning grapefruit. As if a laugh might be a pound of gold.

It was often like squeezing blood from stones: finding the humor in what was more likely tragedy. But we learned a lot from our darkly myste-rious mother, and one of the things we learned was that, depending on your point of view, the humor in a thing could outweigh the tragedy two for one. Humor, she was apt to point out, was harder to locate, so therefore it stood to reason that humor was the more valuable property. "It will save you, too," she'd claim. Humor saved each and every one of us, if at differ-ent times. If we had not been able to laugh at ourselves, putting tongue in cheek, literally, we would not have survived the migrant life we lived. The life we lived made it just about impossible to form lasting, intimate rela-tionships with anyone. It was no accident that my brother and I grew up as close as we did. Now that we are men, there is some distance between us, and that is good, and healthy. We are still able to laugh about it, and us. Mama liked nothing more than a good, old-fashioned, head-tilted-back belly laugh. We called it her whiskey laugh and then she'd throw the bot-tle at us. We were not supposed to draw attention to her drinking. We'd run. Laughing. She called him *T-S-O*.

"Stands for *The Smarter One*," she'd say.

"Why do we need so many names," I asked her.

You had your white name. You had your Indian name. You had your nicknames. *"And,"* Mama would point out as was her way, *"if you were born a Chiricahua, you could name yourself!"*

Now, there was a radical idea. After passing the many tests of manhood the Apaches put their males through, an Apache male might name himself. I asked my brother, Tso, who he would be if he were a Chiricahua. He thought carefully. As a warrior might. Your name was important.

"I would be Stands in Middle of the River."

Now, there's a name. A good one. I liked it.

"I would be . . ." I had to squeeze my eyes some to think about it. ". . . Geronimo," I said.

My brother scoffed. "You're a little late ain'tcha? Somebody already got that name." Eyes to the sky.

I didn't care. When you are five years old, you can be whoever you want. I wanted to be like Geronimo because Geronimo was brave and resolutely able to *see* into the deserts of his dreams. Geronimo was more than a childhood fixation. Speaking as he did of wisdoms and secrets, he was the only voice I knew who had the strength to chase the other voices in my head away. When Geronimo was with me, the cacophony of other voices, everyone telling me what to do, would disappear like smoke drifting out of the hogan and up through the smoke hole, where it mingles with the stars.

I had seen it with my eyes when Geronimo had come to me at night like the Trickster that he was. The cooking smoke would disappear and the voices would recede.

My brother was the only one who knew.

About the voices.

Tso, cool in the middle of the turbulent river. The rivers push, demand, and mandate. Seeking dominace as is their way, having cut through canyons and worn away the rocks. My brother, steadfast in the middle of some icemountain river.

My brother is the real fisherman.

I prefer soaking up the warmth of the rock. As a fisherman, I am usually faking it. I will even break the stupid rules and speak while men are fishing.

Fifteen thousand men in three thousand four hundred and sixty-two boats all trolling off the coast of Santa Cruz got on their radios and angrily *shussshhhhhed* me—ssssshhhhh—*quiet*, don't you know the fish can hear?

Not really. Okay. Okay. The fish can hear. I am always amused by the fishermen who claim that fish can hear you talking. Do they really think the seventy-five-horsepower Johnson engine that got them there was *silent* on the way?

My brother is the better (decidedly more quiet) fisherman. If he asks me to go fishing with him, I always go. No one else especially wants to fish with me and I can't say I blame them. At least Tso knows it will be hard for me to keep my mouth shut *all* the time.

Odd. The two of us have always liked the same things. Even if we are very different. Football in the fall. The volcano our grandmother lived on. Coors before it went east. A Navajo Yehbechai (a sing). A well-drifted nymph (fish bait) on a brand-new line flowing slowly toward the ocean just south of Ukiah, California, as the sun burns the earth again in a rush of blue and radioactive red. Thunder in the distance like a call to arms. Fishing anywhere in Idaho. Fixing truck engines (especially early-model F-150s). Swimming. Girls. Worms. Tying our own fishing flies. Not working. Writing. Reading with flashlights under the Navajo quilts our ancient grandmother made long before her grandsons were due to arrive.

They were due. Those boys. They were overdue. They arrived.

We arrived one one year, and two, the next year, and to an infinity of hands to catch us, and arms to wrap themselves around us, screaming and crying, kicking and fussing, and making sure that the family of singers whose arms we had arrived into knew in no uncertain terms that we were here. All of it was so much bigger than we were.

We were.

That was a story in and of itself.

We were. Singers, too. Singing in Navajoland is not what singing is in the land of the *bilagaana* (white person). A *sing* in Navajoland would be seen as *dancing* or *dancing the dances of celebration* in Anglo culture. To be alive was to dance.

To be alive was to sing with color and light. To be alive was to embrace the night.

Now that we are men, and capable of looking back at those times when we only *were*, we are able, too, to *see* new paths through that deep and wild-with-clover woods. Where we landed into the arms of the People Who Tended to Their Sheep. These were my mother's People. The Navajo refer to Themselves as: the people who walk the surface of the earth.

Those words are the way my brother and I have lived our lives. We have walked in beauty all over the surface of the planet. We have never had a fight. Not a real one. Plenty of pretend ones. Plenty of pushing and shoving and rolling in the grass. We share everything.

Books. We wonder, too, if books have saved our lives. As men, we are always sharing books. We often make our own books. Tso is always sending me stuff he wrote, and I am always sending him stuff I've tried, anyway, to write. I have learned the hard way not to let Other People see that writing.

Daddy always said, *"Nasdijj, you learn the hard way."* He would shake his head. Then he'd turn me upside down and shake me to listen for the loose screws. At the time, I had no idea what he was talking about. I do now though. I am always learning. *The hard way.*

There is nothing I can write or paint that shakes my brother. He is always kind. He is always steadfast in his love for me. His loyalty never wavers. He is always fun to make things with. My brother is the better writer (and the better painter) but he would be far too shy to put any of it into a public context. The good stuff, he claims, writes itself. When we make books together, we make our own covers and designs. Sometimes we put paintings and photographs in the books we make. My writing is instinctual and abstract—most of it has to do with love and loss—and he usually laughs when he reads it, not too unlike the way our mother would have laughed, because he understands the battles of the monsters I refer to.

That is the essence to writing this. The Navajo have a special saying. *Walk in beauty.* It is used as a prayer, a chant, a sing, and in the dances, too. Walk in beauty. You might *walk in beauty* to *hodiyin*, a holy, sacred place. *Allow me to tell you about the man my brother is, and how the two of us struggled and loved to hold the relationship together* is my way of saying to you, *Walk in beauty.* Tso's laughter is a healthy thing. It is, too, his sword in the last battle between good and evil before the day of judgment. Armageddon will be defeated by a giggle or a belly laugh.

When my brother laughs, you have to watch his eyes, for they will kidnap you, and take you places such as *hodiyin* where all living things come with voice. You can lose yourself within those eyes, in the sorrow of history, in the beauty of that eye-catching moment. We were fly-fishing in Canada once and I was asleep in our pup tent. Something woke me up. There he was inside his sleeping bag with his flashlight on. Reading one of my handcrafted books. One I had made just for him. The two of us—the brothers—cannot be divorced from the things we make to express ourselves. We have been taught by *the spirits* that we *are* the things we make.

Someone downstairs (usually our father) would yell: *I said flashlights out!*

Our eyes grew big. We would plunge ourselves back under our pillows. Click. Flashlights out. For now. Slipping under and into the darkness of those Navajo weavings we slept in as children, the rugs of the underworld, and slipping, too, into the strange world I was usually attempting to paint for the imaginary reader, a phantom of the flashlights, who had never seen my world of horses and sheep and volcanoes and the voices that came from there. I want words to be like wings so you might see from higher up.

Tso was my first test audience. He still is.

My brother and I were so close growing up that we were addicted to each other's presence as brothers. We never needed chemicals. We had each other. When he is not with me, I catch myself looking around for him.

"He's not here," my wife will tell me. "He went back to Mexico for the winter. But you knew that."

Yes. I did know that. Still, I look. He could be hiding in a corner some-where reading books.

We have been addicted to the journeys that we found in books ever since we figured out that even with our visual impairments, and our even longer list of learning disabilities, our accumulated inabilities, our perpet-ual struggles to live our lives in such a way as to be able to *deal* with au-thority versus always failing—always, and always, and always failing, the failures of our lives another long list of demented missing links, most of which can be directly connected to the indubitable certainty our mother was inebriated during both her pregnancies, nevertheless—we *could and we did teach ourselves to read*.

We had to. There were no other options. Reading was a matter of life and death. When I am teaching children how to read, I tell them this. *Reading is a matter of life and death.* There is a deadly serious part of any child, buried under layers and layers of the deadening cuteness society as-signs to childhood, that wants to believe it, that does believe it: Reading is a matter of life and death. The beauty to it unfolds when the child asks when does he begin and how.

When do we begin and how?

Here. Now. Let us sit together and read this. Let us write about what we have seen. How simplistic. How complex. The universe the child knew was there—although he was not quite sure where—unfolds. Teaching children to read has been one of the passions of my life.

There were times when I was not sure that learning how to read was going to work for us. Even today, letters appear to me to be upside down. I have this vision of my brother, Tso, and I swimming intrauterine, upside-down insideout mermen, surrounded by a sea of Bombay gin. Olives gur-gling upward toward the ice. Our wrists are bound together with chains. Our mother did not come to marriage with the idea she could control her pregnancies, and the number of babies she might have. Navajo women are taught that the more babies you have, the better things will be. This is not so insane as one might think. The idea of big families has brought the population of the tribe up from less than one thousand individuals to more than two hundred and fifty thousand Navajo. In 1900, the dawn of the twentieth century, the Navajo stood at the precipice where they were ei-ther going to multiply or disappear. They multiplied. They refused to go gently into that good night.

Our mother went through other pregnancies that she lost, and gave birth to dead babies, too. My father and I buried one of our siblings once in the back of a sugarcane field in a migrant camp. The dead thing in a bucket and buried in a hole in the ground. Our father cried as he helped me shovel. Or maybe I was the one who cried as I helped him shovel. I do not know. All I remember is the moon and the cane and the black dirt and the heat like a fervent roasting of our flesh and the river of sweat that poured from my father's hardened body on a night so bibleblack all bodies seemed but apparitions. I do remembering standing there with my father contemplating a mound of dirt, the burying with shovels finally finished. Now, perhaps a prayer. I think that as we stood there in front of that small and buried mount of dirt, my father prayed.

My feelings for the man will always be a contradiction. I wanted him to love me. I did not want him to hurt me. But he hurt me so many times that finding my love for him inside my bones is like searching for the lost city of Atlantis. All we have are rumors that the thing was there. I was allowed to see this *thing*. My father praying. What else did life have in store for me?

My brother being too small to go with our father to do this work. The burying of a fetus. This was the first time I had ever thought of myself as the *bigger* brother. We returned from the nocturnal swamp of the cane field and my father proceeded to get himself riproaring drunk. In the morning, both parents went off to work. Their eyes red-blood-rimmed with an exhaustion that twenty years of sleep could not begin to touch.

My mother did not come to bearing children with the awareness that alcohol was a dangerous thing for babies, and yet something tells me that she knew. That there was a spark inside of her that warned her about the drinking. She did not listen to it.

In Navajo, *dideests' iit* means *I will hear about it*. The word implies a responsibility on the part of the person who is listening *to listen*. *To listen* is not a passive behavior; those who *are listening* must be *open to hearing* things they might not particularly want to hear.

It was becoming quite clear to my little brother and I that when it came to some of the things most people take for granted—like the fact that exposure to alcohol could kill or maim a fetus—often *people hear* only when it is much too late.

It was becoming quite clear to my little brother and I that when it came to some of the things most people take for granted—like the assumption you will be taught to read in school—you are really on your own in trying to decide where to start. We started by simply copying words. We were printing. We weren't going to wait around for someone to teach us because if we did, it would be too late.

Tso and I used to try to read (it was impossible) in the back of the pickup during any of our migrant family's longer moves. We would try to hide our little books in our backpacks although that was the first place our father went on his quests to find forbidden materials. We were not afraid of his finding books so much as we were afraid of him taking us somewhere where they had never heard of books. The long hot rides could be endlessly boring to little boys and we wanted a diversion. The term *far away* had no meaning to us. Everything and nothing was far away. Anytime you got into a truck with Daddy you risked being taken to a migrant camp in Bakersfield, California, or Belle Glade, Florida, or anywhere else that was three thousand miles away. Although it had been endlessly explained to us that we moved around for work, that the season in Florida for picking strawberries would end and when it did we would be driving north to pick tomatoes in Ohio, we did not entirely believe these words. What we believed was that Daddy would move from one place to another because that was who and what he was. Anytime you got into a truck with Daddy you made sure everyone else was coming along.

Or I would jump out and slam the door.

My bravado was an act. I was terrified of being alone with him.

Tso and I could do things in the back of the pickup Daddy could not see.

When are we going to get there was not a question we dared ask. Tso in his exhausted ignorance had asked it once, and Daddy did what he had been swearing ever since we had been able to understand language he would do if either I or Tso *ever, ever* posed that question to him.

I will stop this truck and I will throw you into the ditch and I will beat you with my boot.

Daddy stopped the truck. Daddy threw the small body of Tso into the ditch. Daddy beat him with his boot, kicking him until blood was running from my brother's eye. And then Daddy left him there.

Pulling away and almost into the highway again.

My mother just staring out the window.

Drunk, I think. Anyway, the beer bottles were everywhere up front.

Tso was maybe five.

I had a decision to make before Daddy gunned the truck.

To jump or not to jump. I was six.

I jumped.

As I jumped I could see my mother's eyes like dull mirrors in her head. She was slipping more and more away from us. I knew she would go before she went. There was no way anyone could save her. I jumped off the back of that truck as it was pulling into traffic. I did not want to be dragged down into the depths of death the two adults in my life had assigned themselves to. I jumped from the truck and rolled onto the ground. Stones breaking my skin and my brother running to me. The truck stopped. Our mother flying to us. But it was too late. For her. For us. For the fragments of our memories to do anything more than fly away.

Her going would not be unlike the truck pulling away from Tso, standing there in that ditch, blood running down his face, watching us pulling away. Like one of the fireflies in my mayonnaise jar that in the morning simply wasn't there.

I was on my brother's *side*. You take them or you don't. Even at six. We learned very, very early on, earlier than most children, that you either took a side and stuck to it, or you didn't. Both ways had consequences. We were small children, but we felt as if we had lived forever.

We lived in an adult world with adult consequences. We could see the world of white children, we could watch it on television (even if we did not have television, our friends did) with its advertisements for toys, and we knew it through the eyes of Captain Kangaroo. But we thought of it in the same way we thought of life on Mars.

We were not soft little boys from the suburbs. No. We were *migrant workers*. We were different. Daddy said so, and we *knew* (if we knew anything) that we were different. The way we see the world is different. The way I write is different. The way my brother fishes is different. The truck and the dishevelment and the dogs and the cowboy hats and the shovels and the rakes in the back of the truck and the tangled knots and the bald tires and the trouble and the turmoil in the parking lot and the salsa from the radios in the windows made us different.

Daddy had to go back to pick up my brother. I helped him up into the pickup. I found a rag and wiped the blood from his face and made him hold it to his eye, which turned black and blue and swollen for about two weeks. And then we did not mention any of it again.

There were moves and then there were moves. Broward County, Florida, to Salinas, California. Chico, California, to Yakima, Washington. Bend, Oregon, to Oneida, Tennessee. Oranges to tobacco. Tobacco to apples. Apples to peaches. Peaches to tomatoes. Tomatoes to celery. Celery to cherries. Cherries to lettuce. Lettuce to grapes. Grapes to plums. We picked it all. Nevertheless, there were two kinds of migrants then, back in the nineteen fifties, as there are two kinds of migrant workers today.

There are migrants who read. There are migrants who do not read. Life is hard enough for the migrants who do read. For migrants who are illiterate, life is a familiar place of terror.

We have always said—when asked—we taught ourselves to read, and it's true, we did. But what is even more true is that the *two-of-us* taught the *two-of-us* how to do almost everything. We might get jump-started on a thing by someone else, but it would take the two of us to see it through. Considering the fact that right around the age of six we were essentially motherless—she died frozen long before she died, frozen—and essentially being fatherless for the long haul—he died frozen in his mother's womb—we bumped along as best we could.

We taught ourselves how to wiggle around through truck graveyards. We taught ourselves how to find a truck kingpin at dead truckyards or junkyards, and how to take it and pound it out of the rusted vehicle and use it to connect to your own F-150's steering rod so you can steer the truck and not go off the road. We did not always know the appropriate name for a spare part but we could find it and we could put it on. It only looked like Daddy helped. Daddy never helped. Not really. For one thing, he was drunk a lot. For another thing, it was hard for him to see us successful at anything because it meant he would now have to do something vengeful to keep us in our place (lest we grow bigheaded), and that always included a lot of hurt. There was more hurt in our tiny, troubled, trampled-down straggling mix of innards and migrant homes than fish in any of the rivers we went to as if they were our mother's-in-full-embrace. It was the river and the lake and the creek and the fish pond that could touch us, love us, teach us, and play with us. It looked good when our parents were doing things with us but we knew.

There were programs, usually in churches, and run by the people who ran the church, for migrant children not yet in school. Today they would call these preschool programs. Today there is Migrant Head Start, but no such thing existed then. What church basement programs did exist existed not out of the goodness of anyone's heart, but because migrant mothers could not pick as fast or as much if they had to worry about their children being eaten up by the big machines and farm equipment. Women fresh from villages in Mexico and Central America were forever setting infants in baskets next to the fields being worked, and those infants were forever being run over by tractors. There would be a quick burial and then back to work.

My brother and I only remember snippets of schools. Most of them blend together. Mama barely spoke English herself. She marched us into the preschool, holding the backs of our pants. After Mama died, the person who usually saw to it that we were put in school was the wife of the man who owned the farm we would be working on. It just didn't pay to have us wandering around all day, which was why Daddy was always attempting to draft us into working in the fields. On the bigger farms, no one cared. But on the little farms there was usually a farm boss's wife somewhere keeping an eye on things. Whoops. She spies children. By the look of it, boys. Boys find trouble. In fact, boys will bring the police to the farm.

Crime Number One: bring police to the farm. The sheriff has better things to do than run after shoplifters.

Or migrant criminals.

By the age of eight, we were wanted by the candy bar patrol in about twenty counties in as many states. We figured candy bar companies had our pictures on their most wanted list.

We'd be caught with our pockets filled with Mars Bars and then taken by the ear to school.

We were in the slow group. For Show-and-Tell, we once brought mayonnaise jars filled with dirt, wet cardboard, worms, and fireflies.

We had the facts down, too.

At the time, I was horrified that Tso might forget that he had promised not to *tell* anyone that he had *named* his worm. He did not know if *it* was a he or a she.

We could reduce entire classrooms into laughing, screaming scenes of total uproar.

Wanna see what the worm can do? Tso has just finished a season of picking cherries with the Chippewa where we had lived among a few Chippewa children who spoke French.

Tso's worm's new name was Escargot.

Teacher's eyes to the sky. And that will be enough of that.

School to school to school to school. Until we didn't go to school anymore. I cannot say *we ran away.*

We ran away any number of times. No one missed us. No one realized we were gone.

All I remember about most of those places those yellow buses let us off at is that the teacher would always be with the *bright group* (almost always all girls), and she would point out the *slow group* with her pencil, but most of the time we already knew where *they* were. Usually, the back of the room. One teacher I had used to spend fifty-five (I counted them) minutes with the *bright group*, everyone reading out loud together, and it even looked like it might be fun, and after they had received most of the hour, the teacher would wander over to our *slower circle* with the wooden pointer, whacking kids in the head until she was sure she hadn't missed anyone.

My brother and I concluded we would teach *ourselves*.

The first year of my existence was brotherless. *Do you remember things before I was born?*

Tso has always been curious. His innate curiosity has always been an attribute of coexistent completeness. Versus any self-defeating *obbligato*. Even as toddlers we knew little things: Be aware of the number of liquor bottles under the bed. If they begin to break in the middle of the night expect another *Binge-Nightmare*, most of which lasted astonishingly the exact same number of days or even hours. You could put a stopwatch to them as if you were timing some damaged horse that had once been beautiful around and around the track.

We stole books when we could, and knew to never keep much more than one book, or Daddy would find it, and that would be the end of us.

School libraries were good places to steal books from. They never suspected.

You.

Anywhere near a book.

You were as durable as your agreements. We had a standing agreement written and signed in concrete mixed with blood that one brother would keep the other brother informed of his ongoing crimes. We were major players in each other's crimes anyway, but just to make sure, we agreed that we would always let the other brother know what we were up to. I knew when Tso and his second-grade buddies were going to steal the clapper out of the bell in the middle courtyard of the particular-school-we-were-attending, and he knew when I was going to build one of my forts from building supplies waylaid and scattered all over the fields from a recent Florida hurricane. That spring my fort even had mismatched garage siding.

If I was the fort-builder, Tso was the fisherman. Mainly it was our mother who taught us how to fish, or at least she *jump*-started the process by showing us how to collect nightcrawlers.

By the time we were four we had it down.

By the time we were ten, we had compartmentalized most of the universe. The way we saw it, the universe was split in two. There was the Navajo world of our mother, and this was the universe we loved, but we could not convince our father to let us remain there permanently. For years we could not figure out why he was so intransigent, and then it hit Sa, our grandmother, and she began to question us as to just how much cotton could we pick, how many bushels of apples did we pick up and off the ground? Plums, celery, cherries, grapes, peaches? It went on and on. We rattled off the numbers and Sa closed her eyes and did her calculations in her head.

Between the two of us, we came home with the same pickings as a grown man.

It had to do with money. We brought home the money of another man.

We thought about hiding when he came to get us. But we knew this would not work. Daddy was not beneath spreading his hurt around. Daddy would shoot a few of Sa's best wool sheep, and the pain this would cause would be more than anyone who lived on the slopes of our volcano could bear. My old great aunts still live and raise sheep in this place and by a moral code as unforgiving as death. This is a dry, high-desert place of much magic, and it isn't the kind of place we should have been dragging our father to in his search for us; instead we should have been pulling our father away so he could not contaminate it with his wounded spirit.

It was always best to get him out of there as soon as possible.

We would wave good-bye to our green volcano and wonder if we would ever see it again.

We were ten-year-olds, sitting on the back steps one night in Belle Glade, Florida. Our migrant shack had no electricity so it was always dark as hell. We shined out flashlights on our worm jars. We knew fishing, now. It had been *our* sport for some time. We owned it. And the worms crawling around the dirt and wet cardboard we had put in there. Worms eat wet cardboard. Every few seconds or so, a firefly we had collected would softly and briefly illuminate the inside of the jar with a glow like eternal summers gild them. We had both decided that the best part of living in the South (there had to be something) was the fireflies. We believed they were sending us messages from our mother. Shining the flashlight on the glass of the one jar (Tso having lost his and his current Escargot to a roving gang of bigger boys), we twisted it around and around with our hands, causing us both to *see* into the unsymmetric eyes of our anarchic brother. Me on one side of the jar, and Tso on the other.

My worm homes were always mayonnaise jars. Daddy ate mayonnaise on everything. We could not take our demon eyes off the inside of the mayonnaise jar. Dancing through the dreams of things that were. Eternal summer creates and multiplies in us a small canoe out on a lake. The migrants come here to fish. We see the rat snakes as they go swimming by. Orangish with four black longitudinal stripes. The pupils are black and round. Gathering rays of sun. A brighter ray and more beloved existence.

It was one of those moments my brother scares me.

"What was that?" I asked him.

He shrugged. "A rat snake. We do poems in school—when I go there anyway. I did one about the rat snake."

"Not like that one."

"No. Not like that one. Sometimes they just come to me. Both the snakes and the poems. I don't always understand it, and I don't want to talk about it. If we could get a TV then maybe we wouldn't steal so many books. Sometimes I think I will have to go to jail. I am so *sick* of thinking that! I will have to turn myself in for stealing books from libraries."

"Cuz your brother made you do it."

"Cuz my brother made me do it. Kinda."

Tso was born to it. The poetry of fishing. A certain isolation to who and what he is. Like that one handsome tree set apart in the orchard near the sandy shores of the fishing pond. My brother's mission now is quiet and humility. If there's a river, my brother will want to fish it from the middle, where I prefer the rocks and shadows. From the rocks, the shadows of the river are luminous and liquid. I am like one of the animals from the woods behind us. Darting here and there. Sniffing around for grubs. Busy. Much too busy to catch a fish.

Tso and I had learned early on that words could save you in many, many ways. One of the writers whom Tso and I shared and continue to share as being elected to our Distinguished Literary Pantheon of Diuturnity (we kept you for a week and then we had to throw you away lest we get caught reading books) was and is the Lord Byron. *There is a pleasure in the pathless woods*, Byron writes, *There is a rapture on the lonely shore. There is society where none intrudes. By the deep sea, and music in its roar: I love not man the less, but nature more.*

I frowned my deepest, most serious frown the first time I had to stick a fishhook through the struggling fleshguts of a nightcrawler. The worm, undulating quickly, flipping and whipping his tail about, was an ugly thing even for a nightcrawler.

"A what?" I asked my mom. Shima took me out on a lake that day. I do not remember fish. About all I remember is the worm.

"It's a nightcrawler," she explained. "It crawls down into the deep wet ground where it lives and fish love to eat them and we love to eat the fish."

She smiled. My first lessons in the pecking order of omnivorous ecology were replete with worms, fish, flashlights zigzagging on the ground at night, waiting for the worms to come out, and when they did, we scooped them up and put them victoriously into our worm jars half filled with dirt.

All of this came naturally to the man who is my brother. No worm would ever make him flinch.

I am an idiot who struts and frets about his hours upon the planet attempting to reconstruct the configurations of nothing less than time.

I want time to take me back.

With my fishline tied to my finger sitting in an autumn rain. A rhyme. Wet everywhere. My hook and bobber in the water. Waiting for a fish to come along. Light everywhere between the drops.

Fishing and writing are not too unalike. You must be patient or both will become a misery. In fishing, it is not uncommon for there to be light everywhere between the raining drops. But in writing, it only happens now and then. Enough times anyway to bring you back to fish again.

How many stories does this river tell? My brother laughs. As his voice breaks, too, against the river rocks, I am reminded of my mother's laughing. She would tease us and swear she ate nightcrawlers raw. We would laugh as well, falling to the ground, holding our tummies, pretending to throw up. We did not believe her then. "If she said it today," Tso observed . . .

"I'd believe it," I answered for him.

We were a long way from fishing ponds. The blue water of the Nazko River in British Columbia, Canada, dances, and breaks its light early in the morning as autumn moves slowly as a turtle south, and the wind moves the many colors of the now wet leaves like you have bitten heavily into the rich sweetness of an apple. Can you hear the apple laugh? I hear things laughing all the time. Leaves. Wind. Waves. The dry wheat as you walk through it. Orchards of trees with their heavy limbs bending with apples. Stone-smooth skins and glittering red. Apples laughing like a woman laughs softly from her bed.

The gravel bottom of the river is a brownish gold. Brown-red sand runs like the tannic veins of ravines cutting through the riverbanks and oak roots. My brother's fly line sings. Songs of lakes and moons and dusk and songs of fish and songs of us.

My fishline tied to my finger says nothing. For me, fishing is a muteness. I am not here to fish.

I am here to listen to the silence. I am here to listen to the music of the leaves. I am here to see the stars and—if I am lucky—the aurora borealis. I am only here (the sponge) to soak it up.

That which can be absorbed. The man who is my brother. The apples we carry for lunch. The water and the wind. Perhaps a small piece of liquid shadow from the past. Like a cheap white apple wine. The kind of wine our migrant friends used to steal when we stopped at Groceryway—Mama will chase you out the back door with her broom—and tried to hide the green Boone's Farm bottle in a coat. Only to take off again, burning the rubber on Poncho Ponce's dead Dodge Dart, and throwing stones up in the parking lot. Poncho was sixteen and bought the Dodge in Durango, Mexico. Even then, my brother was intrigued by the engine. It was a conglomeration of the spare parts from twenty engines. We were all of eleven. To hang out with the bigger boys was as delicious as it was dangerous.

Redemption in the fishing life has to do with the fact it can be lived— that life of vanished shadows—alone. Mistakes here are not shared. They are yours to keep wherever you want to keep them.

When he was fourteen, I bought Tso a fly rod with a big black deer-hair moth tied to its leader. It was time to graduate from worms. Deer hair on a hook is light as air. Tso could tie bugs to this leader big enough to catch a bass. Thing was, the fish's head will push the bug away. When a fly fisherman has become pretty good at what he does, he often casts with longer and longer casts. He has done it dramatically a hundred times in his garage. Knowing that his garage is not the river. Knowing but not knowing. Ego. Desire. The ability to control what seems to be chaos. Happens to the best. You are a fisherman now, and you like that clean song the line makes when it whips into the wind. But you're never ready for the unexpected. Not from the safe confines of a suburban two-car garage where one car now sits somewhat permanently in the drive to give you and your fishing junk the room you and your rods need. The unexpected is what brings you to both the desert and the river. The smallmouth with some solid gravel beneath him who in cool water is likely to knock the rod out of your hand. The sidewinder you see slithering into the sage. Rat snakes.

Beware.

Of blindness from another age.

In Mexico (where we do not fly fish much), my brother and I fish for big grouper along the coast of Puerto Penasco. Where the desert meets the sea. The ancient home of the Hohokam Indians. A few Pima Cateno and Arenero Indians still live here hidden in the desert. Their liquid black eyes are quick, and they are beyond humble, hoping, praying you are not the owner of the land their shack, mostly a hammering together of old and discarded signs, is on, and that you will not return, especially with bulldozers, and they are frightened they might have offended you. The babies cry from other darker rooms and everyone is hungry. I can always smell it in the room. Hunger like a corpse rots slowly.

My brother and I have fished this part of the planet for striped marlin, yellowtail, sea bass, yellowfin tuna (my biggest catch of tuna weighing in at twenty-five pounds), grouper, amberjack, roosterfish, and pompano. I caught a sea bass one mile south of Rocky Island that was forty pounds.

Just before the sun sets, and everything is long with sunburn and shadow, I always think I can see them there—the Vanished Ones—I am never really sure of who they are. Or where they came from. No one else (no adult, anyway) I am fishing with ever sees them. But I see them all the time. Infrequently, I can get some of my friends' children or poorer children from the barrio to see them. And when they do, their eyes go wide.

In Puerto Penasco, the Vanished Ones look like Aztecs in their war canoes. There are the warriors who paddle, and there are more vainglorious warriors sitting arrogantly and stiffly in the sterns. In Canada, the Vanished Ones always appear to me to wear a lot of deerskin. In the deserts of New Mexico, the Vanished Ones always appear to me to wear very little. They always seem to arrive from nowhere. Or from a place far away from wherever home is. Their eyes look through me. Warlike. On their way to somewhere ominous and important. I have seen the Vanished Ones vanish into rock paintings. My time and their time seem to meet or collides in some double door where the visible world comes in contact with a world invisible. To us. If a wind moves, there must be a presence coming through. I never know when or where the Vanished Ones will appear. Only that they do.

My brother and I used to pretend we were asleep, and in that space where sleep becomes a basket of leaking images, we would discuss the coming and the going of the Vanished Ones. For a short while, somewhere between the ages of four and five when anything is possible, Tso could see them, too. Even if he was a little dubious. "I saw the deer one jump today," Tso informed me. We were staying with our grandmother. Sa. There were many, many rock paintings around the Anasazi paths that crisscrossed the sides of the old volcano where Sa lived overlooking the ancient canyons of Chaco. Today, as men, grounded and secure, we no longer articulate the vision of moving animals that leap into the rock. Today, as men, we fish. Knowing what we know.

In Puerto Penasco, we give our fish away to the desperately poor Indian people who live in shacks set back not too far from the condominiums that are now beginning to define the place. These are the people who would eat our bait (pieces of squid and perfectly delicious if cooked appropriately) if they could.

A striped marlin is a ridiculous fish to eat. It is almost entirely bone (which is why it is called a bonefish). I gave one away in Puerto Penasco that weighed in at the shrimp dock at two hundred pounds. I gave away a dorado there that weighed all of thirty pounds. I could always give the fish away to hungry people at the shrimp docks, but to find the children, and the women with the babies, you have to drive around north on Balboa, and then *behind the trees* you will find the shacks, the cardboard ones, and the ones made from signs. The children will peek at you from behind palm trees, which do not hide them well. Every family has a pot to cook a fish in. The first time I ever did this, I cut the heads of the fish off.

My brother rolls his eyes.

He brings a separate plastic bag filled with grouper heads.

Enough said.

I suppose I could eat a fish head if I had to, and there have been more than a few times in the past when I have had to (I try to block that memory out).

In the States, we catch and release. In Canada, we eat them all. It has something to do with the air being cold, and we were always hungry.

We were always hungry. As boys. It never really goes away. Hunger. Like a canoe at night, it eases through the bulrushes until they have thinned enough for a man to cast.

Who whips his cast where the bulrushes and the weeds are thick as snakes?

A glutton or a fool.

I have asked my brother not to come to my house in North Carolina. I do not want to see him there. I have no desire to fish with him in North Carolina. I want to picture him in my mind fishing with his wife (we call her Dancer) in Canada. I want to picture the two of them in Mexico fishing for big grouper. I want to keep the image of my brother giving his catch of the day away to soft Indian women who are nursing babies. I want to picture the two of them in their Airstream in Puerto Penasco eating shrimp and drinking beer and walking sunsets until your legs ache, and your toes go pink. I want to picture him fixing trucks, which is what he loves. I do not want to see my brother anywhere near a buzzing, busy town or city. Tso does not do well in such thickly populated places as the American South. There are more people here than birds in Paradise.

I do not want him to see me. Like this. No longer able to walk or do much for myself. It always seems to be the end with me. Like some small-mouth that has jerked my rod into the lake. The hammerheads are always coming.

My bones are dying. All of them. Fingers. Toes. Shoulders. Elbows. Legs. Hips. Arms. Wrists. Knees. Human beings are of a complex structure. They are known to fall apart like the shacks made from cardboard boxes at the maquiladoras. Those City-States of Shacks that follow the corporate assembly plants of Mexico around like cancerous lesions with names like Ford, Motorola, General Electric, Amana, Frigidaire, and May-tag. Entire cities made from the cardboard boxes used by factories to pack-age television sets. This is how the body ends. It rains. You are exposed. Your nakedness a sore upon the land. You float away. A cardboard box now undone.

My bones have been attacked by avascular necrosis. There are cysts on the bones now. Some bones are dead. The pain is horrific. My wife and I make a ritual out of going to the hospital every day. The blood draws. The INR counts. How quickly does your blood coagulate? Too quickly I am told. My pulmonary embolisms are killing me. When they stick the needles in, I close my eyes. I want to go off somewhere almost cold. I want to see my brother in the canoe fishing. I do not want to see him here in this room with me. Him waiting. Pacing like he does. Worrying.

He still bites the skin on the back of his right hand.

Only I knew about that hand.

Tso did not want me to tell his wife. About the hand.

"Fine," I said. "Then stop biting it."

It took a long time for Tso to reach the point where he wasn't biting the hand. He would disappear into the bathroom (Dancer and I both listening for the sound of water), and come out smiling having dried his hands. The right one having skin just below the wrist the color of a cooked lobster.

You've been biting your hand again.

No, I haven't. No. I'm really not biting myself anymore. I'm not. I'm not.

My brother was, too, biting the back of his hand red again. He was wor-rying and I have ordered him in no uncertain terms to stop it. But he frets. About his brother the hysterical hypochondriac.

He is a much better fisherman than he is a writer. I was the one who wrote the journals. Tso was the one who hid them if he could.

We never wanted Daddy to read what had been written.

We were never entirely sure that Daddy was a complete illiterate. Daddy could fake it well. We *knew* he could not read, but what if this was just another ruse? What if this deception was just another way for Daddy to *get us* and hurt us?

But I was not capable of *not* writing about what went on all around me all the time. I was not capable of that kind of silence. I would write some-where. Anywhere. I still write on my hands and arms.

Illness and brotherhood have been metaphors ripe for the writer since

the dawn of written language. The worst part of it—being a vegetable—
is the being handled roughly by the people who see you as a thing. An ob-
ject. Not human. They will and they do hurt you. "Now, what do we
have here?" my orthopedic surgeon asks as he picks up my chart, thick as a
dictionary.

He is one of the good guys.

Now. What. Do. We. Have. Here.

I wonder, too. About what there is to have. About all you really ever
have is the past, and the songs made there. That place of shadows and the
Vanished Ones. My own past is like a Navajo Yehbechai. The Night Chant
Ceremony. Where the dancing illuminations of the past leap around in
masks. I can and do prefer to keep many of those masked characters there.
Chained to the past where 'adaazbaa (they who went off to war) have been
tamed by time. I no longer care to unchain them to study what they might
do next. I have seen that war, too. And understand the past can come back
to destroy who you are today.

There is much about my past I do not know. There is much about my
past I do not want to know. As I have tried to peel some of that bark away
and off the tree so I might know the middle of the thing, the light and the
soul of the tree have been unleashed in such ways as to let me know unerr-
ingly that the old soul of the tree has placed its bark here for a purpose. It
is his skin and it holds him to himself, and, yes, his secrets in. For they are
his, and don't I know it, from beyond space and time, a mirrored showing
off of the mystery to the art of loving madness.

My brother is the real fisherman. Light everywhere between the drops.
Time. The stuff that has happened. You eat it for your lunch like an apple.
Put it in your pocket. It will be warm when you bite into the thing. Do you
hear it laughing? You are your history.

2

This *Is the Story*
I Have to Tell

The Third World was a place of light and contradiction. There were oceans one way and mountains another way. Changing Woman and her sister (who had yet to be named) came into this world up through the tender shoot of a living reed.

There were other worlds all around.

Everything was moving. Some things up. Some things down. Some things in circles. Tomorrow, Changing Woman would give birth to twins.

Only Coyote knew. His grin told him.

Changing Woman and her sister would hold hands and see where the wind would take them now.

This is the story I have to tell. My father was a white man.

I do not know much about his past, and, now, knowing him like I do, as though he were a ghost because he is one, I want to keep him there.

Inside the coffin. Beware.

Of plunging sharpened crosses into the heart of the dead. Digging him up even in the literary sense makes me feel as if I am back there with him again. He swore he loved me. But it wasn't true. You cannot love the thing you would destroy. I do *not* believe it.

My mother was *with the Navajo*. That is how the Navajo define themselves.

The people who walk the surface of the earth understand that you have to be *with* someone. Somewhere. She loved us. Imperfectly. *But she loved us.*

My mother would look hurt and confused when white people would laugh at her answering the question: *"Where do you come from?"*

"I am with the Navajo," Shima would say.

There would be laughter.

I would take her hand and gently lead her away from there. I would not want her to be anywhere near where the people laughed. People are dangerous.

I am not with the Navajo.

I am not Navajo.

I am not Indian.

I make no claim to such a sacred heritage.

The world I come from is the world of war and darkness.

The fact that I lived with and among the Navajo only has meaning to me.

The world I come from believes that ancient man came to North America over the Bering Straits at a time when it was cold, and the snow-pack had sucked the oceans up. Thus uncovering enough of a land bridge for human beings to cross over.

The Navajo listen silently to this theory. They try not to grin too hard.

The Navajo *believe* that they (the People) have been here forever. Their creation stories tell them this.

I walk among them as though *I* were the one who was a ghost. I try my best to not disrespect things among the Navajo, knowing, as I do, that I fail almost all the time.

I am *with* the White World. Meaning *I have arrived from the bleeding mouth of chaos.*

My mother and my father met in a Gallup, New Mexico, bar. After my mother died from alcohol poisoning my father fell apart and we were homeless for a time. We lived under a bridge. I looked around at what I could do.

Pop bottles. Beer bottles. You received a few pennies for returning them to the store. I collected bottles people had thrown away. At first, I had an old bag. And then Tso and I dragged a shopping cart we had found in a parking lot over to the bridge that was our home. Now what I collect are the stories people have forgotten that they knew. There are stories everywhere. Some of the best ones are found under bridges.

I am like that bridge we lived under. Tucked in between the concrete struts was shelter. The people who lived there sat around defeated mainly and told the story of what had brought them to this place. They had lost everything and they wanted you to know this. They were the people of death (at least that is how a small boy of seven saw them) and they were blind.

I watched them closely every day we lived in our blankets under that bridge. Their skin was red like burned meat and their eyes were slits. They could not *see* the world as anything other than a place that had cast them here, and here they would stay, forever.

We could not have stayed there longer than a few weeks. It was not a life. It was more a death of almost everything around you. Today I have no idea where this bridge was. It could have been anywhere. But where it was *is irrelevant*. Eventually my father would find his way out from under the bridge, and he would move on to other migrant worker jobs. For that is who and what he was—a migrant worker, and so were we. My brother and I still (in our own blindness) see ourselves as *migrant workers*. It isn't something that can be washed away. We were migrant workers and we liked it. It was what we knew. What we knew of the real world—the world I write words for today—was infinitesimal. Tiny. Small. Microscopic. Although we had seen an awful lot of geography. Now, as our father would attempt and attempt and attempt to reconstruct his life, we would spend more and more time with our mother's people. Our father would give us to them. To take in until he might return for us. We had a lot to learn.

To *see* among the People of the Volcano—a place I am told my ancestors crawled out from with their own brotherhoods—is more, oh, much more than what you do with your eyes. To *see* means the way in which you perceive the journey that is your life, *and to see* is what you do with that life.

A couple of years ago, I spent a year on the Navajo Nation collecting stories. I was writing *Geronimo's Bones* and wanted to know about the Athabascan stories of the War Twins. Not that I thought of myself and my brother as them. No. We are not twins and we have no magical powers. People either took me into their hogans to tell me what they knew, or they shut the door in my face. As with many of the myths handed down in oral cultures, the story of the Navajo War Twins, and how they found their father (who rejected them), varied hogan to hogan. In some of the hogans, the myths were told in the traditional way using as points of reference many of the holy places on the reservation. But many times the story of the War Twins changed, as did the places the War Twins supposedly emerged from and went to on their many adventures defeating monsters.

The only monsters we knew were fish.

On the first part of the journey, I was drinkin' up all the sky. There were gods and myths and lips that kiss and I have no idea why.

Lose everything. Our grandmother said it and she would hold us up when we were small to see the sunrise. Her door faced east. You have the sunrise, we were told. Such richness.

The sky is breaking. I can remember the first time I saw the sky. I was on my mother's back in a Navajo cradleboard. There will be people who will insist that no one can remember back that far. But I do. We were at the top of the volcano where my mother, Shima, grew up among the grama grass, sage, and sheep. The sky was breaking blue.

The sky in this place is a sky of many visions. Visions that allow you to *see*. The sky in this place of high altitude is always breaking blue.

My father broke us all. He did not discriminate. He broke everyone he could. First, he would break your bones.

I do not know what the connection was between his overt violence and his love. I think he did love. Something. Once.

The sky was not the only thing that was breaking then. Our father was breaking into pieces, too, but there was not a thing two little boys could do about it. At some point our father was no longer able to distinguish his love for us and his attraction to us from his need to portray himself as a significant authority figure within our lives. He had no idea where the anger left and the love began. The very first time my father ever came into my room and crawled into my bed, I did not know what he was doing. We were living in migrant housing and my brother and I were sharing a small room. At first, I thought my father's coming to me was a loving thing, but one with a few question marks. It was a huge and deeply black mystery. Complete with feelings where you are falling off from some great height, or you are being chased by trains. When he put my small penis into his mouth, the only thing I could think to do (or not do) was *do not* pee in his mouth (I was terrified I might), and since I had no idea what came next, or what *to do*, I did the next best thing. Do nothing.

Maybe if I do nothing he will not kill me. I knew in my bones he would kill me now.

As his penis was ejaculating in my mouth, I was letting go of my life. And yet the horrible taste and gluelike consistency of his ejaculate was so utterly disgusting it brought me back to fighting, gagging, and screaming for my life. I had (have) this intense will to live.

I fought him. It seemed to rise up in me like vomit in my throat.

But as he came to me night after night, I grew tired.

I gagged his sperm down and screamed, *"No!"*

I pushed him away.

I bit him hard. Everything about him—*us*—was hard. The life we lived. The forgiveness we sought. The poverty we sought to avoid.

My mother was still alive then, which means I was not seven yet. She came into the room where he was beating me and she pulled him off. Screaming. Crying. Weeping. He picked me up and threw me down the stairs. I remember the stairs. They were dark and the paint was peeling. I remember looking up at the single lightbulb swinging in the stairwell and wondering if it was a star. I needed something in my life to be beautiful. I would take anything.

The spell had been broken.

We all knew who and what he was. Then. *And yet he would come back into my room time and time and time again and beg me for my silence.*

Ssshhh. Do not speak.

The fish can hear. He was phyically imposing. Yet I had something he needed but I was never sure how to use it.

My silence.

I learned how to write it down. In *spite* of dyslexia (still with me). In *spite* of Fetal Alcohol Syndrome (still with me). In *spite* of *him* (mercifully no longer with me). Writing things down confused and threatened him. I believe my father was terrified I would write the story I am now going to tell. Now that he is no longer standing there breathing on the other side of my bedroom door. In my nightmares, he still comes for me.

Me. Surrendering power to him he does not have. The power of any corpse is only contained in how we remember.

I forgive him. I can do that now. Now that everything inside of me is dying.

Every horror perpetrated on my person was, too, perpetrated on the person of my brother. We were in this thick and horrid soup together.

There are different ways to see the same life. In this instance, my life. But my life mixed up and connected to the life of the man who is my brother. The rat snake and the worm. One: There is the lens that sees backward through the mythological past. This is the lens that *sees* the legend of the War Twins, and the fact that we are not so terribly removed from whence we came. Two: There is my life in freeform where I want the reader to know and feel what it is I know and feel. What I often feel is a great falling from the earth, a maniacal fearfulness that I am falling down, down into some great and debilitating black hole. Three: Finally, there is the road trip. My brother and I stole a car, picked up a girl, and drove the car, with the girl, to California. To find some other life only to find the mirror of the past staring us down again and again. My whole life has been one road trip after another. We were never simply migrants picking food. We were migrants seeing great and vivid dramas unfolding in front of us. I am here to tell you all these things: the mythology, the falling down, and the we-were-living-on-the-road.

The houses changed. The bedroom doors changed. The names of the rivers and the fish changed. The nature of what was silence changed. The damage was the same.

At the end of the day, we were kicked into the dirt if we had not picked enough. We were required to present Daddy with our *migrant buckets*. It is the dirt I first remember tasting as a child and you remember that first time of tasting things. Grit and mud and the leather from a boot.

Most everyone else—especially white people—referred to him as *the Cowboy*.

Hispanics called him *Patron* or *Padron*.

Mama referred to him (when he was not around, which was a lot) as *That Rodeo Son-of-a-Bitch*.

Mama was not all that different from children on the *migrant ladder of importance*, and at the end of the day she was required to present her own bucket or buckets to him, too. If he determined that she had not been working as hard as she should have been working, he would kick her into the same dirt into which he kicked us children.

When I see my mother in my mind, she is always rising painfully from the dirt. Not the dirt of some southern field where the rain keeps almost everything a little wet. When I see my mother in my mind, she is always picking herself up from the Navajo dirt, the western dirt where they grow things like potatoes. There are vast potato fields in northern Navajoland. Where the dirt is dry, and the wind sweeps it up in gusts. This is where I see my mother rising from the dirt and I always close my eyes to this and pray for her a set of wings.

The words we use to teach children *how to see* other human beings are important. Our father may not have been able to read and write *much* (or much more than we knew), but he knew how to use words as a weapon. Something he could use to wage war against us. Daddy called our mother *That Navajo Cunt*, and then he would laugh, and the men standing with him—looking at Mama trying to raise herself from the dirt—would laugh with him, albeit sometimes nervously. You never really knew where you stood with the man, and you could find yourself on your hands and knees in the dirt, with your butt and your back screaming from having been kicked. *Anyone under* Daddy's sense of self was liable to be kicked, punched, sworn at, and thrown through the wall. *Anyone above* Daddy's sense of authority could lord it over him if they wanted to, and they could reduce him to the status of a crying, snarling dog.

Dogs that have been kicked all do one thing. They bite back. The Cowboy's entire migrant camp existence was the life of a slinking, snarling, kicked-into-the-dirt migrant camp dog that would bite at anything and anyone that came too close. I will never know the answer to this, but I suspect he was abused as well. It makes me sick to think about it. I look back at my life and I shudder. It was so dysfunctional. Dysfunctional. Difficult. Detritus. Debris. Detached. Desolate. Despicable. Why would anyone with such neurological *decoupage* pick writing words as his *work*? There is something about words that is like the light at night to me. The light from passing cars. The light from bigger trucks behind you as if they might eat you up. The light from trains with all the strangers staring out. The carnival lights that lit up the county fairs and swept by you like a comet.

I want time to change. I want it to take me back. Back to the time I knew when everything could be explained by what came from and what went into the throat of the volcano. The volcano we lived on the sides of with our horses and our sheep. I want time to take me there and leave me there forever. In a place where my father would never show up to take us back.

Nevertheless, the man was a *human being*, and as such he came into the world like the rest of us, naked and with needs. We are not born into the world alone. We are born into the world dependent. All human infants have a need to be fed and a need to be held and a need to know they are safe and loved. As the human being becomes an adult, it still needs to know that it is loved, and that it can love back. It needs to touch, and it needs to be touched, too.

I am not cognizant of the developmental stages that eventually cause a man to seek not the human kinds of contact he needs to restore himself to himself, but contact with human beings over whom he has authority, who are vulnerable, and who cannot fight back. What drives a man to twisting them? I do not know how this works. I do know this: There is a murderously dark connection between the violence a man exhibits within the social context of his life, and the violence a man exhibits within the hidden moments, the still-life snapshots of ordinary couplings, the eye contact his or her eyes make to his or her children. These infinitesimal moments of light slowed down count for something, too.

We did not dare look up at Daddy. You looked down. You averted your eyes into some hidden, humble place where you fervently hoped that within the next second or two he was not going to tear into you. Some humble place not unlike that paint-peeling stairwell where the stars swung on wire. His fear and his secrets came at you like an animal with rabies finds its way out of the woods. Creatures running everywhichway in front of him attempting to avoid the unavoidable. The light in the stairwell rocking back and forth.

I kept the memories of his arrivals, his demented craving for that human touch and companionship he never had in the real world, only in the world of our warm beds, as secrets locked forever within a tomb, mine mainly, knowing in my heart that if the tomb were ever opened, if light were to ever penetrate this place, not only would my universe implode, but my chances of ever being really loved by my father would be nonexistent. I forgave him and forgave him. I created nonexistent real fathers. Men in my mind who would save us and take us in. Men who never left us for three days and came home with whores. Men who never left us locked out of the house for the night and sleeping in our jackets on the porch. Men who did not stop the truck and tell you to get out.

Just out.

I forgive him now. My grandmother would hold me up to see the rising of the sun. *Lose everything*, she said.

I see him alone. Standing in the rain at the edge of a migrant field. In the dirt. Wet. In the rain. There is no sun. Only roiling clouds of grief. He kneels and touches the dirt.

We needed someone who might save us. Someone who had both the power and the authority to defy my father. Someone with a voice so unmistakable, it could not be taken for another human being. I have known Geronimo all my life. For a small boy, he was an extraordinary gift. My mother and my grandmother were not a physical match for my father. He could beat them up and did. They found it difficult to see themselves as people who could physically protect me. But they gave me something spiritual to protect me.

He was a warrior, too. Geronimo.

"What is it you *see*," he asks. "Of the past. Of passing images from some *other* time, some *other* place?"

"I *see* us migrant boys jumping into rivers. So we could swim the day away. I see that image of us a lot. Jumping from the riverbanks. Holding your breath, and then gasping down, down, plunging into water. I would still be underwater and listening to the other boys breaking the sound barrier as their brown, migrant bodies hit the deepness of the water like a bunch of naval underwater depth charges and the whole world down there just exploded with our invasive plunging."

Geronimo's eyes roll up toward the sky. "You were always in the water if there was any around," he tells me.

I see my brother, Tso, and I picking in the fields.

The Smarter One. You are what the people call you.

I was happy to have someone else take on this name. It meant I would not be blamed for everything.

The long hot hours of our bending. The river was waiting for us in the heat, but the river had to wait. We had jobs to do. We started working in the fields soon after we had learned to walk. Our job at three was easy but not to us. We picked bugs. We went up and down the rows. Potatoes, tomatoes, it didn't matter. They all had bugs and worms. Our job was to pick the bug off the plant and put the bug or the worm into a can. Our father showed us how. We were not afraid of bugs or worms. It would have been a little self-defeating to be afraid of the things you were surrounded by.

We picked bugs and worms off plants until we were so bone-weary, we had to stop. The long brown fields of dirt stretching far away and disappearing as they do at the end of the horizon. As we grew older, we learned how to pick, not the parasites, but the things that would become food. I see Tso has filled his picking bucket, but I have not. This was usually the case.

"You talk too much," Tso would say. He shakes his dark Chiricahua-looking head.

Tso was my external friend.

Geronimo was in my head. Geronimo, the Trickster. He who dreams.

He who has taken me inside the languages of those running, sometimes turbulent streams. Of languages? More than one? Assuredly. More than two.

There is always English.

There was Spanish.

There is Athabascan. The Navajo speak one version of it. The Athabascans of Canada speak another. The Apache people speak a third. There are other Athabascan-speaking tribes, but I do not know them. The heritage of any Athabascan person is the heritage of a language-in-migration. Always moving. In many ways, it is the language of dreams. It is made of a complex poetry.

It has been suggested that as a language it made the adjustment to jumping continents and straits. It is the language of movement and adventure. As far as the Navajo are concerned, it has always been here.

It was probably Mama who introduced us to Geronimo first. Every night she told us stories. Not just stories of adventure but stories of adventure and redemption.

Geronimo has always come to me with his visions. Schemes. What is that of love? Some hand. That reaches to you from the past. Pulling you closer and closer to what the future is.

All my life pushing me and pushing me toward the people I *ought* to love. And more often than not, did. Love them.

"As well as I could," I tell him. Defending myself. I am always defending myself. To him.

"As well you should be so lucky, boy." There is a light in the eyes of Geronimo.

"You mean to have them in my life?"

"Not really. No. That is not what I mean. I mean, how lucky they didn't walk away from you, Nasdijj, when it became obvious to them it was going to be hard as hell, this loving you. Hard as hell, boy. In time, it becomes painfully obvious to anyone who knows you, that loving you, should they take that leap, is going to be . . ."

Often, when he speaks to me, he ponders. Slows. Nothing pushes him. Geronimo. I am privy to his haunted whispers. That leap from idea to idea.

"Perhaps more than they have to give. Oh, they do it. Leaping to that precipice you strut around on. As if they might save you. So pathetic. Only *you* can save *you*, and your willingness comes and goes. Your *children* who have no say-so in the thing. They are stuck with you."

If I do my standing on the precipice, he does his standing looking outward from the eons. My children. Gathering them around me is much more difficult than it would appear.

Come, children. Gather round. There is so much I want to tell them I have never told them.

It is the silence that will resound.

Death takes too many of them. My children. Off to that tomb of resurrection and defeat. How is it that if we have died, we have been defeated, too. How is it that we have come to that?

I have kept my daughter pretty much in the background. As far as any of my writing goes. She is so vulnerable.

Come, children. Gather round.

"You know, they love you. I do not know why. But they do. Your gathering of their prettiness will be something of a feat," the Chiricahua dreamer tells me.

"I thought you said—*how many times, old man*—we could do anything if we put our minds and our dreams to it?"

"So. Let me say it again. My Chiricahua whispers like the desert in your sleeping ear. *We could do anything if we put our minds and our dreams to it, boy.*"

What are his whispers to me but the wind at night as they speak of love. His wives loved him, and divorced him, and stood by him, and died for him, and bore his babies, baby-after-baby, most of whom died in childbirth. But if you made it as an Apache to the age of ten—*like he did right up to the time where his father would test him and test him and make his mettle hard for it required not-so-much-as-tenderness to be an Apache warrior back, back, back then, seeing him as I do in dreams*—chances were good you would make it, too, to adulthood.

Yes. Male children in Apache culture were tested and trained. To be a warrior of the wind was no simple thing. It took incredible endurance. Most modern human beings simply could not do it.

I can see them now, half naked, running around in their Apache villages. Being chased by grandmothers. The children. Out with you to the horses and the dogs. Wigwams everywhere on the banks of the Gila. Water going by.

In some ways, it was idyllic. The lovemaking and the courting of the girls. An Apache warrior was obligated to offer her father gifts.

Gifts that would measure not just his worthiness as a male, but also his standing with the tribe, and that would mean the accumulated wisdoms of the elders for their wisdoms would not be spared. "All of us were children once," he tells me. "To understand the man we will become it is important to remember who we were."

I was angry and hard and unyielding and lived in some black space where I spit at life. Being surrounded by the creatures of insanity as I was.

~~~~~~

Often, I wonder if my children are afraid of me. Looking up at me as they do. Trembling.

Children. Come. Gather round.

We must test our voices to the stories found. In our veins. Through time. The ones that make us laugh and the ones that only rhyme.

My children are the children of the sun and stories. I have held both—the children and the stories—close to my heart.

I asked my children to set my bed by the window so I might face the coming of the sun. I see him there. On horseback. Waving.

Outside on the old dirt road. Armed with nothing but a loincloth.

I do not think I want to see the sunset yet.

I know he would be in there as well. That sweating dripping from him. Death is like a shadow that slowly spreads itself silently into the corners and the windows of my sunset cabin.

They say he died in an army infirmary.

This is historical rhetoric. The reports of his drunkenness are lies designed to make you continue believing in an assigned recklesness that was never, ever his. No. It was *assigned* to him, but it was never him. He was not reckless to see escape in dreams. And it did keep his people hidden away from those bluecoats who would come after them for the slaughter.

There isn't a single Apache alive who believes Geronimo died in an army infirmary. In fact, *there was no army infirmary within five hundred miles of where Geronimo died.*

They make these stories up to suggest a generosity that never existed and does not exist now.

Today Fort Sill, Oklahoma, is an almost placid place. I went early in the morning to visit the small museum there.

The sergeant who had been assigned to the museum was asleep at his desk. I walked around quietly.

It was eerily silent. The place did not have another single visitor. I knew the way to the grave. And to the place where the small cabin Geronimo had lived in once stood.

Now bulldozed under.

Fort Sill is a place of bones.

We still think of Geronimo's bones as being Apache bones, and we are not entirely wrong to think that. But what an Apache is to us today is not what an Apache was back then. When Geronimo was alive, Geronimo's bones were Bedonkohe bones. The Bedonkohe were, of course, Apache, as were the Chiricahua, and the Mescalero. But Geronimo would have thought of himself as *being* a *Bedonkohe* who was *riding with* the Chiricahua long, long before he would have seen his bones as *being WITH the Chiricahua*. In Geronimo's time, people thought of themselves as being *with* their familial subtribes, and the concept *they were all Apaches* was incommensurate with how they saw themselves in relation to not just the earth, but also the beings who walked the surface of the earth *with them*. If you had asked a Navajo man at this time who he was, and where he was from, you might have been told: *He was Coyotero Nayenezgani born to the Water Flows Together People Clan for the Mexican People Clan.* You were born to a clan before you were born to a tribe. In most Athabascan-speaking tribes, both men and women (while it was unusual for a woman to ride and fight among the warriors, it was not something unknown or even looked down upon) were allowed to ride and fight with whoever moved them most. You were not required to ride with Coyotero if he did not *move* your spirit. Tribal leaders were typically elected, and while Geronimo and his bones rode with the warrior Ju and the Chiricahua, Geronimo was valued not because of his shooting skill or ability to plot, but *because of his dreams* that lent themselves to the necessary question-of-survival: *What will the Apache people do next?*

Entire clans, entire families, entire herds of livestock, herd after herd after herd of goats and sheep and horses, entire ways of life waited for Geronimo to wake himself and speak.

Where to go today?

Where to go today? No Apache worthy of the name would be caught dead pointing his finger at anything. For years, now, linguists have been told that among Athabascans *pointing* is rude. That is like saying feeding the king of Spain sheep shit for lunch isn't very nice. *Pointing* assumes an awful lot of responsibility in that *if you point to it you therefore know what it is.*

When, in fact, no one ever can. If you point to it you not only must assume you know what it *is*, but by virtue of that you better damn well know exactly what it isn't.

~~~~~~

Geronimo hated the last years of his life in prison.

He says so in his memoirs (always translated). Geronimo was constantly petitioning the government that had convicted him to set him free.

Geronimo's bones were very old. Nevertheless, they had something most men never have. One: because most men do not live that long. And two: because they had lived through more war and peace than most men see in twenty lifetimes. Geronimo's bones were the synthesis through which enormous change would pass in the twinkling of a human eye. In 1905, Geronimo was making a sling of arrows. He had found the perfect stones all around the small Oklahoma cabin that while secluded was still within the prison that contained him. *Him* and the spirit that held his bones inside his flesh. Geronimo found his perfect stones and the perfect pieces of quill and wood he would need to make his arrows, which he finely crafted in the Bedonkohe way, and sold for twenty-five cents apiece. At the same time Geronimo was crafting his "Apache" arrows, Albert Einstein, a clerk in a European patent office, was making important contributions to quantum theory in his special theory of relativity.

The old and the new would collide in a time frame that would extend itself all the way from the making of an arrow to the splitting of the atom. In 1879, the year Einstein was born, Geronimo was still being hunted down by both Mexican and American war machines.

You might think Geronimo's home would have been a place of historical interest. But all we are left with is the jail cell they say he spent time in.

I have searched the spot where the old cabin was, but you won't find any-thing there. It has all been sifted through. More chiefs of more tribes are quietly buried in the silence of Fort Sill than any other place in the continental United States. The Bedonkohe are there. The Chokonen are there. The Nedni are there. The only concrete proof of their existence is the row upon row of small white gravestones. Now made smooth by weather.

Small-arms fire can be heard in war games from across the river.

I sit among the chiefs and eat apples and tie gifts to trees. I always come here to seek my dreams. When even my dreams have left me, I come to this place to find them.

The graves in this place speak in the synthesis of embrace.

People have left many reading glasses, the kind with black, plastic frames, tied there in the tree as bundled medicine gifts for Geronimo who never was a chief. The wind makes the reading glasses in the tree tinkle like music. The red brick of the fort itself bakes, as does the military jail in which Geronimo is said to have spent a lot of time.

I go inside. The place is empty, as haunted as places come.

I walk down a flight of dark stairs (there are no lights here, but I have come with a flashlight) to the basement where I suspect the *real cells are*.

"Yes. They kept me here. Chained like an animal."

My hunch is correct. The real cells all have doors on them at least four inches thick with no windows whatsoever, and bars on the doors so the jail-ers can see in. I walk into a cell. There is a small bed here. The walking space is as big as the bed. I am unable to stand upright. The sense of con-finement is overwhelming. *I must get out.*

No one stops me.

I open the huge upstairs doors into the sun.

The *real* cells are downstairs in the pitch dark. I cannot breathe again. *Coffins.*

Geronimo, being at least a century, or close to one anyway, was thrown from his horse and found by his wife. Old. Worn out. Dying. Bones.

THAT is how warriors die, you know.

There is nothing mystical or cosmic to it. They are found by their wives. Wounded. Maimed. Broken. Bleeding. Burning up with fever. Internally injured.

They are dragged home—by their wives—and put to bed.

Where they die.

In bed.

When the battles were done, and the smoke had blown away like fog, and horses were limping about everywhere, it was the wives who descended. To find their hus-

bands and their lovers and their fathers and their brothers and to drag them back past reason, past all this the world knows well, past emptiness, and the ground is soaked in blood and hell.

I have worked with terminally ill children who have seen their own deaths quite clearly, and I have held their little hands, not knowing, really, that I believed them.

Their complacency. Their acceptance.

I believe them now. Your death just comes to you.

I want to see the sun as it begins the days. Begins the days. Yes.

The arrival of the sun. Mine comes to me about six a.m. and the dog stirs. Another sunrise. I no longer take them for granted. I value each sunrise as it comes. Held together by my bones.

I fell down the stairs and could not breathe.

The ambulance came to take me away, and my dog had to be carried into the bathroom and locked in there because in her mind *these were the men who had come to take me away.*

She was willing to die defending me. Her own life was nothing.

I had to convince them that as my service dog she not only had to come to the hospital with me, but she had to come into the hospital as well. I meant it. They relented. There she was, standing guard in our little cubicle of hospital curtains. As long as they were not hurting me (they were) she allowed them to take me away.

Slow motion: I was coming down the stairs. My office is in a loft on the second floor of the cabin. About halfway down the stairs, I am falling and falling and down and down. A tumble of bones and flesh and crutches, and a nice butt people used to look at but not anymore.

Things go.

But not my Navajo. She guards me now day and night. If I wake up and look over at her she is always wide awake and waiting for those men—she will growl them away—who might arrive in that car that screams. She will not allow it. Enough is enough.

She has allowed too much.

We share these sunrises. My window overlooks the forest and the meadow. Deer abound. They come to the window to taunt the dog and to see, too, who would sleep here like this among them.

I would. In numb thrombosis. They call it a pulmonary embolism. It is a blood clot the size of a T-bone steak, two of which reside, now, in my lungs, and one in my right leg.

The hardest thing about being on a respirator is that you cannot speak. My intensive care nurse was a drag queen. I loved her. "Sucking cock," she assured me, "helps to teach you to tolerate the tube, honey."

She called me honey, and kept me alive. It wasn't easy. Now she sits with me on her days off and insists I have to get back into life, and finish this book.

"Oh, you're okay," they tell me, "but if you feel any pain be sure to get to the hospital fast."

Any pain. Right.

I have reached that point where if I can't breathe, then I can't breathe.

I do not want to go there again. No. Please. No.

Why is it we see death itself as having disgraced ourselves? My children often arrive at night as ghosts.

Oh, they did this, they did that, they died.

I could not prevent it. Warriors all.

There is perhaps nothing more foolish in the universe than a warrior.

My two dead sons sit in the shadows of the sun.

They never speak.

Nor acknowlege one the other. I cannot go to them. I cannot do it yet. It is not time. Nevertheless, they wait.

And fear no more my words of rage.

The wars they fight I cannot wage.

Today I see a family of bald eagles. They have a huge nest way up high in one of the old oaks out by Jordan Lake. Sometimes I can't believe I live here. It can be that softly beautiful.

The mist on the lake obscures everything but sound and so the plump fish jump. With abandon. Down here in Crow Hollow. The cabin I live in was once a slave cabin. Northwest end of the lake. Not too far from the landfill that from time to time burns underground. The smoke driving everything including me away. The eagles dive-bomb for fish, and catch them, too, one after the other, feeding chicks up there. Both Mom and Dad are very busy. Before the eggs hatched, they used to sit on logs at the lakeshore and cavort in mud. Big wings like stilts. Boy eagles and girl eagles making the fiercest quacking sounds like *Craaaaack Craaaaaaack Craaaaaaack.*

The calls of childhood are demanding. *Feed me! Feed me!* And so they do. Never stopping really to do much else. Don't think for a moment the fish don't know it, too, because they do. There have been days when I have tried to catch the eagles goofing off or napping. But no. They are up long before the sun arrives. Their eyesight is that luminously spectacular.

I stand with my crutches at the edges of the lake early in the morning and try not to wonder too hard at all I have lost.

Lose everything? Wondering if he did this, too. Geronimo. The jester and the witch.

His first wife and children butchered by the soldiers where they stood.

I walk slowly, painfully back into the house.

The coons have been here, too.

They are the court jesters of the woods. They love to sit on top of my jeep and gossip about which of my neighbors has the best garbage. Doing their nails and primping. *Really, Duella, last night the Stones had the most excellent Chianti. I dashed it off with steak, and blueberry ice cream.*

This news is enough to make the other coons do backflips.

The coyotes down the hill stay in their cave with their pups mainly. They are very skittish and so afraid. The foxes are more brave. The foxes somehow (no one knows how) manage to sneak themselves up to my tin roof where they love to simply scamper around and make noise like haha. There is a grand potbellied pig that comes by and eats my acorns. Head bent, he is most intent, and simply goes about his pig business. I wonder where he lives. He has a friend. A tiny goat, which follows the pig everywhere. My children just think I should behave but it hurts to behave.

Geronimo comes. In dreams.

Hangs there. Like baggage. Dust.

Geronimo has come to rip the coming of the day with his teeth. We speak together consistently. As a child, Geronimo would rescue my little brother and myself from the talons of that great beast who was our migrant father. I am absolutely positive that the abstract *image* of Geronimo was given to me by our mother's mother who could *see* (she did not have to be there to know) what was going on.

Dreamers see.

Through the worst of it, I could sense her with me, too. She who dreams.

They found my mother frozen solid and I knew she was dreaming in there. Hard as marbles. Our father would go mad. They who dream so the People can find their way and not be destroyed. In the early creation tales of the nomadic Athabascans, these would be known as the Holy People. They who dream. I am not one of *them*.

The sun comes up. The lingering clouds drench the lake and wrap our air in a fine mist. My neighbors must be burning wood or the landfill is on fire again. The smoke snakes about the ground and slowly curves upward in gray scarves and down in the ravine the ferns are wet and glitter in the sun as her sun eyes touch them in sparkling-green illumination.

Grandmother was an elderly Athabascan-speaking Navajo although there were some in the sheep camp who intimated she had Apache blood as well. The old men almost giggle at this news. Hands cover mouths. Eyes averted. They have a hard time not smiling too hard and they share some private joke. You paid that price (or the women did) in those old days if you did not subscribe to the notions and institutions such as marriage, and she did not.

Subscribe.

Sa was just too fucking independent to marry some warrior she would be compelled to drag home and feed soup.

It was hardly unique among the Athabascans to have blood from other tribes. Sa lived among her sheep on the slopes of an extinct volcano called Ak'i Dah Nast'ani. They who dream know the volcano well. While she could not physically stand up to our father, she could imbue her two grandsons with stories and legends and myths that could sustain their inner lives. Inner lives that would be rich, indeed.

"And Geronimo got away again," she'd say on those nights we stayed with her. Beginning each new story about Geronimo with last night's "Escape Impossible." We were not the first nor will we be the last to sustain our inner lives with the image of the hero. Geronimo was that hero.

When he was alive, Geronimo (whose Indian name was Goyathlay) was a great seer who led his people through the deserts (for years of freedom from the whites whose military machine pursued them) via his dreams. Geronimo's dreams told him what to do and where to go and when to stop the tribe even as they were being chased so they might hold many of the ceremonies such as the puberty ceremony, very important to Apaches, together. Imagine stopping an entire army for a puberty ceremony.

They say, too, that some army brats, spoiled little officers-in-training, Prescott Bush among them, snuck out to Geronimo's grave to despoil it, stealing the skull, and sending it back to cohorts at the Skull and Bones Club at Yale.

Do I, someone who has studied the life of this great warrior, believe this nonsense?

Yes. I do.

Every word of it. I also believe that it was in the final analysis the Yale Skull and Bones Club (and more specifically Yale itself) that was made a fool of, for what has been stolen can, in fact, be stolen again, and look closely, lads of Yale and privilege. For the skull you hold is not the skull you think you hold. The dreamers have come and robbed you of it.

Do not drop the thing you think you hold. Beware.

During his lifetime, Indian people everywhere hung on every word spread about Geronimo, and people of every ethnic possibility lined up to touch him at such "celebrations" as the "World's Fair" in St. Louis, when Geronimo was an elderly man, and had been defeated. Yet even then, his image rejected utterly the notion of defeat for, after all, he was still alive, and so were his people. Embattled, yes. Defeated, never.

"I will go back," he said. Geronimo meant the Gila and the mountains there that had saved him so many times from being shot by whites.

The landscape of his birth.

He never made it back. But there *are rumors*. Of bones and skulls that sweep the desert wind like Crazy Horse somewhere near Little Big Horn Creek.

Beware.

You might find secrets in the places where you grieve. The secrets of yourself. You just might find Crazy Horse and Geronimo among you—inside you—even as you breathe.

Our grandmother also knew to combine the image of the hero with the image of emergence, and she told us night after night, year after year, the entire Navajo creation story, and how *we heroes, her boys* would fit into this, in much the same way any white boy raised by a television would want to be the heroes found there.

Armed thusly, we would survive.

Armed thusly, we would also learn to read and write.

What compels a man to live the "heroic" life? How do we measure the impact our *oneness*, as individual grains of sand, has upon the desert wind?

In the emergence myths of many indigenous tribes of the American Southwest, *time* breaks, allowing *the People* to emerge from their various states (insects being one, animals another) *as their warrior journeys take them from one world up to another. It is time that rips the fabric of the universe, and that allows Coyote to play his tricks upon the travelers.*

Coyote was an entity who stood between the idea of community and the idea of the cosmos. How could a culture as ancient as the Anasazi understand that time has held the fabric of the universe together, and yet "heroic time" symbolizes that which stands apart, thus allowing altogether the existence of life in the universe?

~~~~

How are we our history? Let us immerse ourselves in what is living myth. Two warrior brothers in full warpaint survive a planet that would see them dead.

We knew we were not them.

But we could play at Being Them. The power was in the play.

The legend of the War Twins is one many tribes share. Representing nothing less than hope itself, they will come (Monster Slayer and Child Born for Water), and save the People, and with their *powers* (such as the *illumination*, which I translate literally from *his lightning bolts from which he sees*), they will save the People by *illuminating* their ability to see, or, again, translated literally: *the ability of the People to translate for themselves the symbols that surround them, put there by the light and dark forces of the universe.*

I walked all around the volcano on and off one entire year, interviewing old people about how they *saw* the creation story. And then I wrote it down. Not having the slightest idea what I would do with it, which is why the Navajo would even speak to me. My interpretation of this ancient text is that "to live the heroic life, one must teach the People how to read."

Reading the weather is one way to read. Reading the behavior of animals is another.

Reading rocks.

This is my interpretation of the Athabascan concept: *hodeeshzhiizhgoo naas.*

Meaning: *illumination in the course of time.* Will be *seen* as the ability to read and write. "Reading and writing" not necessarily meaning an understanding of a written text, *but an understanding of symbolized abstractions.* Time itself will break the fabric again, allowing the people to transform themselves from preliterate cultures to literate ones. Or presented in a more contemporary "light," T-I-M-E itself will break the fabric of emergence again and again in the form of brotherhoods or sisterhoods or alliances where within the context of the alliance, one brother (Monster Slayer) symbolizes sacrifice where the other brother (Child Born for Water) symbolizes the environmentally fundamental, or chemically elemental, sets of conditions (positively charged particles at high speeds coming into contact with negatively charged particles) necessary for change to occur.

And not just for change to occur. For the sake of change to occur. But for the making of new elements. For the Navajo, the following is elemental:

Johonaa'ei is the sun and the father of the War Twins. As such, he is not just light, but he is all elements from which he can choose to take apart or put together. Johonaa'ei is the Big Bang who gave elements to his "suns." With the concept of Navajo creationism, Johonaa'ei is a complex god, and not necessarily benevolent.

The People were always curious. Always in movement and never static. As their lives were lived out-of-doors, they were much more cognizant of the horizon than is modern man who lives within walls. It is not an accident that modern man adorns many of his walls with representations of the sun.

Of the People it is also said that they circled up toward the top of the mountain until they reached the smooth, hard shell of the sky overhead. When they could go no higher they looked down and saw that water now covered everything. They had nowhere to land either above or below. Suddenly, someone with a blue head appeared and called to them: "Here! Come this way! Here to the east there is a hole!"

They found that hole and entered. One by one they filed through to the other side of the sky. And that is how they reached the surface of the Second World.

How do I explain my migrant past to my own children? A creation story of endings and beginnings—a conversation with Grandmother Sa—where time as a circular phenomenon swallows the mythic tail of the not-so-mythic snake. *Snap!* It is the past that *is* Geronimo's bones. It is *the now* that pulls us through the soft mystery of moans.

The migrant nomad seeks the stability of homes. Built in places considered *inhospitable*.

We never had one that lasted for more than a few months—a few lasted less than a minute—we just kept going and how many times did my brother and I just stand there in awe of the children who were home and delirious like yellow candles in their windows, and snugly tucked into beds by parents who loved them.

For us, everything was ephemeral. We lived under a bridge with our father who had lost his mind and the trucks went by so fast and the fumes were gray and we would wipe the snot from our noses on our coatsleeves and sit on the concrete and put our heads down, down, down into our hands.

It was Geronimo who came to me in voices.

Great curtains of mud-hole water would come screaming down on us, and I was no longer able to tell the shivering from the craziness. Perhaps it was coming from us in horizontal rushes as the big interstate rigs plowed a bitter agony in the terror of the grinding night.

We see!

We see!

Migrants. Apples. Picking pieces of the sky. I pick stories. The dirt knows why.

3

〜〜〜〜

I Am in Blood

Changing Woman would call her sister White Shell Woman.
   White Shell Woman who could hear.
   Her ears knew all the sounds a universe might make.
   "What is it that you hear now, dear sister," Changing Woman asked. She was
fat with twins. They were not of Coyote's making, but he would pretend they were.
   White Shell Woman looked all around the universe. Her face grew pale.
   "Monsters," she said. She could hear the coming of the monsters.

I am in blood.
   I am my father's murderous image. *Hang him.*
   Hang his indifference. Hang his fists. Hang his lies. Hang him.
   To stop. My dreams. From leaking. I had a little brother, too.
   Tso, oh, little somersault-of-warriorness, always looking up to me.
What are our responsibilities to our brothers? Mine is to his heart. I had
seen exactly one movie where the cavalry had wiped out the Indians. Some
male movie star hero like Cornell Wilde or Robert Taylor (blue hair, both,
perhaps it was the film) was dressed in fringed deerskin and he had a magnificent black bullwhip that could make everyone do what the hero wanted.
Forget the cowboys and the Indians. We wanted the whip.

This was in Traverse City, Michigan, and we were there to pick black cherries with the Chippewa. The smell of cherry trees mixes with the grass. Picking cherries with the Chippewa was something we did every year. The lake. The beach. The sand. The huge, sweeping Ojibwe dunes. Always and always, the wind. Oh, Grandfather. This was the closest we ever came to anything like a vacation. The term *vacation* and the term *migrant worker* definitely do *not* go together. But the Chippewa as the People of the Big Woods did. They would laugh and push and fool around in all the cherry trees. The connection to the Chippewa was one of lake as blue as the turquoise we wore. And sand as soft as the desert sand we flew over with our feet and moccasins. And fish! The coho salmon of the Big Blue Lake. You filled your lungs and spread your arms and sailed like wind upon your skin.

The Salvation Army of Indian migrants mingled with the Latinos and the celery-pickers from as far south as Kalamazoo. The cherry crop was regular, dependable, and the money was decent as decent goes for migrant workers. We could (and did) eat all we wanted. The results of which made for late-night treks to outhouses in places like Torch Lake and Kewadin where Tso would cry because he did not want to wade out into that strange night on strange paths with strange snakes. The woods. I would hold his small and warmer hand and we would find our way. The Chippewa we shared the migrant housing with would chuckle and wave their noses at us: *Do not eat the fruit, you hungry boys!*

There was a brick alley at the side of the Michigan Theater downtown, Traverse City. I do not remember what my brother and I were doing messing around downtown Traverse City in the middle of the afternoon on a Saturday. Although Mama loved to shop the Woolworth's there. I saw her once pop a small lipstick into her purse. She saw that I had seen this. I knew her heart sank some. Like a pebble that causes other waves to form those circles of echo and perfection that have lives of their own. We pretended it never happened. What would have been the point? *That all your spook is, honey, stealing lipstick like loneliness?*

There was a rock that sat in the bottom of our bellies knowing we were the thieves.

It wasn't too hard to give her the slip, but there would be hell to pay. Hell-to-pay was a pretense, too. It came with the territory. She did figure into all her social calculations what she called: *the damn Picture Show.*

She gave us a couple of hours anyway. To hang ourselves. *That all your spook is, honey, just stealing time like it was one of those pretty pictures they printed in the Bible, but you didn't want the Bible. You only wanted the picture and so you ripped it out.*

"I KNEW you boys would sneak in there!"

Eyes to the ground. We were sorry, Mama.

Like shit we were. She would sigh like the cynic, Diogenes. *"Nasdijj, you will try the soul of reason, boy."*

Yes, Mama.

I have often wondered if Mama meant I would try the soul of treason. Her English sometimes slipped like those bras she always wore. Women wore bras in the nineteen fifties. Mama's came with straps, and like Mama, they were always falling. She'd reach around and pull the strap up, but in a nice way.

That all your spook is, honey, hours and hours scrunched down at the picture show?

We had figured with our evil, criminal boy-minds that when the folks who were coming out of one picture show opened that alley door, with the Coke sign on it, and the picture of Maureen O'Hara, we could slip in soundless as a shadow. Piece of cake. Slink down some in the seats. Pretending to be a Saturday-afternoon set of brothers behaving themselves in the coolness of the air-conditioned theater.

There was work to do. There was a whole floor to investigate for pennies, dimes, nickels. No one *ever* lost a quarter. There was candy to confiscate. Milk Duds we had to find. Truth was, we'd scrape up the floor for popcorn, too. Like voracious vacuum cleaners, a vast sucking sound could be heard. We were children, and even if so much of our lives was lived in desperation, we liked our lives. There had to be something good inside of us and we believed that, and hung on to it, even. Even if we did not know what it was, and maybe we would never know what it was, but it had to be like the light.

Even in the darkest bowels of the night in that jail they built for Geronimo—I was there, I saw it—there was a light that snuck in through the bottom of the door. Like stars. There will always be men and some women, too, with mainly darkness in them. But that wasn't us no matter how many times we might sneak into a picture show.

Them movie star white folks in the movie could hide inside their moving stagecoach, and shoot up the picture show Indians one-pop-at-a-time. Arrows sticking to the stagecoach like it was a runaway porcupine.

Ava Gardner in *Ride, Vaquero!* She talked to us. Us not-entirely-white boys, and we wondered, too, at how dark she was.

The white "ladies," crack shots all, wearing hats worthy of a Parisian designer, Yves St. Laurent, never moving a single hair out of place. Everyone on the stagecoach seemed to be newly arrived in the West. In search of riches. Never grace.

A few people had it anyway. We just figured that was why they were movie stars. Like Ava Gardner when she would free all of Texas.

We knew Texas. We had picked cotton there. It went on and on.

We knew Indian women who would have turned these couture females into so much steak tartare, too.

We knew Chippewa women who hated the French priests.

We knew Apache women who hated the Spanish priests.

We knew Navajo women who hated the Anglo priests.

The word has spilled more blood than can be mopped up by women on their indigenous knees.

We knew migrant ladies who would have stolen all the white women's jewelery and pawned it by the time the stage rolled into downtown Denver. The bloodthirsty Hollywood Indians are on the top of the stagecoach. Climbing in.

It is a wonder the Indians lost. Nevertheless, the Indians were obviously brave.

Too bad the Chippewa led them west.

The Sioux in front of them.

To take on a portentous enemy such as Debbie Reynolds. Her rifle was entirely fake. Like us, they were the outlaws. My brother and I were always the outlaws. My mother pulled her hair out we had seen that movie. *Ride, Vaquero!* And the one with the whip. She prayed and chanted to her gods for days. In Navajo, we call this *singing*.

"But, Mama, Geronimo will save us!" From adversity. Adversity was real. And so was hunger. And so was tuberculosis. And so was alcoholism, which was probably on a par with smallpox. It was smallpox that got the Chippewa. Not war. Had the Europeans and the sacks of priests been limited to their conquests on the merits of the wars they waged, we would all be living in tepees by now. A tepee being a house of some not-too-small sense of harmony. No. They needed disease. And so was the extraordinary sense of loss our father lived with in his inability to support us very well and sometimes not at all. More and more. Not at all. More and more. Down the beer drain. We would find them passed out in the truck cab and covered in each other's vomit.

We blame him—not her—not because it's right, or because it's wrong, or because of any moral imperative whatsoever. We blame him—and not her—because we know like that rock that sits solid in the bottom of our bowels that were we to blame her, it would rip whatever we have of ourselves to shreds, it would. And we would be destroyed. No. We blame him. So we might endure.

My mother, Shima, could not save herself. She could not bridge the gap between her connection to the earth, and her marriage to the black storm that was the wind that swept through my spine anyway like encephalitis. I could not save her. I could pull the hose out in the morning and wake her up with water as she frequently passed out from drinking where she stood. I knew we needed food. My brother would be back in the house crying.

Because he was hungry.

And the hose and the water was the only way I knew to wake her. And feed us, please.

We would try to feed ourselves from the water in the hose but all it ever did was blunt whatever pain was coming. The pain would come, and even hunger made your bowels move like water, and that is how children at those edges hanging on with their fingernails die of dehydration.

Lose everything. It all just comes spilling out.

That all your spook is, honey, hunger spasms?

Her bed the ground. Her struggle to provide us with a good and steady life just slipped from her not unlike the way in which it was slipping from our father, too. Sanity as slippery as a fish. They would work hard together, and harder, and impossibly hard in the fields and the rows, saying not a word between them, but picking and hoeing and getting by and dripping sweat and muscle in the sun.

I sleep now in my bed that faces the window and I can see them through the shadows as the sun does its dying time. Soaking through bandannas. Their vision all but floundering before them. Their eyes melting into rivulets of pupils. Drinking all their pain away at night. They just went dead inside. How to live beyond despair and still live. Do not kid yourself. It doesn't happen. Once you die inside, you are the dead.

We boys had found our new *God*. Geronimo was full of spit, git, and fun. Mama was, however, not buying it this week. The cinematic versions of porous history took a backseat when it came to the portmanteau of histori-cal analysis to which our mother subscribed. Leastways, cinema was a struggle. Mama found it immensely entertaining. But just plain wrong. She would crackle with the joy of it. And clap in lieu of popcorn (who needs popcorn, watch the movie). But she was smart enough to know when she was being bamboozled, as her entire cosmic existence depended upon the legends and mythologies she had set up to revel in as a portfolio of richly-imbued-imagination that could and did coexist side by side an eight-by-ten signed black-and-white glossy of Cornell Wilde that Shima, our mother, and Sa, her mother, had sent away for in a moment of what Sa called "sheer Francis Albert Sinatra madness."

The women cackled.

Sa's understanding of history as an oral powerhouse was breathtaking. But Sa came from a world where history was sung.

Word for word, and remembered.

Francis Albert read his music. The world was a complex place and growing more so. Mama and Grandmother confronted it with the humor that marked their people who walked the surface of the earth.

There was "the movie" Geronimo. And Mama wanted so much to enjoy him. Like the Robert Taylor Geronimo. But the "real" Geronimo was a much more serious affair. And she could, if she tried, separate them, and keep them separate. The real posse from the pretend posse.

Bang, you're dead, Nasdijj!

Am not! Am not!

Run. Wherever we went as migrants, there would be the local boys. Run, Nasdijj. The common static, and the local noise.

Bullets and arrows are zipping past my head. I can feel the small wake of air as the bullet passes inches from my ears.

You're dead! You're dead! Am not. Am not.

Quick, draw a cordon round. To my forts. My hermitage. My rabbit holes of necessity, and the banishment of the down and down. To my hideouts. To my secret arroyos. To my dark and river caves. To my hiding-in-my-hiding wilderness where I was free to scream and rave. I would dive down and down and down into these places of the dreams.

Into myself. You sure as hell hoped it (you) would not be completely empty when your bones like stones hit bottom. When all was silent but the wind.

Scream. Scream.

Sometimes the marginal people said the screaming scared them. I would do my best to stop. Stop, Nasdijj, please, please, stop.

Let *them*—the other migrant riffraff—enforce the army rules. Let the other little boys decide who's in. Who's out. I'm the renegade. The pariah of the fools. Bullets do not touch me. My magic ribbon shirts. Arrows cannot pierce my sacred flesh. I am impervious to death.

I spent hours in the woods screaming.

It wasn't normal.

I heard voices. I talked to Geronimo. I was not a *normal* kid.

Teachers would look at me in horror like: Not in my class, he isn't.

I smelled. I had worms. Lice. My clothes were rags, and my hair was something people wanted to set a match to just to see the explosion.

On my way back to the migrant camp from school once—I did not often go to school as I was apt to work in the fields as we really did need the money—I had to sit down on the curb, and put my hands over my ears to make the voices go away. The voices were a plague of sheer and utter misery. He was always around. At the darker corners of my vision where the shadows danced. Geronimo laughing.

Geronimo will save us, please! I knew he would. He would. He had to. It was what heroes did. They saved you. I was drowning. *We're hanging the Indians in Dodge!*

When the movie was over, it was back to scarfing up the floor again for trinkets. Gum. Yaaa. We were the kind of scumbag boys who became joyous over the discovery of gum under the seats. It was a wonder some microbe did not do us in right there in the theater.

Catch me, catch me. One, two, three.

You better run fast this time, Nasdijj.

It terrified me that the bigger boys who were often out for my ass—as I did not play subservient to their posturing too well—would find out I heard voices.

It's like having a tongue so large it drags itself around on the ground and everyone can see you as another freak at the freak show.

~~~~~~

4

The Freak Show Was a
Serious Business to Me

Changing Woman gave birth to twins. Monster Slayer and Child Born for Water.

In two days, the boys were able to run and shoot arrows.

In three days, they had many questions they would put to their mother and their aunt who was White Shell Woman.

This amused Coyote greatly—he would hide and hang out by the windows of the hogan the women had built. So he might hear everything.

White Shell Woman heard the monsters first. They would be the Naayee and Coyote would run and hide. It was Changing Woman who would know what to do with the boys and where to hide them, but they must learn to be very quiet.

Their mother told them ssshhh . . .

She would put them in with the brooms.

They were suddenly plunged into a darkness they did not know.

A falling down as if into a great volcano. Plunging and tumbling.

Even as they fell, in the distance they could see what appeared to be a great underground kiva. Spider tracks led there and smoke curled up from the ground.

The *freak show* was a serious business to me. I could not let the other children know I heard voices. I could not let teachers know I heard voices. The Chippewa taught me how to speak to white men.

In French. They will not know it well and this will shame them.

Some. Then you just walk away. I got it.

Un averti en vaut deux. A person warned is equal to two; forewarned is forearmed. I carefully planned my hiding places so I was never more than a minute from one. Time flies through the world. *That all your spook is, honey, that ticking you hear?*

Vis à fronte.

Force from in front.

My craziness and my dirt and my mean strength and my fears and my voices all combined now like they had never combined before to make something that could both write and run and run and write.

I would run to my hiding places. I would write once I could get there. It was the *getting there* that seemed to be always so horrendously impossible. My father and his grabbing hands would be right behind me.

Local farm boys do not like being called white boys and they will call you one, too, in about thirty seconds.

White boys! White boys! One, two, three!

I taunted the other migrant boys, too. They could not catch me.

Blood in my lungs. Run, you worm. Run. My muscled legs pounding through the forest paths hard. Pounding through the Midwest farm-paths hard. Stopping suddenly to see the sunset. Set. Pounding through the tractor trails hard. Pounding through the high-desert mesa paths hard. Pounding the paths wherever we lived. The Mojave Desert. The cornfields of Nebraska. *That all your spook is, honey, I lived every fucking where?* Hard as hard could go. I was on fire and with wings and harder than Geronimo. Before you hang me, you dim-witted little fucks, first you have *got* to find me.

I am breathing hard up here in the tallest tree in the migrant camp. My skills at knowing how and where to build my fortresses were unmatched by any kid. Mama knew. She would watch me build them. She knew I built them to keep whatever sanity I had. My tree fort is my castle.

There is always a pecking order among the boys.

The boys who had been in the migrant camp the longest had the best assign-ments such as where you played games, who got to use the one rowboat down at the lake, who got to use the basketball hoop (no net, just a rim) at the basketball court (parking lot). It went on and on.

Then, there were the local boys who tended to see us comers-and-goers as their personal slaves (hey, spicboy, I want my truck washed, you wanna quarter?).

We all wanted the quarters. Every group and subgroup strove for superiority. It did not matter if you lived there or if you came from just be-yond the horizon.

If pushed, I had an attitude.

You wanna hang me, you local farm boy motherfuckers(!), then you gotta go for it, and none of you emaciated scroungy migrant crows look up to the job. Hang me? It will never happen. Geronimo will come, and he will beat the bloody shit from your crumb-cake mouths.

I was maybe all of six.

They all had houses and homes and moms and dads and food and I hated them. Guns and swords and bows-of-woe. I am from the land of blood and lava flow.

I knew we were different. I knew I had to find the things my brother and I had that those other kids could not come close to. Okay, so you have a car and a house and a mom and a dad who has a real job but we have the wind and we have heard the fires crack at the black hag of midnight. We have seen the gods themselves descend from the top of the mountain at night to reveal themselves to us (in their magic masks) in illumination as powerful, and what suburban boy on his baseball team could say as much? My grandmother had shown me the dried blood from giants and how it flowed down as lava from the mountain we knew as Tsoodzil. Our gods had blood and bones and you could reach out and touch them they were so real. They were no Sunday-morning ritual in a suit and tie and shiny shoes. We did not always have shoes. Our secrets were as tongue-tied as they were inviolate. From the power of our secrets, we knew, too, something of the power of silence. There were times when I understood at some deeper level than the guts of any boy, that holding forth your tongue and going into the solitude was a far, far better thing, now, than shutting down. Solitude was visitation, and as such, you came out of it, not only intact, but often rested. Solitude was refreshing where the process of shutting down was a deep and dangerously desolate landscape. Too abandoned to be let in. Too provoked upon the wind of change. No. I could go into some safe place of hiding where I never spoke to anyone. Better that than to confront the piece-by-piece of the shutting downs. The breathless agony of the drowning marks and the running with the hounds. There was a world of difference. Our hiding places, too, that my little brother (when he was finally big enough and o-u-t of diapers) and I built every time we moved to a new spot upon the earth, were places we would treat as sacrosanct, inviolable. We knew from the wisdom passed on down to us by our grandmother, Sa, and our grandfather, Nilch'i, that a place was often a thing of landscape as you had made it.

Dook'o'ooshif was a mountain fastened with a sunbeam. This mountain was covered with a yellow cloud. It was decorated with black clouds and male rain.

〰〰〰〰

We were living in an Airstream trailer at the Louisiana rodeo. It was a job as much as it was a way of life. We played war with the other boys in swamps.

I could see them in the swamps. They had come to the swamps seeking refuge. The Vanished Ones. The *Desconocidos*. The unknown dead. Light everywhere between the drops.

We all had sticks and we ate frog's legs. All the other cowboy Airstreams, and the trailers of the folks connected to the traveling, nomadic rodeo, were lined up in row upon row—divided by thin oyster-shell roads—on the blackrich alluvial-plains-of-grass that made for a vast Louisiana parking lot (where submergence was often little more than optical illusion, especially when it rained) of eighteen-wheelers, engines on and hot, cotton candy machines, hot-dog caravans with the ready-to-eat East Texas hot dogs dripping in mustard rotating on a rotating machine that made *stra-a-a-nge-sounding* machine-noises like a corpse is having problems snoring: upupupupupuUUUUpppp, and pickups weighed down with bales of hay for animals.

Come seeeeee thenakedwomanwithfivebreastsonherbellydancingonatabletopwith-theheadlessman. Step right up. Come seeeeee theseveredheadofAdolfHitlerinajar.

It was not a carnival but it was.

When there is a Ferris wheel, it is a carnival. Zuni to Nashville.

It's a carnival.

We were not supposed to go anywhere near the rides.

Can you imagine telling two dusty ragamuffins they are not to go anywhere near the rides?

We shook our heads in submissive agreement. Our eyes wandering.

Most people came to see someone truly mad—like my dad—ride a Brahman bull for maybe all of ten seconds before wise-old Zeeboo Boozer knocked his cowboy ass into Chinese noodles—all the way to Shanghai. *Who* would *ride* a Brahman bull? Nobody. Nobody sane. My brother and I would go to the rodeo show and cheer for old Zeeboo. The carnival could pack them in. But so could the livestock, and the real rodeo events.

Our daddy was a bullrider. Hadn't had a complete thought since the hogs ate Grandma. He rode Brahman bulls, but he also wrestled several tons of bellowing cow meat down to the ground. Those cute little baby cows only look cute. They were usually mad as hot spit about it. Being hog-tied. You hoped to God no animal hooves would find their way to your face or your head but they always did. My dad's face looked like the fine topography of an asteroid. It was badly scarred and made him appear to be the bad guy in a John Wayne movie. Our bad-guy dad (even the bad bad-guy kids would take one look at our dad and run) was with the Clancys who were buying up the town and throwing the women and the children into the streets, where they would ravage them. The arrival of John Wayne was a given. Our dad would be the guy with the knife in his teeth at the poker table in the saloon where all the saloon hall girls cowered in fear.

And sat on his lap.

Their arms around him.

And staring at his cards.

Old John would surely shoot that fuck and the sheriff would come limping across the mud.

Movies were horseshit mainly.

As someone who had always been around animals, I did not feel compelled to *love* every animal that walked out the barn door. I liked most of them. I was not *afraid* of animals (I was up to my neck in them at my grandmother's), and this endeared me to the rodeo veterinarians. I would assist them and I was free.

"Here, boy, hold my bag. Walk with me."

How hard could those directions be? I was the boy who got to hold the veterinarian's black bag. It was a big deal among the boys.

When the bulls were angry, all the wailing places would descend within these worn barn walls. But when the bulls were sad—their purpose for existing can be found in their sperm—every cow in the meadows and the arroyos made them wait to take their turn. I lived in a world only I knew about.

In the barns with the animals unless Daddy found me, and he would pick me up and sling my carcass across his broad shoulders and take me home.

At least we had one.

For however long it lasted. Not that long.

Our Airstream was a shiny aluminum bubble called a Bambee. It slept four if everyone turned in the right direction at the same time. We parked on one side of the rodeo arena. The animals were quartered in a long row of temporary stalls for the horses. Or horses could be quartered in horse trailers parked behind the long row of stalls that were used, too, for livestock during carnivals, and 4-H competitions. We liked this rodeo living far, far more than we had ever liked living in a migrant camp. Not knowing or understanding that it never paid its way nor could it because quite simply it allowed my father such close proximity to gambling his future (and ours) away in spit.

Having grown up, and having lived as migrants literally in barns, neon motels, migrant camps, flophouses, Quonset huts, and bunkhouses inhabited by cowboys and hookers, all our lives, my brother and I knew more about the handling and the ailments of livestock and Brahma bulls (overweight killing machines built more like a Sherman tank than an animal) than your typical local lint-head college-graduate veterinarian.

Any boy invested with the sacred carrying of the vet's black bag had to know certain things. Like how cows gave birth.

The *young* college-grad lint-head veterinarians who knew mainly some book-learned folderol had no idea how to stick your hand in there all the way up to your shoulder blade, and gently pull the calf *o-u-t of the mother and i-n-t-o the world.*

I am in blood.

Daddy knew everything there was to know about the life and death cycles of the animals. But he was losing his grip on it. I keep searching for a time when I loved my father. I do think it did exist. Once. I remember sitting on his lap and he liked that and I liked that, too, but not the way he did.

Daddy would set me up on a wooden chest that held his saddle and things (it smelled nice like leather in there) and he would take my clothes off and kiss me everywhere. I did not know what to think of it. It confused me. I never came in his mouth like he did in mine, but when he sucked me, now, I knew enough to hold him behind his head. He would get angry when I could not find it to be erect. My holding his head meant I could control him some, and I would take any symbolism I could get, and would have *gotten* hard if I could have, which I could not.

Once, Daddy walked home with us through the carnival section of what was supposed to be "the rodeo." Daddy liked the rodeo part of it and detested the carnival part of it. *Come seeeeee thetwoheadedwartbabyfeeditselfwithspoons and step right up . . .*

We got to where the carny guy with the rifles tried working his oily self on the wrong man. You were supposed to take the (slightly twisted) rifle the carny man gave you and try your luck at shooting moving ducks in a row.

Daddy paid the guy whose wavy hair was blue as axle grease a dollar, and took the rifle, and examined it. He then handed the rifle to me. Daddy stood behind me with his .45 Smith & Wesson, his cowboy gun, and every time I pinged the back of the duck pond with that so-called rifle that would not allow Annie Oakley to hit a barn door, Daddy (directly behind my left shoulder) shot the duck to broken smithereens. Duck woodchips flying everywhere. The carny guy ate dirt.

I was a kid and did not understand that what Daddy was shooting was the romantic cheapening of the cowboy.

Daddy *was* a cowboy, a real one, and it was becoming harder and harder to make anything of a living at it. Our mother had only just died, and Daddy was still in some kind of perpetual alcoholic stupor over it. His sweat was sweet like bourbon.

I remember, too, that when he came in my mouth, the sweetness of his cum was one of the only ways I could deal with swallowing that stuff and you best swallow every drop because the gun that was dropping carny ducks would be pointed at the side of your head and when he ejaculated it pressed so hard into your head, it hurt.

At the sound of that gun, the carny came to a grinding, slow-motion stop, and everyone with cotton candy on their lips was staring at the man who had dropped those ducks dead as pieces of plywood, which is what they were.

A deal is a deal.

I was elated to bring home a huge teddy bear.

My brother laughed and we played with the teddy bear.

One of Daddy's whores, a nice woman by the name of Dorthea, was staying with us then. What those whores saw in Daddy and his Bambee Airstream with his two little boys is something I will never fathom. Dorthea was the Big Tent Woman With the Pussy That Went on Backwards and Ate Corn on the Cob. Apparently, it was not Corn on the Cob Night in the Big Tent. She had been playing cards with my little brother, Tso, and she was quite solemn when we got to the Bambee.

"You know they will come, Cowboy."

They did come. They took him away for three or four days.

Dorthea took us to see him at the jail.

We liked the idea of talking on the telephone to someone you could see through the window.

He was in a mood when he got out of jail, and shot the teddy bear.

They did not come for him this time.

~~~~~

Daddy taught us everything he knew about animals, and it was a considerable dark and bloody ground. Daddy knew, too, he was losing it, bit by bit. He was always looking over his shoulder, now, looking for the bone man. The bone man sneaks into your home. Hides in your closet. And watches you dress yourself in life. It didn't take the bone man to fathom Daddy had lost his ability to *see*.

The birthing of a race colt (where everyone we knew had a share, including our share of two hairs on the tail) was worthy of a Shivaree. A Louisiana down-home-front-porch carnival (our front porch consisted of a picnic table but we liked it) and all the boiled crawdaddies you could eat, and all the Texas Red Star beer you could drink. Drinkin' mash, and talking trash. We loved a Shiveree. In those days you needed a church key to open a beer can and we could open a hundred beer cans each at a Shiveree. Big men would scoop us up and sit us on ponies. Daddy needed us to know as much about animals as he could teach us because Daddy himself was like a limestone statue in a suckswamp. Sinking slowly to the bottom.

It was becoming harder and harder for him to even keep a job because he kept screwing things up like confusing atropine for insulin. I may have been all of eight years old, but I could *read* (Daddy lied and *claimed* he could read, but what Daddy did was called *winging it*), and I knew the difference between *atropine* and *insulin*, and I could give subcutaneous vaccinations. A veterinarian in Pecos, New Mexico, had taught me how to give shots to dogs (mine died anyway after a rabid coyote had lit into him), and I was always at least attempting to piece together and learn as much about the universe of animals as I could.

It was not uncommon in those days for people who lived in "The Remote" to handle their own large-animal veterinarian chores. I was only a little bit past the feed them and water them (the animals) stage. I was a very small potato at a very big fish fry. I figured I would be a vet when I grew up. I had assisted a local vet who used to travel up and down to all the migrant camps and reservations performing neutering and spays. We turned an old teacher's desk into Surgery #1, and we were set to go.

When it rains in Louisiana, it rains bullfrogs, and the entire parking lot of Airstreams, and cowboys, and oyster shells, and Harley-Davidsons, and poker games, and kids, got turned into a sea of Louisiana mud.

A little rain did not deter us. There was no way my brother and I were going to stay cooped up in that Airstream with six men, two hookers, and a poker game. Just hook us up to a nicotine drip. My mama would have taken her broom and whoomped them suck-egg cowboys bald-headed. Them whores, the door.

With Mama dead, there was no one around mainly to tend to two very rambunctious boys in their new and sassy cowboy boots. My little brother and I were as happy as two chuckheaded catfish all fired up and full of ten-gallon-git. Our hats were ten-gallon-Stetsons. I got the white Stetson because I was a white boy, and my little brother, Tso, got the black Stetson because (it was said) he was an Indian.

Navajo are born *to* their mother's clan *for* their father's clan.

Since our daddy did not have a clan, we were outcast bastards. Mama was born to the Water Flowing People Clan *for* Salt *(Ashiihi)*. Tso and I did not then, and we do not now, look anything alike.

How I could be a white boy, and my brother an Indian, was not a problematic configuration when you are seven. Eight. Nine. Ten.

You can shrug it off. When you are nineteen, however, the configurations change.

When we were around nineteen, my brother and I drove over a Texas bridge into Mexico to visit with a great discovery we had made.

Our father's *other* family.

That he would have one in Mexico did not surprise us.

We were taking our time with the introductions. And reeling just a bit. There were so many new faces (that looked just like us) to account for. Names to learn. I needed air.

These were nice people. They were kind and generous, Daddy. Why couldn't we have known about them? Why? Why? Why? Maybe they could have helped keep at least some of the loneliness a-w-a-y. I do not understand.

Why did they have to turn out to be so nice?

Why couldn't they have been monsters, Daddy?

Like you.

Outside on the porch was an older man (when you're nineteen, an older man can be forty) who looked an awful lot like my brother.

We shook hands. It was the feeling of the hand. I knew I had met this man before in another life.

My Spanish sucked then, and it sucks today. Fortunately, Ernesto spoke English, and rather well.

"You don't remember, do you?" he said.

Remember what?

"Fishing for catfish at night in Louisiana."

It came flooding back like night air as the Whisky Chitto overflows in spring not far from De Ridder, Louisiana. It was the middle of the week and no rodeo. There was the poke boat. The flashlights. The cane poles. The chicken heads for bait. The gators in the water roaring. That black, black water shine reflecting swamps and moons. The catfish as big as my brother—maybe thirty pounds.

We were there the night.

Morning broke as the tropical sun licked the swamps in red.

Our small poke boat was filled with fish.

Ernesto had been a rodeo clown, and we were quite taken with him. He was a friend of our father, which could be both good and bad. We were wary. We did not want to be caught out in some Louisiana swamp in the dead of night with a raving drunk in the boat. Been there. Done that. There was no way that was going to happen. If it had been Daddy, we would have quietly poured the whiskey out into the lake and accepted the consequences. We loved to fish but not to the extent that we wanted to be eaten by gators in Riverhappy, Gumbotown.

To this very day Tso and I are on the alert for alcoholism.

We sort of feel as if we have done our part. Got the watch. Gave the speech. Gone fishing. We are suspicious of alcoholics. It is a horrible disease. We are prone to it, and we know that. In our late-to-arrive adulthood, we are not drinking. We cannot afford it. From time to time we fall off the wagon. With a drink. Or a beer. But nothing more than that so there's really no good reason to beat ourselves up too badly for having committed a crime. We know where we stand. Like the man said: It is a day-to-day proposition.

Ernesto was not Daddy. He was a rodeo clown. He was fun. His Bambee was always neat, and picked up. It was maybe six steps from our Airstream. He went way out of his way to do things with us. Two little boys he barely knew parked next door at the rodeo trailer park. His alliance with our father went so far, and we liked that. "Your daddy," Ernesto claimed, "sometimes ain't got enough sense to flag a freight train."

We laughed. We knew that, too. It was a reality you articulated at your peril.

As a rodeo clown, Ernesto had to know his trade, and better than fully half the cowboys who arrived full of gloat. A Brahma bull will deflate you shortly. I was sitting in the stern of the poke boat. The Whisky Chitto River ran slow and as deep-black in this sad slave-swamp as it ever did.

"I knew your mama," Ernesto said.

"She died." I was eight. It choked me some.

"I heard that, too. I heard it when I was in Arkansas." Ernesto threw his bait back into the water.

"We were in Arkansas," I said.

Not really sure where the hell we were half the time.

"No, boy. You were in Texas. I hear you lie like a sieve about your age, too."

I did not lie about not really knowing what state I was in when something happened. I thought it was all more or less the *world* if you asked me.

I understood the states were different. But the *migrant camps* were the same. As far as my age was concerned, it wasn't that I was consciously not telling the truth, I simply did not always know how old I was. It wasn't like we exactly celebrated birthdays with cake and candles. By eight in the evening, Daddy was usually three sheets to the wind.

"Were you a rodeo clown in Arkansas?"

"I reckon, I was."

"Mama died, then we were hungry. I think we were in Texas."

"You were in Texas."

"They had ladies who danced there and they swirled all around and their dresses went out like the wings on wind."

That was about what I knew of Texas.

We were all of nineteen, now, and men.

Now, I remember Ernesto.

"You took us fishing?"

"If I remember correctly, Poco, you filled the boat up with catfish. We took it home and had ourselves a . . ."

"Shiveree," I said.

He laughed. "A Shiveree."

"You don't want to know who I am, do you?" he said. His smile was warm and genuine. *Let it lie, Nasdijj.*

They are only bones, boy.

Mexican lowriders—homeboys—went riding by the house. Ernesto waved. This one was going to really hurt.

I was wearing my hair long then, and he moved some of it from my eyes. It was an intimate gesture, and one I probably would not have tolerated in just about any other context. This was touching, and much too close. But I allowed it. From Ernesto. I do not know why. He looked exactly like my brother would look in another twenty years.

There are instincts people have. Like running from the dead. The dead could not catch me, no. *That all your spook is, honey, the dead are catching up?* The hot and yellow floodlights of the Mexican moon articulated ecstasies up there beyond the wedges of Ernesto's soul, and his face, a peeling sulfur, now, rippled, split upon the lattices of cowboy pain. Everyone has pain. Pain is the juice that runs the world.

I do not want to know. I knew Ernesto's Navajo eyes. I knew it would be okay with him.

To not know the pain he would come with.

To not be that painful sword. Ernesto loved me but he did not know me. He loved me like you would love a valued family member. But I barely knew him. No. I did not want to know him.

He kissed me on the mouth. Right there in Mexico.

I was a little surprised.

Shit.

I was shaking.

I took my brother's hand, my soft brother's hand, my dark brother's hand, my *Indian* brother's hand, and we drove back across the river.

I am in blood.

Who gave *me this sack of bones for a body? Who* did *this to me? I want them brought before judgment.*

When I drag myself into the frostcold bathroom early in the autumnal mornings-of-lament to look into the witching-morning mirror, I see the haunted image of my borne-down migrant father—bent and suffering, mean like a kicked dog mean, the jinn of the desert storms, his warlock eyes the undersongs of a ruined masculinity, licking his bloody wounds.

Daddy, do you remember that night you came home from the bars late, and you had wrecked the truck? That was always my worst nightmare.

Not that you would die some prince of death upon my breath. You would get drunk some night in town and wreck the truck and the sheriff's car would pull into the drive.

Two little boys home alone in their underpants.

The cops are at the door.

Putcher pants on, boy. You and your brother are being put in foster homes.

Notice the plural, Daddy.

We wouldn't be in the same foster home.

Do you think Tso could survive that? I do not.

No. You only wrecked the truck. The tree died.

Coming upstairs to hold me. Weeping. Asking for my forgiveness.

How. How. How do I do that? Again?

The wretched always have lovers but they have no friends.

Even then your *hands and your hands and your hands* are all over me, touching and touching and touching, and your lips on my body like some law of servitude invoked, and you have removed everything I use to keep the distance between us. The great horror and the darkness. You breathing on me. Ejaculating in me and I am vomiting again and again. What is this guilt you call despair? Is mine. Is mine. For you have betrayed me, too.

Muchos pocos hacen un mucho.

Many littles makes a much.

"Nasdijj, please, I love you, I don't mean to—hurt you, honey."

I no longer listened to the words. They weren't even words. They were the distant feelings of a drunken man.

Lost in his own torment. I did not want it.

Then or now.

Our father was the man who loved us—my little brother, my mother, and myself—almost desperately for the first six years of my life. Coming to our beds.

Then, Mama died.

The black cat jumped softly in the night to the night and through it. We lived under bridges for a little while. In the rain.

Having touched death, having held it in my hand, having held it like a squirming baby in my arms, I fly no ephemeral judgments against any man. We come to death like we come to birth. Naked and ourselves. He was going to deal with Mama's death or not. This, too, was the woman he shoved around, this, too, was the woman into whose face he threw coffee if it was not perfection, this, too, was the woman he beat, this, too, was the woman he raped with her bent over the kitchen table, and weeping, her sons and the adolescent boys from across the street for an audience, this, too, was the woman who had died on the inside long, long before she finally did the numbing of the deed.

Just before she left on that long walk into town for whiskey, she rocked us for a long, long time, and we fell asleep against her sweat. Even then, it was an alcoholic sweat. She smelled sweet like bourbon. She put us on the bed, and I do not remember her leaving the house, but she did.

The Mexican women in the migrant camp cared for my brother and I. We slept with the Mexicans for about a week and they had food. We were so impressed that anyone would have food right there in the house. We wondered if we would ever see him again, or would we live with the Mexicans. We prayed like hell we could live with the Mexicans but it was not to be. In his own faithless way, he would eventually show his migrant face. The face I see now in the mirror whenever I care to look, which, quite frankly, is not that often.

His truck would pull up in that cloud of cold dust in which he lived. There being, of course, only one way to do things, his way or the highway, and it was neither a joke or a metaphor as he had kicked the two of us *o-u-t* of his truck (he hated our fiddling with the radio), which pulled up into a freezing cloud of limestone at the very end of her funeral—not that anyone there had missed his royal presence. He gets out of his truck and unzips himself and pisses in the parking lot. Dead drunk. People just looked away. We all knew he wanted to piss his life away and the rest of us with him if we would go along for the ride. I did *not* want to. But I was tired, and the voices were getting strident. We were always, and always walking home at the side of some road, fatherless. He was always absent unless he wanted something.

Love. Sex. Whiskey.

Forgiveness.

That was about all he ever required. She could give him all three and when she wasn't there to put out for him, he turned-in-our-horror to us. His sons.

Forgive him? Never.

I would try every mental trick in the book—staring at the wall—to not cum in his mouth, but he always had the better of me, and reduced me to tears and rage.

Her medicine?

Her answer to the dilemma of her life: acute alcohol poisoning and frozen in a ditch. She had given up. His promises were lies. *Things* would not get better. *Things* were only getting worse. *Things* were disintegrating, and no matter how much money you tried to make, picking, and picking, and picking crops, *things* simply slipped away, and turned into that slipping dust we held in our hand, wondering *how good things* could *do* that like they had never existed.

When they had. There had been good things in our existence.

No se conoce elbien hasta que se ha perdido.

"One never recognizes something good until he has lost it."

Cervantes (1547–1616).

Who rode his Arabian stallion onto the world stage in the middle of all that European chaos. At that time my mother's people were still arriving from places north in the vast, nomadic migration of the Athabascan-speaking peoples who would follow their ancestors' paths and trace secret routes through the Rocky Mountains, south. To arrive in the American Southwest filled with dreams—how many people have done just that since 1547—to find cultures before them abandoned, gone, and long forgotten. Only their kivas and their descendants—the Hopi and the Zuni and the Tewa—remained. The Anasazi were otherwise vanished.

My mother's people, the Navajo, didn't know whether to call our father a *bilagaana* (white man) or a Skinwalker—a pale spirit who comes from the north, the not-dead-yet soul of someone who has died—or a Souleater, who desires to inhabit the body of someone living. Time and time again, I saw Navajo who took one look at my father, and their faces fell, and they'd turn around and put as much distance between themselves and my dad as their pickup trucks could travel. There were some contemporary Navajo who didn't care. But there were just as many Navajo who could *see*, and what they *saw* in my dad was a vacant soul who preyed upon the souls of other people.

The modern Navajo laugh at this old stuff. The modern Navajo wants to shop at the mall, buy new cars every other year, drive on paved roads, have running water and a toilet inside the house, and have enough money to put in a bank versus cash inside a coffee can tied on a rope and hung high in a cottonwood tree, which is where my grandmother kept her money. The traditional Navajo, the elders, understand there are rare and precious pearls of wisdom that extend themselves like flashing comets as they travel the universe from one end to the other. There is wisdom and there is knowledge. One is not the other. Knowledge is the ice, the degree to which the ice is packed solid, and knowledge is the speed at which the comet travels sun to sun. Wisdom is the circumflexion that the comet takes, the degree to which angularity flings fragments of the universe itself into dark matter in the disk, creating the illumination of halos, and that exotic *thing* we humans refer to as *beauty*, which we walk through as the people who walk upon the surface of the earth. Or not.

5

To Walk *in Beauty* When it Came to the Cowboy Who Was My Dad Was an Enormous Contradiction

The horizon shimmered as Monster Slayer and Child Born for Water walked and walked.

For days they followed the trail of spiders across the floor of a vast desert. There was nothing to drink except each other's sweat.

Two enormous crows landed in front of the War Twins.

"Do you seek your father?" the crows inquired.

"Do we have one?" Monster Slayer asked.

"Oh, yes! But he is very mean, and he will make you perform many tests."

"Will you take us to him?" Child Born for Water asked the crows.

But no. The crows did not fly that high.

"But if you get on our backs, we will fly you across this dangerous desert," the crows offered.

Soon the boys were aloft, and, looking down, they could see Coyote panting with the biggest grin on his face anyone had ever seen.

To *walk* in beauty when it came to the Cowboy who was my dad was an enormous contradiction. Knowledge is the ice. Wisdom is the recognition that as the ice travels along its predetermined course, the luminosity is what causes us to look up, and wonder at the smallness of ourselves.

Now he was coming to our bed, and spending the night. He used to leave after he came inside one of us. But now he spent the night with his arm wrapped tight around me. I would stay there like that for hours frozen in terror.

In many respects, my father *was* a ghost who sucked on the souls of those of us *alive*, and he bled the world dry, *dry*, dry as dead birch bark, dry as oyster shells set out in the sun, dry as week-old bread, dry as vodka cut with coyote piss, dried like leather until there was nothing left of you, and he could then inhabit the inside of your skin. He was a parasite. A worm. Just knowing him was a bondage of the soul.

I saw coyotes slink in silent pain to him. Heads held low-to-the-ground. Snarling. Spit drooling from between their teeth. Him. Standing there ramrod-straight. Like a beacon. The dog slowly wipes his length along my father's leg. And takes a piss the other way.

My father was a cowboy who could not make his living as a cowboy.

There are men who can do it, but by and large they are single. They don't usually have families who depend upon them. But my father never, ever saw any of it in that context because he could neither add nor subtract. The man lived by what he would will to happen. The day of the cowboy had been over for a long, long time.

My father was a cowboy who lived tough, rode tough, and died as tough as the Brahma bulls he wrestled to the ground at the rodeo. That you could be this tough and yet find it difficult to put enough food on the table in the migrant kitchen to feed your two boys was more contradiction than my father could fathom. That he had failed was not something he could live with. So he died. My father may have been alive as he was beating me and throwing me into plows but the *man* who was my father was dead. The *men* who collectively took us in, some of them even taking me, the difficult one, the smart-ass, into their hearts, became the father we did not have. The man died. So he goes out with a hooker and does not come back for four days. So it's not our fucking business, and what does it mean *to us*! *O-u-r* fucking business. So the father I have constructed in my head, the man who allows me to paint something of his image here, only fails because his reality is one-dimensional. That is *all* I dare lend to him. I dare *not* give him, the dead, more power than they (or he) deserve. The man failed because he took the easy way out and it crashed in on him because it does that. The man failed to love us because he was a failure at loving us. Only now that I am in my fifties, and my bones are dying, and I am facing surgeries that are more than a little frightening (to me), am I able to put together some of the fragmented pieces of the puzzle of who he was.

The man lived by will alone. He could do this on a dry day at a hundred degrees, or in the snow, or in the mud as the rain pelted him, and not a single sane soul was in the rodeo stands to see this act of selfless stupidity. The problem with following the rodeo circuit with two little boys is that the flophouse whores could be amazingly maternal, and there was always one who wanted to turn his randy ass in to Social Services. Daddy simply could not keep up with what was and what was not abuse and neglect. They kept changing the rules out from under him.

Why did he want us?

I know why.

To prove to those disapproving eyes (like my grandmother's) that we were *his* property. What was his was his. It was that simple.

We were *p-r-o-p-e-r-t-y* . . .

Daddy would see some hooker crying and gagging on the guilt on the pay phone and he knew it was time to go.

They were always turning him in. Shrieking child abuse.

They saw themselves in us.

Local law enforcement for the most part wanted as little to do with him as possible. For our part, my little brother and I loved those rodeos, and the dust, and the cowboy boots (we usually got ours around Christmas at the Gallup Flea Market). But what we loved the most about the rodeo was grape cotton candy, and we would walk around the rodeo eating grape cotton candy, which the rodeo grape cotton candy people gave to us for free because we were walking, talking purple advertisements for the stuff— about as happy as a pig in a purple pig barn. Someone big would pick us up and set us on his shoulders. The view alone was Byron on his beloved Bridge of Sighs. A palace and a prison on each hand as death is a river of gore and being gored and what eventually dies inside.

We are our bones. Our Bridge of Sighs was a set of shoulders and our Venice was a small town in Florida we passed through going south on old Florida 41. That was the old way to the sugarcane. Around old Immokalee. Our Bridge of Sighs was a set of hands that could pick us up and let us see the world from the perspective of a safer place our father could never invade or be a part of.

Our father never picked us up to pick us up. It would not have happened. Our Bridge of Sighs was a Venice populated with men who did not want to hurt us.

Without these men, I am not sure we would have made it through life at all.

They were Boy Scout troop leaders of troops we could never join but they would let us in for a week or two and then we had to leave. Always to the next migrant camp. Always before we could get attached to anything. Until Daddy would tire of us and leave us in New Mexico where we wished he would leave us forever. These men were bus drivers for the soccer team. They were the men like my ninth-grade journalism teacher who allowed me to be an editor for a month and then I had to go again. They gave me chances. They took chances giving me chances. They were men like the young Michigan State Police trooper who did not arrest me for the alleged theft of those official (they had a seal), black, state police diving fins.

That had disappeared from his car. I took them.

He had been diving around Torch Lake in Michigan looking for the body of a Chippewa girl who had drowned there.

I thought I might help him out. We were there picking cherries, which was decidedly more boring than looking for bodies in lakes.

The troopers thought they saw something in a bed of reeds and cattails (turned out to be a thrown-away old coat) and they completely lost their focus on the police car with the trunk open. It happens in crime scenes. As I went for those fins in that car trunk my brother started biting his hand off.

"Don't *do it, pleeeeze,*" he begged.

But I had to.

Those were the best fins you could get. You could not *buy* fins like that. They would make you go really fast in the water.

When I got the fins home, they were far, far too big for me. But I swore to myself I would find a way to make them work. *For me.* My pocketknife could turn the trick.

"Okay, now you can return them," Tso pleaded.

Return them? My own brother had gone completely mad.

I made Tso hide them. I was always making him *hide* everything.

My grandmother Sa had Spirit Sisters. Auntie Verna was one. She did not approve of how I *dominated Tso and everyone could see it* (her words). Auntie Verna maintained (and she was absolutely correct) that Tso just looked up at me and gave me all the trust he ever had for anyone and anything. And I, for my part, returned none of it except for my facetious and *not amusing* and flippant grin.

It was obvious (that word again) that Tso loved me and I loved me, too. Perhaps a bit too fucking much.

The fins made me very fast under the water (my knife "adjusted" them, making straps, and of course ruined them in the process) and under the water I did not have to listen to Verna carry on like a snowstorm in the mountains. She was right. I was not considerate. And seeing as how there were very, very, very *few* people in the world who were going to be there when I needed them (as this is what happens to moral scum such as myself at the end), I was going to have to refigure *out* some things so my brother could at least *stop his hands from bleeding long enough to get the blood out of Verna's white rug* . . .

Verna was a lot more scary than the state police.

The young man who had not arrested me came to the house one night.

Would I like to go to the big state police post (it was on a college campus and I had never seen one of those either) and take some beginner lessons in skin diving from a state police expert who was going to help in the recovery of the body of the girl who had drowned?

Swimming lessons, really.

My father was hardly going to say I could not go although he was a bit nervous about what I might say.

To people.

When I explained to the trooper, who had to be no older than twenty-four, that I could not leave my brother alone, he grinned and included him.

We spent two days in a huge pool with cops. We slept in a barracks with younger cops-in-training. It was a slick training post and people there smiled at us. There was a camaraderie Tso and I had never seen before. No one was mean and no one pushed us around.

We learned not just how to swim, but the basics to saving drowning lives. If we had wanted to continue, we could have become lifeguards. Someday. A real job.

We were kids. It was grand and glorious. These men were saving us.

And they knew it.

Two days was not enough time to become proficient at swimming. But it opened doors for us. It allowed us to see that groups of men could do more than just pick crops. There was no way we would be allowed to stay long enough to get our Red Cross lifeguard training, and we weren't old enough for it anyway (we did not know that). Now we had more swimming skills than we had had before. We had been shown another world of men and no one hurt anyone. In our world, people were always being hurt right and left. This was another universe.

Our Bridge of Sighs could have been another migrant neighbor like Christobel Romero who already had a dozen boys. But in our younger days he would pick us up and set us on his shoulders and roll around in the grass with us at the end of a working day and released from the imprisonment of the fields. He would open his family just long enough for us to feel some of the warmth they knew and they were strong enough to be able to share it. Our father thought strength had to do with one's physical ability to instill fear in a child or any other form of life smaller than our father. Christobel Romero was a migrant and had about the same kind of education our father had. The education of the board. But Señor Romero *knew*. About the strength in sharing.

The guys here were mechanics, cowboys, migrants, air-conditioning repairmen, roofers, teachers, auto parts supply technicians, and they were all magnificent. They drove trucks, and made things move. They were ordinary men who kept the extraordinary world glued together, and it was important that chaos be kept at bay, and that *things work*. That Bridge of Sighs had nothing to do with being anyone's biological parent. It had to do with Christobel Romero's ability to look into our eyes and seeing the hurt and numbness there *do* something about it.

He picked us up.

Our Bridge of Sighs was simply an effort to pick us up and set us down and on our own two feet. He said *this is the world* and we looked all around.

And sighed. Things worked. Things worked so well, in fact, it was clearly safe enough for us to take a temporary break from worrying about how all of it was going to become unglued again. We could relax and let someone else be the guards at the door tonight.

The rodeo chute would open and my father's horse would come flying out of there like a comet whose straightforward destination was three tons of malicious Brahma bull. The Brahma bull's head would be lowered, and the animal would be scruffing up the ground.

This violence only held us for so long. Violence was nothing new and it was not unique. I was maybe four and even then, the sight of my cowboy father fresh from the rodeo shower—naked and done with Brahma bulls for the night—was enough to compel me to turn my head and look away from the sight of flesh that had been gored time and time again. I had seen my father's body littered with black stitches that would wrap themselves around his torso like a tiny set of train tracks. My father loathed physicians—they cost money—and he was always removing his stitches himself except for the ones he could not reach.

"Just pull it out and clip it," he would tell me, and he would close his eyes.

He never gave this horrible task to my little brother, Tso, seeing as how I was *the bigger brother* and as such my responsibilities were numerous. I took Daddy's stitches out. I bandaged his wounds. I read to him (as he could neither read nor write) the directions on bottles.

Taking his stitches out was terrifying because if I hurt him, Daddy would slug me clear across the room. My hands would shake. I was obliged to use the same clipping instruments we used to clip the horses with. You grab the thing *and clip it off*. My father would jump and clench his jaw. Pain was something a real man just had to tolerate.

One winter's day, Mama walked into town. It was not unusual for Mama to walk into town. I was old enough to know that Mama was a heavy drinker. In the summer, when Mama was stone-cold unconscious, and asleep on the ground outside, and had, in fact, been there the entire night, I could always wake her up with the garden hose. Mama sputterin', and coming back to life in torrents, at once shocked and attempting to push the onslaught of water-from-the-hose away from her. Mama might be drenched but drenched was better than dead.

As the hose was pouring water on her, I remember thinking: *Do not die here, Mama. I will not know what to do.*

Summer was one thing, winter another. Navajo winters are biting, dark freezerburns of finite mass and primordial decay. The gloom threatens to become one with you. In the summer, groups of us—my mother, myself, my little brother, my mother's mother, and Grandfather Nilch'i—would go out into the mesa, get flat on our backs, and stare straight up to see the clouds today, and what patterns they might be making for us to re-create on looms. Our Navajo grandmother always had big bags of wool around the hogan, wool that would be made into weavings. This was great stuff for kids in the summer. But it could not be done in the winter as there would be too much snow, and the clouds for their part hung too low, roiling as was their way from a black grayness into an even lower, and blacker grayness like the eyes of supersymmetric windstorms, not too dissimilar from the whirling spots of Jupiter. If summers were a looking up, winters were a looking down.

The direction people *see* has great significance to all Navajo creation stories—and to the emergence legends of the Ute, the Paiute, the Zuni, the Hopi, the Acoma, the Pima, the Havasupai, and the Sioux.

In order to go up you must look that way—up. The Navajo have only been a formal tribe since 1923. For centuries, they were a loosely knit *band* of Athabascan-speaking clans who were surrounded by the Utes to the north, the Mescalero and the Comanche in the south and the southeast, the Tewa to the east, the Zuni in the immediate south, the Chiricahua to the southwest, and to the west what hemmed the Navajo in were great rivers, enormous deserts, and imposing mountain ranges such as the Mojave, the Colorado, and the Coconino Plateau. The only way to go was *up*.

Which is exactly what the people did.

This tradition of *seeing up* is difficult for non-Indian people to understand. *Up* is not a direction as much as it is a *place*. A *place* where *seeing* occurs. Within this precept that connects time, life, history, and death, all four concepts become more than an objective sequence of events. I cannot explain my life as an objective sequence of events because that is not how I know it. I can only explain it using the analogies and the symbols I understand, and while some of those symbols and representations are *different*, they are not so foreign or alien as to defy the European eyes, ears, and ability to articulate music.

Now not only was he taking to spending the night, but when he was done having sex with us he would want to talk. What I did was talking but it was not talking as I was much too numb to talk. All language to me was a numbness now. It kept changing, too. Like we did.

Nasdijj, do you love me.

Yes, Daddy.

(What was I going to say, no, you dumb fuck.)

Nasdijj, I am sorry if I hurt you.

Yes, Daddy.

I knew this: The words that came from his mouth were more ephemeral than the grape cotton candy I loved.

They melted.

The melting of history itself can also be the story of personal identity. For the Navajo, blueprints for conducting a moral life are constructed in this complex realm. Chronology is not the connective tissue that holds our technological perspectives (designed around getting as much work done as humanly possible) bound or tethered to our preliterate roots. In fact, our preliterate roots have over time created a vast repertoire of song-and-dance reflecting the mythologies of emergence. We emerge from a past toward a future imbued with (versus shackled to) *time as an arrow that flies in endlessly repeated cycles not unlike the way in which the particles and atoms of light are projected* not as a straight line but as an angularity.

Like the comet that flies around the sun using the gravitational fields of enor-

mous nebuli to fling itself back and forth between deep-space stars we never see and
the sun we see every day we are alive and walking upright upon the earth.

I did not know where the voices I heard came from.

Especially Geronimo's.

"Nasdijj, you are attempting to explain to *bilagaanas* a life, and how that life has been superimposed against a bedrock of strange happenings. It cannot be done."

"You, Old Indian, who says: It cannot be done. It can be done. But not in the old way, and not in the new ways, either. It takes both the old and the new. It is a story ripe for confusion but only if you are confused."

We knew the earth, too, was *a body*.

We could see it.

Often, in the morning, if we were staying with Grandmother Sa, she would take us up to the top of the volcano she lived on.

From here, you could see all the earth, all the planets, all of the moon and sun even as they rose and fell.

It was another place to *see*, the volcano.

We had stayed with Sa for a whole summer once. Mama and Daddy had followed the crops. Secretly, we hoped (and we prayed) they would not come for us. Perhaps they would forget us. Perhaps they would just *keep going*. But no such luck.

They arrived. And we fell apart. Mama wanted us to hug her but we would not. Daddy pretended not to care in the least about any of it. Come. Go. Stay. It didn't matter to him.

We cried.

We wailed.

We threw our cowboy boots at the wall.

Sa gathered us. She pulled us to her like ducks.

"You are the warriors," she reiterated. "Just like Naeenazghani who would be Monster Slayer, and Tobajishinchini, Child Born for Water. *Remember?*"

Yes. We remembered. We were like them but we were not them.

It was so hard. It had become *our* volcano, too. We wanted to see the sunrise from the top every day.

We wanted to play with the sheep every day.

We wanted to ride our ponies bareback (Daddy was shocked to see it and he had to sit his skinny butt down on the ground) every day.

It would be here. The volcano.

Our home!

Daddy could NOT take it away. No!

It wasn't going away. Now we had work to do. There would be monsters.

"So. Did the old witch put any of her spells on you?"

Daddy could have used a few spells himself.

We watched the old volcano fade away, and we were more than a little silent. We had been taught, now, how to work with it.

Becoming the silence, and the sword the silence walks in on.

As we left the shadow of the volcano, looking up, there was the deep red body of the moon that seemed to be flying down.

The crippled body of the father was the crippled thundering of the man ringing and ringing in my ears. After our mother died, his was the boiling body that broke our bones with baseball bats, his was the body that would throw the smaller bodies of his sons into his bed with hookers and his whores who were as terrified of him as we were. His was the body that beat us up for imaginary crimes. His was the body that forced us to go with other men hand in hand. His was the body that stripped off the flesh from our backs with his whipping and his oiled bullwhips. And his was the body that inflicted violence after violence—throwing me through entire windows of glass—and leaving *me* the cripple that I am.

I blame him.

The twisted pain I live with is his fault.

For years, I didn't want to see it. I didn't want to articulate what went on there. I didn't want to relive a single moment of it.

But I have gone down into that rug of blackness, and I have faced him there, and as warriors, I have won.

Daddy died. His pauper's grave is surrounded by a field of wheat. I have walked through the music of that wheat, too.

I am still here, and I am still breathing, and I have not succumbed to the suicidal pit of Mesozoic acrimony he would have me fall into.

I have had children, and they are my heart. I have neither destroyed them nor provoked them with indignity. I have nurtured them, and in so doing I have found the warrior way. Of its own beauty is the mind diseased. Mark! Where his carnage and his conquests freeze. The music of the voices in the mind cannot cease. He makes a deafening solitude and calls it peace.

There was one thing, though, my father had, I do *not* have. Blue eyes. Eyes as cold and blue as the New Mexico sky in winter. I have my mother's eyes, and they were brown as was the desert and the reservation earth she came from. When things hit bottom, and they do, I've been around long enough to know that none of us is immune from hitting that hellhole hard—hell being neither fire nor brimstone, but just plain hard—I am able to remind myself that nothing is forever by seeing into the eyes of my mother's wisdom. Paradise lost. For now the light has gone into the darkness, nor is it becoming to sit about at the feast of gods, but better to go home.

I understand that the ride I have so-far given to the reader—so we could arrive at this desert house together—has been a difficult one. I have so-far allowed you upon a journey that has been disjointed and hard.

But that is *exactly* how I see those early years. They're disjointed. They're difficult to understand. I hear voices. I see Geronimo.

That *was* the journey through those years. Difficult. Hard. Disjointed. My father's eyes were indifferent. His was the wisdom of indifference.

My mother's eyes were the world.

The edge of the cliff I walk is always there.

Even then, I knew I would die in pain. You become the warrior pain, and the sword the pain rides in on.

Geronimo (supposedly our mythic savior) is often called an Apache or a Chiricahua, but Geronimo was a Bedonkohe. At a time when fighting wars was changing from an agrarian militia-in-combat to a more industrial mass killing machine—as, indeed, the world had changed, too, from an aggregate of agrarian cultures to a more industrial urbanity—here was a little, wizened old man dressed in a loincloth with a stovepipe hat, who single-handedly led his people out of reservation bondage, as the entire U.S. military machine gave chase.

It wasn't just Geronimo who eluded them.

It wasn't just a people creeping about the desert in the night that eluded them.

It wasn't just a strange and different language that eluded them.

It was an entirely different way of thinking and seeing that eluded them completely.

The cat jumped and landed on his feet. There was a rip in the fabric of time, and Coyote saw his chance. America had spent twenty million of its dollars attempting to slug its way west to subdue the last of the Apaches. Twenty million dollars and twenty years. Geronimo's final surrender came in 1886, and was the last significant Indian guerrilla action to take place in the USA. At the end, Geronimo's *vast tribe of warriors and horses and guns and bloodthirsty visions* came down in reality to sixteen very tired old men, twelve women, and six children. Upon his surrender, Geronimo and his *"army"* were shipped like cattle to Fort Marion, Florida. Geronimo himself was kept separate, as it was thought that if he were to be in close contact with his *people* there would be another tidal wave of blood and revolt.

There wasn't.

There was however an outbreak of tuberculosis. Men, women, and children died as medical care was slow to arrive. The Apaches were settled in Mount Vernon, where a quarter of them died.

Fort Sill, Oklahoma, would be their final incarceration.

"I hated that place they put us in like animals in a cage. But we had vowed not to fight another day. Or they would have crushed us. I would lie in my cell and attempt to look past the bars on the windows out at the moon but I had been enclosed. All we wanted was to go home."

"Do you feel as though you had given up?"

"Oh, we gave up over and over and over again. Giving up is nothing. What is hard are those long nights where you wonder if you might have won. I can see nothing that we did that might have been changed so we could have won our freedom. I cannot think that we Apache people are utterly useless. Or why would Usen or God have created us? We are all his children, are we not? The sun, the darkness, the winds are all listening to us and to what we have to say."

It was Geronimo the seer who led his people across a desert of cactus and jackrabbit and sun. It is said among Athabascan-speaking people that Geronimo's age at this time of chase was right around seventy. Out of sheer embarrassment military historians have placed Geronimo at around fifty at this time of "eluding them." Yet when Geronimo spoke of where his people lived (he never bothered to learn English), he used the term *wigwam*. By 1830, the *wigwam* had been replaced by the *wickiup*, which was nothing more than a structure made from sticks. A structure that could be abandoned easily where a *wigwam* was a more significant investment, and could not be so easily left behind.

That a seventy-year-old man (who had had nine wives and a subsequent number of children) with his loincloth and stovepipe hat could outwit the U.S. military, and then go on to live (imprisoned) for another thirty years, was a significant story that white historians felt obliged to smudge with the historical paint of alcoholism. It has been said that Geronimo, now a hundred years old, fell off his horse in a drunken stupor, and was taken to a military hospital at Fort Sill where he died in 1909.

And yet there is no evidence of such a hospital ever being built at Fort Sill, and a more likely explanation is that Geronimo had a stroke, never once having been observed inebriated by anyone at the prison where he was incarcerated. It is much more likely that his wife found him—not all that far from the log cabin where they lived—and this is probably where he died, again, not too far from where he's buried beneath a towering oak that reaches toward the sky with many medicine bundles tied there to give his spirit strength.

Geronimo is the past.

And yet he lived in our minds and our stories and our imaginations, and in our house of migrants-always-on-the-run, and often from the men who would come in the middle of the night to beat our father up for unpaid gambling debts that my ten-year-old brother and I would always have to pay with our work in the fields.

By the end of a day after hefting two or three hundred melons, you will learn to hate them, as they will break your back as efficiently as a baseball bat ever did.

There are pictures of Geronimo in the fields at Fort Sill where he worked and was imprisoned and attempted to help his people by picking melons. Melon after melon. Geronimo stands blinking in the sun. Holding a melon and managing even then to seem defiant. Defiant to the end.

Holding his melons was his last stand among the white men who would never grant a one-hundred-year-old man clemency, as he was considered to be far too dangerous (especially to women) everywhere in the West.

The good citizens of Tucson put a price upon his head. *How an elderly and frail man was a threat to Tucson, Arizona, in the early nineteen hundreds is anyone's guess.*

In order to prevent an uprising, and to protect Geronimo, the American government refused to release him from Fort Sill. Geronimo petitioned them again and again. He was even invited to lead the inaugural parade of the newly elected Teddy Roosevelt. The image of Geronimo dressed in full Apache war regalia, and carrying the American flag down Pennsylvania Avenue, was said to be worth the price of the inaugural, the most expensive event yet borne by an American government. Geronimo was convinced that *now they would let him go.*

They never did.

We saw him everywhere. We saw him in the migrant camps we lived in. We saw him in the fields we worked. We saw him in the stories our mother told to us at night. We would be safely snuggled down into that thick Navajo rug Sa had made. Safe from wars and monsters. Sa was a creature of the old ways that are mainly gone today. Sa told us stories, too. Stories painted with her voice and with her hands. When she told a story, she looked like a conductor at the Philharmonic. Sa only spoke Navajo so we understood a little of *how* a story falls or stands.

Sa was *very close* to an ancient Navajo gentleman who lived in his own hogan among the sheep camps. Sa would walk as was her way down the goat path to share the sunset with him. She would vary this routine, too, as she did not believe in routines (*hodeeshzhiizhgoo naas hadeezbin*—in the course of time, things change, become full).

Young Navajo run at sunrise. As the sky is breaking.

To see them, it is not unlike seeing a lone warrior running with the deer. Sa and Nilch'i would speak of their times of running with the sun, and then they would be quiet for a long while. As the sun rose in the east over Mount Taylor, they would sing long Navajo poems to the accompaniment of the wind's deerskin drums. If Sa was the poem and the running with the deer, Nilch'i was the wind that pushed up against her skin and made her fast.

We called him Nilch'i—*Grandfather*—although he was not formally married to Sa. Still, we referred to him as Grandfather because that is who and what he was.

Even though these two sweet old folks were well into their eighties, their liaison of some sixty years continued to make the village tongues cluck.

Clickety-cluck. Sa's considered opinion was *to let them cluck until their tongues unstuck.*

Sa might be older than the moon but she was still capable of giving them something to cluck about.

Tonight as I lie here in my bed that faces outside the window, I can hear the eagles play.

Craaaack. Craaaack.

They remind me of Sa.

As little boys, we didn't think it odd that Nilch'i and Sa had never married. It was something that simply was. Sa lived with her goats and sheep, and Nilch'i lived around the goat path in his own hogan.

Only as an adult have I finally realized that Sa and Nilch'i were deeply bonded, yet Sa was much, much too independent to be married to any man. For his part, Nilch'i had one great love in his life, and that was Sa. He really believed that being allowed by his god, Begochiddy, to live in such close proximity to the woman he loved was such good fortune, *no man* could ask more from life.

Both Sa and Nilch'i believed that they had been given so much to be thankful for. Tso and I would stare at our feet. We knew what this meant. We little ones with our whining and complaints. Most of which could be erased by a kiss but who to kiss us? They would. Two wizened little old

Navajo among the sheep on a volcano where no one had anything, and the
sun rose and fell with the regularity of life and death itself upon some pale
horse ridden brazen through the throat's doubt.

They did not doubt. They had somehow carved in ice the image of
themselves upon that pale horse, one clinging to the other, the world before them, and providence as a guide through their years and winters of
their solitude. The world was all before them. As was the eloquence of language that they shared. The volcano they lived on overlooked the sweeping deserts of Chaco, and they could see all the way to Coyote Canyon
where *the old ones* had built an entire escarpment of roads, none of which
could even be recognized as roads from ground level. One had to be above
this to *see* the virtuoso spirit or creative genius who had made these roads—
trading pathways but spiritual connections, too—crisscrossing the valleys,
the deserts, the mountains, and it took your breath away to know other cultures had been here with their own technologies, their own sets of kachi-
nas and gods, and their own ways to *see* the world.

We had our sitting rock that looked north past Crownpoint toward
Pueblo Pintado. Tso would wiggle and sit on Sa's lap and she would rock
and hold him and hum. I sat leaned up against Nilch'i who never seemed
to move (even if he was the wind). Nilch'i would explain in Navajo how
Chaco was a city many, many, many years ago, and if we allowed the sun
behind us to set as was its way, we, too, would be rewarded with the sights
and sounds of people moving, speaking, running after dogs (we liked this
one very much).

The way Nilch'i explained it, about a thousand years ago Chaco was the
center of Anasazi life. The Navajo were still coming in vast bands of clans
and families, but they avoided the Anasazi, and went around them. The
Anasazi lived in great houses, some of which were more than four stories
high. Nilch'i put his huge hand over my eyes and shut them.

Grandmother and Grandfather began to hum together.

I could see them. I could touch them. I could hear them. I was there.

It was almost terrifying. I was like the crow. Pine-covered mountains to
bare sand dunes. Flat plains to deep canyons. Sandstone cliffs to lava flows.
The bare desert floor to cool springs. A village was composed of row upon
row of contiguous living with doors (as the Navajo would adopt) opening
in an easterly direction so the warm effect of the winter sun could be felt.
A short distance away would be one or more kivas.

I was with the Old Ones. I was with them on their roads. I was with
them in their kivas. I was with them as the women ground the corn.

They wore hide cloaks, shirtlike garments, and fur blankets. Many people wore nothing more than sandals. People liked to decorate their bodies. The men wore their hair long and braided. Young women were wearing their hair in elaborate fashions. Living rooms had central fire pits. Living, eating, sleeping, making love—was all done on the floor. There was no such thing as furniture. There are smoke holes in the roof, and wing walls extending from fire pits to the walls on either side of entries. These wing walls, from a few inches to several feet high, obviously serve to partition a room, with the major household activities taking place in the larger portions of the house.

The heavy wing walls themselves serve, too, to dissipate cold air, but their main function is to keep crawling babies, always curious, inside the house. In the main part of the main house, halfway between the fire pit and the rear wall, there are small holes that serve as the representation of Sipapu, the mythical hole where one's ancestors emerged into this world from the one below.

Volcanoes. Holes. Reeds. On the wings of birds. Emergence being both a religious, an architectural, and a literary theme. Grandfather, Sa, Tso, and I are sitting just below a rock where the image of Kokopelli is seen playing his flute. There are spirals, snakes, dragons, daggers helping mark the movements of the sun. Infants are crying. Toddlers are getting into things. The dogs bark.

And the black cat jumps.

It was up here where the four of us liked to play or watch the sun that Grandfather brought out a particular jish. A jish is a leather pouch in which a shaman (though owning a jish is hardly limited to shaman) keeps his sacred objects. This jish was filled with old bone dice. What a find! Eight to ten oval bones about an inch long and two or three circular ones made up a set. The oval bones were incised on one side and coated with pitch or ocher, and the round bones had a small hole drilled partially into the center of one face.

Grandfather's ancient and arthritic hands suddenly became quite ungnarled and lithe as sparrows. Grandfather showed us how there could be forty-four possible combinations in the lay of the dice alone. Tso could sit there and play dice for hours day in and day out.

Sa and Nilch'i took many long, long walks around and around the volcano's rim lost in thought and even deeper contemplation. She was something of a scandal among the conservative, traditional Navajo. As children, we never realized the new paths Sa blazed for Navajo women. As a grandmother, she loved ferociously. She loved us harder than anyone I have ever known.

She did not approve of the man Shima (our mother) married. It wasn't that he was white. A *bilagaana*, as the Navajo would say. Sa was quite capable of seeing beyond the context of a person's skin. Sa simply knew somewhere in her soul that our father, Patron—or, as people liked to call him, the Cowboy—was an abusive and tormented man.

He was.

Beyond anyone's capacity for imagination.

Our mother met our father in a bar in Gallup. I happen to know the one. Just off Route 66, you can still see Indians being kicked out of there, and landing facedown in the dust. Indian men leaned up in silence against the outside walls. It is a place of sadness for the Navajo, the Acoma, and the Zuni who come in there to drink. My father's line was classic: *Let me take you away from here.*

Our mother jumped at the opportunity, if you can call life in the migrant camps of America an opportunity.

My mother and my father took off for the migrant camps of America, and as a family we lived virtually everywhere. We picked tomatoes in New Jersey. We picked cherries in Michigan. We picked oranges and strawberries and burned sugarcane in Florida. We picked artichokes in Salinas. We picked cotton in Texas and New Mexico. We picked apples everywhere from the Pacific Northwest to Maine to North Carolina. We picked peaches in Georgia, and tobacco in Tennessee. We were always from the land behind us.

But things did not always flow perfectly for my mother and father, and when she finally couldn't take another minute of his bullshit, she would load my brother and myself into a pickup truck, and drive us back to the volcano she had been raised on.

My grandmother's sheep camp was nomadic. Nilch'i's sheep camp (smaller than Sa's) stayed where it was. In the summer, the sheep were driven to higher ground. In winter, they were penned at a lower elevation, and frequently fed feed. The sheep were sheared in the spring for wool, and they were often eaten. Just when we boys would get settled in at Sa's, our father would arrive to spirit us off again. We hated the migrant life, and wanted to live on the slopes of the volcano, but it was not to be. We wished fervently that someone would stand up to our father and let us live on the magical slopes of Ak'i Dah Nast'ani, but we were always creatures of the wind.

Nevertheless, we saw Geronimo everywhere, and prayed that he might save us.

I am in blood. History, too, is liquid, and pumped in rhythmic intervals, the scribe sets his tribe upon and in the running of that long and timeless river we know as culture and society.

My brother and I—now that we are men—have this strange habit of coming back to the places we have lived. I do not know why. Perhaps deep down in our souls we still cling to the hope that life might have worked here, and here, and here.

Geronimo was born in a wigwam on the Gila River. I have tracked this place down with my black cat eyes. We were living in the desert. The Chiricahua desert. The desert where the Apache had once lived among his gods.

My mother would open the migrant camp trailer door, and I would run outside and clomp around in my too-big cowboy boots and underpants. To play with those Apache gods.

Look there. Look quickly. For he disappears not unlike the way in which water, too, evaporates. The naked Apache warrior on his horse moves the earth and makes it rumble. The Chiricahua desert was a place of family, babies, homes. Life, and with it the ephemeral, can crumble.

As soon as our legs were strong enough to carry us, my brother and I would run around to all our secret hiding places—the topmost branches of cottonwood trees, a rock cave by the river, an arroyo called Arroyo Seco, underneath the trailer with the lizards, snakes, and scorpions—and we would play *the hunt for Geronimo's bones*, and we would find them for we would be warriors, too. After all, our artwork was everywhere. Now the Chiricahua leaves no footprint of even a moccasin in this place of cats and horses.

We were little boys. We had always lived in migrant camps. But now we were living in a real house (it was a trailer but we thought it was a house) and we liked that place very much. There were old abandoned trucks rusted up on cinder blocks we could play in and drive, and drive, and drive. We would play spaceships and drive into the sky. It was in the middle of the desert with cactus all around. We had a Christmas tree that year in the trailer and we made paper candles that our mother set into the tree. Our mother cooked a turkey outside in a hole in the ground. The Navajo way. Snow fell softly in the desert like a kiss upon a nose. Wild horses came to see us, and we fell down attempting to chase them through the sage.

Daddy wanted us to come to work with him. We were so excited. Daddy was a cowboy. A real cowboy. We grinned in the pickup all the way to his work. We knew he had tried so hard. To find a job. To keep a job. We were hoping this one might be it. We sought what stability could be had. We were proud to be his sons, then. We were excited, too, because we knew he was working with horses.

My brother and I loved horses. We loved everything about them. We had cowboy boots! We had some plastic Apache horses we kept in our pockets.

The horses where Daddy worked were kept in a corral. We petted some. Their noses were soft and wet. We liked these horses very much.

There was a ramp. The horses went up the ramp.

Daddy was in the shed at the top of the ramp. Waiting. This was where Daddy worked. He joked and said it was his office. He was the man who bashed the horses' heads in with a baseball bat.

We stood there stunned.

It was as if a light had gone on inside your legs and traveled up and down your spine. Trying to escape. I could not breathe. Someone had stuck his hands inside my bowels and squeezed. The smell was bad. The plywood place was evil and the cold came in bitterly. No one had articulated this. His crusade to let us know in no uncertain terms that life was a falling down into a long dark tunnel had hit home again and again and again. This conflict between his universe and the universe of our Navajo mother had taken us by our arms and pulled them until they had nearly left their aching sockets. Blood was splattered on the floor and on the walls. I held my brother's hand. He was fragile and small. He bit down on his lip so he wouldn't cry. He stuttered, and his jaw shook.

"This is the dog food place," Daddy said. "Your precious horses are turned into dog food. Wanna see?"

There were bloodstained baseball bats in the corner of the shed. Daddy wore a slick yellow raincoat that was covered in blood.

"You boys go get a baseball bat."

We shook our heads no.

Please, no, Daddy.

He would *learn us* is what he said.

The first horse of the night came up the wooden ramp.

His eyes were wide and his nose was flared. That horse knew. The swinging of the bat made a crunching sound that brought us to our knees, too. No, Daddy, no. We had to put our hands over our ears to not hear the screaming of the horses. And then we ran into the night.

We had always loved the night. It surrounded us with thick black shadows and he could not always find us in the night.

It was a long walk home in our cowboy boots.

We knew the way. We made it a point to always know the way. To watch carefully when you are in the truck because you never knew when he would stop and tell you to get out and drive away. Leaving you. He had left us in the desert once. All by ourselves. So that we might learn the lesson that when all is said and done—all you really have is yourself. We walked and walked that whole night he left us by ourselves. Holding hands. In our pajamas.

This time my brother cried loud and long, and coyotes in the distance could hear him, and we were glad coyotes were there, but we were afraid, too, because we thought they might be wolves. There were horses there, too, and when cars went by we could see their eyes off in the not-too-distant distance, and we knew not every horse got turned into dog food. This time, cars would go past us very fast on that blacktop highway we were following, and a few almost hit us, and honked their horns in anger at us as they went whooshing by. Every car who was that wind felt like another horse, another passing death, and when the cars and big trucks went by we wanted to put our hands to our ears and not hear it. We desired silence.

This time, when we got home, he was waiting for us. Sitting there with his beer and his cowboy hat and his cigarette. How did we like his office? And who did we think we were with our fancy hope that *he* would find a job. If we wanted a job so bad, we could go get one. He beat us with the same baseball bat that he used to kill the horses.

We knew the feel of a baseball bat when it crunches bone. He pushed us in the chest with the baseball bat, and we fell down.

We knew the feel of his belt when it whips strips of skin and meat off our backs.

We knew the feel of the willow whip.

We knew the feel of a hot cigarette glowing at the purple end of our tit.

He stuck kitchen matches inside my penis and the penis of my brother. It hurt. He would light it, *y-e-s?*

No. No. No, Daddy. No. We would promise to do our chores and not ask for food and never be a bother. He was our cold, mad, cold, mad, and raving, raving father.

For more than forty years, those horses have been inside our heads. The sound of the nervous hooves up the wooden ramp. The eyes. The screaming. We always knew horses had sad and faraway voices, too.

We were criminals. There was no fucking hope for us. We had very surly attitudes, and we hated everyone and everything.

We were the eleven-year-olds who in their torn T-shirts leaned against the porch post of the general-store-slash-gas-station and with their surly cigarettes, too, they blew off the entire adult population of the world, and anyone else who might have or might have someday any authority over them whatsoever, and fuck you, too.

I hated those cigarettes. They were props and so were we. It was the theater of the absurd.

I am unsure that anything has really changed all that much. I know I feel fourteen. The ages jump around some. But the issues are the same. We had been plotting our escape and constructing our escape mechanisms since the day we had arrived on earth. There just had to be a way out of here. We would find it. We would find it and avail ourselves of any way out of this existence we could put together, buy, steal, beg for, grab, and *run* with. If there was anything we knew how to do, it was *run*.

We had been running since our dark eyes had first seen the light of day. Even when our father broke our legs, our eyes ran behind places no one could ever see so we could hide, and if the only place you have to hide is quick behind your eyes, then quick, boy, get there.

When you are born into a world of utter hopelessness, and there is no point to being here, still, you scan, you search, you do not give up, you refuse to buy it because the day arrives when you understand that's where they want you. They want you dead and silent. They want you soft, compliant, broken, and so vacant you wouldn't dream of asking questions.

Questions. We had questions. Like *why*.

If you want answers, you're on your own. We were on our own. But we could still laugh. We could still sing. And we could still make the kind of silly music most adults did not want to hear. We had something they could never figure. They knew it existed because we could always see them looking at us as if they simply had to know what it was that prevented us from being worn down and we knew what it was if they did not and they did not.

Know.

~~~~~

6

In the Summer of 1963,
My Younger Brother and I
Stole a Corvette

Changing Woman often came to the desert to be alone and think. She scanned the horizon for monsters. But there were no monsters. All was quiet.

Changing Woman worried. What would become of the twins?

And so it was that Changing Woman found herself alone in the desert—she liked to listen to the softness of the wind—but she was not alone.

Coyote was hiding behind a rock. As was his way.

Changing Woman knew this. She could hear him breathing heavily behind that rock, but she ignored him. And there was that smell. Of dog.

"You don't have to hide, you know. I am aware you are there. Watching as is your sneaky way, you Trickster," Changing Woman said. She was determined not to be fooled by Coyote or turned into the subject of his jokes.

Coyote emerged from wherever he had been hiding and spying on Changing Woman.

Coyote shrugged.

"You do not know everything," he said. Miffed. That he had been found out.

Changing Woman laughed.

"You do not know the future," Coyote said. Now it was his turn to laugh.

"How could knowing the future be something of value?" she asked the Trickster.

"Your children," Coyote said. "I know a great river where in reflection you may see how it is they live out their lives, and what becomes of them."

Coyote had always fancied her.

He knew what she desired.

Changing Woman scooped up handfuls of desert sand and let the sand fall gently from her fingers. She said nothing.

"I could take you there. I could show you something no human has ever seen before."

"The future," Changing Woman said, "will happen soon enough. For now, the monsters are not here and the day is beautiful. The wind speaks of peace to me. I will be content with that."

"But we could run away together."

Changing Woman looked at Coyote incredulously. "Me? Run away with you?"

Coyote hung his mangy head.

"There must be a future that will never happen." She patted him on the head (poor, pathetic dog) and went inside her hogan, where she bolted shut the door.

From behind his rock, Coyote could hear the sound of Changing Woman singing.

In the summer of 1963, my younger brother and I stole a Corvette Grand Sport II Roadster four-speed with a three-hundred-seventy-five-horsepower high-performance engine, side exhaust, knockoff wheels, angle head plugs, and the cutest little foam dice . . .

Superimposed on the foam dice hanging from the mirror was the image of a naked woman. The dice itself were only dots. It was every adolescent male's fantasy, that car.

In those days, there was no such thing as a car locking mechanism other than the one that came with the car.

All our father's migrant friends were criminals. Most of them were harmless and benign. A few were simply men who thought they would find some kind of shortcut through life and if they lived their lives at the horse track or the dog track they would eventually make that one lucky bet that would pay off in six or seven figures.

Some of these guys had a few screws loose.

Migrant criminals are guys who *do not* want to be found. Ever. They have the perfect environment for it. In the migrant life, you can have (our daddy did) a family on each side of the border with Mexico.

The passageways are not there to connect one life to the other. No. Communion is *not* connection. Daddy had his Mexican family. Then, he had *us*.

It was not necessary those two dissimilar worlds be connected. The house of prayer was the migrant fields and the bending and the bending and the bent shapes of human beings with their agony and their bones. Rows and rows of human beings.

The altar was the back of a pickup truck, and the box the cabbages go into. *We* were the penitent forms below. *Life* is not *either–or*.

It only is.

You are immersed in it. Or not.

Teaching us how to pick locks and hot-wire cars was pure sport. Daddy usually passed out by the time a party got well under way, and the whores were especially eager to teach us their talents. The men would teach us what they thought we needed to know. And the women taught us what they thought we needed to know. Our education was complete.

Most whores I have known despise sex. We *liked* the whores Daddy brought home. They were our friends. And they liked us, too. We knew (and understood) something Daddy did not know (or understand and never would): Whores were not *born* to a life of sexual bondage. They did not care all that much for men. Which we were not. Yet. And they liked us because they understood we had something in common with them and that was the act and the art of survival. You survived or you floated facedown in the river.

When Daddy was done with them, the whores would sit by the window. Staring. Smoking cigarettes. Motioning for us to come sit by them. We would do this if we felt warm enough, and the whore would run her fingers through our hair and ask us questions like did we like school, were we good in school?

We would sigh and tell her. We did not go to school. Much. We were never there—anywhere—long enough to go to school.

They thought this was sad but we did not.

We thought of it as a fringe benefit owed to us.

For tolerating him and his abuse.

We hated him—our cold, mad father—and always remembered the sound of the horses going up that wet wooden ramp. Where do you begin your life? In an odd way, *mine* began the night of the death of horses.

One hooker we liked tremendously showed us how to steal food. This skill came in very handy time and time again. We had our "stealing clothes," which were our nice clothes (lots of elastic) layered and a little large. Our "seedy" clothes would only attract attention. I would hold the elastic back of my brother's butt open, and drop steaks and chops down there. At some point we just stopped being hungry all the goddamn time. Because we took responsibility for our hunger. When you are as hungry as we were, the only thing that was going to touch that hurt was food in your belly.

"You stole things. Food?"

"We did. We knew it was bad."

"We stole cattle. From Mexico. But the army made us take the cattle back. A man was only worth how many cattle he might have. Our warriors were starving. But we had to take the cattle back to Mexico. To return it to the ranchers there who wanted to hang us. It was all to humiliate us."

Geronimo should be a bitter man. But sometimes he laughs like a lunatic.

Hookers thought we were cute. Especially Tso. Now, there's cute. He was a dark little imp. Me? I am not dark. I am light, and look like my sometimes almost blond father whose hair (like mine) burned lighter in the sun.

Not only did the hookers teach us how to steal food, they taught us how to cook and eat it before Daddy got home from the fields. When Daddy was around, he ate everything. When Mama was alive, she was obliged to *make his dinner* although she had worked the same number of hours he had, and just as hard. But once he walked through that door, he was the King again, and never offered to lift a finger. He ate like some voracious machine. You'd never find him in Safeway ripping off hot dogs. It would have been beneath him. But he'd eat the hot dogs we stole.

It took a hooker about three minutes to size up our entire situation. If there was nothing to eat at the migrant shack, Daddy would take off for town. He might not be back until late. Especially if there was a bar in town and there were usually a few. They all knew Daddy. Daddy would arrive home late and usually with a woman. He liked the new ones fresh from some other town. She was often surprised to see us. Daddy would pull her into his bedroom, and shut the door. Tso would say, "Don't be too shocked to see us because in about an hour he's gonna put us in bed with you."

He could be bad enough when Mama was alive, but after Mama died, he pretty much disintegrated. I did my best to give my brother the room to say whatever he had to say. We had all kinds of games we would play so we would not get dragged into bed with the hooker and her gentleman-of-the-evening.

Sometimes we pretended we were just too drunk to join them. Daddy would get all rank about our drinking his liquor but when he checked it, there was never anything missing. He never figured. We would drink enough tequila to rock back and forth when we walked, it was play-acting, and we'd spill some on our pajamas. You had to reek before he let you out of it. Our *stud* duties. Tso would squinch his face like some giant had pinched it when he tasted tequila.

Yuck. Sometimes we pretended we were too far gone down into sleep to leave our beds. This was dangerous. He would pick you up and throw you against the wall or—worse—through a window to wake you up.

I have the scars.

I learned the art of making bandages from a school nurse who probably saved our lives because she understood our situation, too. She spoke Spanish and she was from Belle Glade, Florida. We were there burning sugarcane. We were always coming and going to and from Florida. She showed me how to bandage something so as not to lose too much blood under the assumption you were *not* going to be *gotten* to a hospital where you might receive stitches. There is an art to it. To the application of the hydrogen peroxide. Daddy threw me into the talons of an upside-down plow once. The kind of plow they use to rip open the earth for cotton fields. Texas sod-busting cotton fields. These are the curved-metal swords that cut into the earth to open it for planting seeds. I was impaled there for some time and struggling only made the wounds worse. All I could do was hold very still and hope I didn't bleed to death before someone came. I don't even remember who pulled me out of that plow. What I remember are the infections. My leg turned green and hot. But I kept bandaging it like I had been taught to do, and I did not lose the leg. It was a miracle. That was the first wound I would have (it would not be the last) where I could look down into the thing and see bone. I learned how to spell femur.

Violent sex with Daddy was a dangerous business. Sometimes we pretended we were too sick to do it. Mix mustard and eggs together. You will vomit sooner or later. We would both vomit on him and he hated that. It ended sex rather quickly, too.

The whores who knew us and who liked us refused to have sex with us. They were our defenders and sometimes our defenders-in-absentia, and Daddy would stop bringing them home when they began to argue with him over his treatment of his "children." They would come over on their own, though, to check on us, and we so appreciated it. If he knew someone might come over, he was less apt to beat you black and blue. The whores knew this.

But there were always whores new in town and broke.

It is a mistake and a stereotype to assume that this underbelly-of-life existence was morally and economically confined to major urban centers. Go to Belle Glade, Florida. A very, very small town at the edges of the Everglades. Belle Glade is a migrant town. Strawberries. Tomatoes. Sugarcane. It is a farming environment. It now also has one of the highest rates of sexually transmitted diseases in the country along with corresponding rates of HIV infection—almost double the infection rates found in Harlem. On

Saturday nights, downtown Belle Glade is full of hookers when the migrants get their paychecks. The hookers are transported in from Miami on
a caravan of Trailways buses. Heroin on the streets of Belle Glade can be
purchased wholesale.

Dying scum is where you find it dying.

The migrant life is no little mom-and-pop farming operation where the
happy migrants arrive once a year with their salsa and sombreros.

Industrial farming operations like the ones owned by General Foods,
Quaker Oats, and Pepsi are twenty-four-hour-a-day, seven-day-a-week operations with warehouses and loading docks that light up at night, and
night trucks, the big rigs, eighteen-wheelers, all lined up and waiting to be
loaded.

The kind of trucks that growl late into the night. We always fell asleep
with the sound of them creeping like big cats crawling into your skin.

Even some of the new-to-town whores would get dressed quickly and
fly out of Daddy's bedroom like dazed crows with their eyes flaming yellow
when they realized children were going to be part of the scene. These were
few and far between. Hookers with the heart of gold and the decent stan-
dards of decency (because they remembered their sister's children at
Christmas) were a 1942 Paramount lot fantasy starring Chris Kringel and
Natalie Wood. My brother and I had developed little tricks we would do to
get it over with as soon as possible. Fake orgasms were nothing.

We could do that.

Truth is, we did not know what an orgasm was for the longest time. This
business confused us, and we never had erections. We never "came" in any
of the sex scenes with hookers and our father. It was like having sex with a
bomb that might go off and you with it and *blam-the-lot-of-us-into-a-thousand-
tiny-pieces*. Usually we were so scared it was quite impossible to know what
to do next. It was not about sex. It was about domination and power. We
found these scenes intimidating and horrifying. But we would lead the
whore (by this time she is quite willing to let us take the lead) into things
we knew he liked. It was touch and go. He enjoyed seeing us go through
our paces. In that respect, he was waiting and waiting and waiting (you
could see it like a film that covered his eyes like glass). We would lick and
suck her breasts while he put his head between her legs. We would pretend
to fuck her and the louder she was the better it went. All of it was pretend.
I think he knew that.

It was the pretense that mattered. It was the *waiting*. He actually
thought he was showing us what it meant to *be* a man.

He would learn us.

Later, much later in life, we would discover that *being* a man had to do with generosity, and forgiveness. How could he teach us things he did not know? What we three—the hooker, my brother, and myself—were doing was trying our damndest not to get beat up. He was quite capable of it. He would beat us all and we knew it. The women he brought home could at least begin to figure it out. The more often he brought you home, the more familiar he was with you, the more relaxed he'd get, at which point he would show his peacock colors, and all of them were violent.

We wanted to tell them: *Whatever you do—do NOT cry*.

Weeping *always* got the whore beat up and bad. Women never learn to watch or defend their kidneys. They don't come to it with self-defense skills because they are kept powerless. Daddy's fist would break their nose. Daddy would rip huge patches of hair right out of their heads. Daddy was vicious.

The hard part was having no clothes on in front of people you wanted to like you. Now they would know you like this.

My brother and I are over fifty, and yet we are still pulling up memories, and we are still weeping.

Now that Daddy is dead.

~~~~~~

Conchita Flamingo was a seventy-five-year-old bartender (she owned the place) in Fabens, Texas, who almost fell down the day my brother and I walked into her cantina. A neon flamingo blinked on and off out on the gravel road to Fabens just past the bridge to Guadalupe. We sat in our truck for some time before we gathered our courage to go in there. The door was wide open. Cowboys leaning over drinks and smoking cigarettes. Oblivious to the heat and one another. Johnny Cash oozed out the window. "How many bars just like this did we drag his carcass out of?" my brother wondered.

A few. A few in snow and gravel. His boots digging pathways.

The feel of gravel under your cowboy boots is always the same. The sun was up and the gravel parking lot glimmered dust and white.

Conchita Flamingo was behind the bar.

Fabens is a town about the size of a book of matches.

I was eighteen, and Tso was seventeen. We had been directed to this bar by friends in Las Cruces who knew Daddy. We were looking for Daddy because we needed him to sign off on a deed to that trailer we had once lived in as babies. We wanted that cash. It was not a fortune, but it gave us an excuse to wander around a part of his life we had never known about but had suspected for some time.

Conchita knew who we were immediately.

She put us in her truck and drove us to Guadalupe herself. Her black raven-eyes lost in crags of dark skin and darting at us like woodpeckers.

In those days there was no immigration fence. People went back and forth across the border mainly as they pleased, and it was not a problem. Today that area of Texas is an armed camp and a war zone of desert, drug smuggling, coyotes, and desperate illegal migrants.

Conchita's truck pulls into an old adobe home that looks like any other old adobe home. Two junkers in the front yeard. A Chevrolet for parts. A Mustang for parts.

An F-150 that worked.

Dogs everywhere.

A twelve-year-old girl, barefoot, out on the front porch sitting on a couch, with babies crawling all around her.

A man walks out of the house.

He looks exactly like me.

An almost blond Mexican. The man behind him looked exactly like my brother. Long dark hair and all.

They were as surprised to see us as we were to see them.

These were warm people. There was food. But it took a while to get to the place where you are comparing notes.

Did he . . .

The eyes that stared at the floor said it all. Had he done here the things he had done to us? What made us think this place was any different?

The floors our eyes sweep and sweep again, the years and the same centuries of grief. I want him to pay us all. He will not do it. And my roiling in this wind just makes the corpse he is smile like a china doll. I don't know what we were. I do not know that we were ever really little boys.

He was the devil.

What I love about my *Mexican* side to the family is that there are few abstractions. He was the devil. *Dios que da la llaga da la medicina.*

Anyone who knows the shadow world of the sexual underground knows that not everything is what it seems to be. Carla was a hooker Daddy brought home who had a bigger dick than Daddy. Bigger balls, too. When it became obvious that Daddy was going to bring his two little sons into the bed, Carla made her gender-secrets known. Daddy was furious. The Coyote had been tricked.

"Honey," she spat. "That's why they call eet tricks. *Quien te cubre te descubre.*"

"Fucking *spic!*"

"Carla donn like you call her names, no, no, no." She waved her finger. "Such nice boys, too! Doncha *know* whatcha *got*, Puta!" She was furious. It was the only time in our lives we would see him humiliated. She was a rage machine. She was not afraid to fight. But what really elevated her to another level was the fact she knew how to do it well. She never wasted a single move. It was like watching a straight razor cutting butter. It was worth a million and one hours in therapy. The *sight* of that man who had hurt us so many times getting what he deserved. From a woman who was a man who was a woman. Tso and I both savored those images and we pulled them out when we needed them.

We have needed them.

Right around this time, one of my more esoteric fantasies involved Gina Lollobrigida. Daddy had pictures of her, too, in a magazine. Carla reminded me of Gina. Carla had great red nails. She waved them. "No. No. No. Aunt Carla want little boys to *see!*"

She was stronger in a quick, strange way than any man we had ever known. She slapped him around. She beat him silly. She knocked a tooth out of his head. *She fucked him,* and when she came she screamed loud enough for the whole migrant camp to hear it. "Come on, Daddy. Carla's dick is gonna fuck that *big ole hole!*" And she would slap his butt with a leather strap he kept around to slap us with like she was riding an Arabian. Whoopin' and hollerin'. "Carla came like a hurricane! Woooweee!"

She tied him up. With his legs and hands up and around his back, and the Cowboy on his belly. Like a calf at the rodeo arena. She gagged him. She put him on the bed. Then she did her eyes and lipstick in a mirror while she talked to us.

This strange, deeply moving event was the beginning of my seeing myself *as a writer.* Odd as it is to say it even here. It was dramatic. It had color. There was a resolution. *And if I held the mirror of it up while I remade who I was in the reflection of the event—I could re-create with some power the reflection of what I had seen, heard, smelled, tasted.*

People ask me: *When did you become a writer?*

I became a writer in the holding of a mirror as an infinitely powerful instrument. "You boys see'd some bad bad things, surely. I am so sorry. Really, I am. Come sit on my lap."

She was big and strong and safe and she had a very, very big black dick. Daddy struggled on the bed. We ignored him. Tso called her pretty. She smiled. She, too, knew fragility when it was before her.

Unfolded. There.

"Munchkin, I am definitely *not* pretty, but I try real hard, I do. I want you boys to remember what happened here tonight. People can surprise you."

We nodded in enthusiastic agreement.

"I sure surprised you, little peanut, huh?" And she tickled my brother, who giggled and wiggled on her lap.

"Oh, he's just a bad bad bad bad old man, and that's all he is. You boys know the world has truckloads of bad bad people. They're everywhere. But we get up every day. We do our nails." She painted one of my brother's fingernails red. "We put our panty hose on one leg at a time just like everybody else. And we get on with it, we do."

"What does *get on with it* mean, please?"

She combed his beautiful hair for a long soft moment. "It means our tits are on straight and we walk right out there into the world, honey."

"I get it, I do."

She kissed him. "I know you do."

She sat down on the bed beside my naked father. She spoke to him very matter-of-factly, softly. "I am taking your money, Cowboy. I do think I earned it tonight."

His eyes bulged red. He would find her and kill her. He would.

She opened her purse, and took out a very big gun. Our eyes bulged.

"I learned how to use this in Korea. It's a country in case you didn't know. They had a war there. I was a marine. Sergeant Major Carla Consuela Lamatalatata ands you better believe it cuz I put this *gusto picaresco* gun in your gringo mouth to blow you, Mama, into kindom cum. And if I hear one whisper you hurt these boys, I come back, and I fuck you in the middle of the street and charge admission, Papie. You get it? Good. Cuz these boys no untie you. I take them with me to next bus stop. Put them on the bus back here. That gives you time to be discovered all tied up nudie like a warthog, Papie. Tata."

She fed us first.

A huge gut-splitting fucking meal of rice and burritos and all the cracks of the migrant shack smelled great and dripped with grease.

Hot lard.

"Papie" had to endure the whole thing.

She put us on a bus and we never saw her again. Daddy never mentioned how he got released.

We developed a respect for hookers. The hooker sky was always breaking. The good ones had great survival skills. Whenever I have had extraordinary downtimes in my life, plunging into the bowels of the depths of suicidal *hell and back again*, I find the community's hookers, I find out where they live, and I move in with them, *baby*, because they remind me that no one is alone unless they want to be.

~~~~

It was always a question of surviving him. You never saw two boys learn to wash, and wipe dry, and put away the dishes faster than we did. It was a small thing, but not to us. We wanted to eat, be safe, and not participate in this with him. We did not care to save ourselves for him, or with him, or know him in any way. We never fought. It was always in our best interest to cooperate with each other, *our best interests* were mainly in our face—like food, and freedom, and the flowering of fait accompli.

Daddy would have been *(less than)* amused to know we were eating without him. The ghost of an enormous symbolism resides in the shadows here. The father's role in putting food upon the table. The actualization of responsibility. It was *not* our responsibility to feed him. It was *his* responsibility to feed *us*, but we were doing that for ourselves in a fluid universe where responsibility was a flytrap. Hunger being perhaps more symbolism than an aching gut. We in our innocence (we had none) wanted him to ache with it, and us.

And he did.

We hungered for a father. One who could put food on the table. That we could (and did) feed ourselves pushed him into a corner where his viciousness lay in wait, and had been waiting for some time, and now would lash not unlike that snapping of the snake's tail. People here and there gave us food. We stole food. We hoarded what we stole. We had a nice stash of food. We became like squirrels. He would have wanted his cut of the take, which would have been just about all the food we could steal. Stealing food from grocery stores was hard enough. It took planning and some nerve. The last thing we needed was responsibility for feeding that cheap low-life son-of-a-bitch.

~~~~

Stealing cars was easy. I remember thinking he could see us as we broke into the Corvette. Now I had something he could never have.

My brother and I were forever looking into the Corvette's rearview mirror so we could see who and what was behind us.

I would turn the mirror and time itself seemed to be on horseback like Geronimo. The wind in his hair.

The same rearview mirror my brother was always combing his hair in front of. He kept that damn comb in his front shirt pocket. The white girls liked to call him cute. They'd sigh. He'd die. And then he'd say: *Awww, shoot.*

My brother was hypnotized by those stupid dice.

As the torque of the car increased, the foam dice with the superimposed image of the naked woman (my brother had this bad habit of taking the foam dice and squeezing and unsqueezing the naked woman, who seemed to move in ecstacy) swayed back and forth.

Back and forth.

As though she were in tune to time.

"Where are we going?" my brother wondered. He was combing his long black hair in the rearview mirror, which meant he was leaning over into my space. The Corvette could handle two people, but it really only had a headrest for one. The driver.

That would be me. I was a pretty good driver if I didn't have to go backward or park or drive too fast. I was conservative and drove like an old woman. I was usually under the speed limit and scared to death. But I was tall for my age and could pass for being sixteen in a pinch. I knew a place in El Paso that made fake Texas driver's licenses but we were a long way from El Paso. We were in New Jersey. Picking tomatoes.

A Grand Sport Roadster is a race car. Not a luxury sedan. My personal space was mine. I gently placed my brother back into his personal space. You gotta be firm with your kid brother. You gotta set an example. This is my space. This is your space.

The reality is that Tso could not even sleep unless I was next to him. His arm around me. Finally, finally, he sleeps.

I touch his heartbeat with my fingers.

I hear it pressed against my ears.

It was going to be a long drive to Half-Moon Bay, California. Tso was thirteen. Thirteen and breathless. His long black Navajo hair attracted girls who had never seen a guy with long black hair. He had only cut his hair a few times in his life as was the custom of many Indian men. He had kept it short as a little boy, but it grew long and splendid. In 1963, this was pretty radical.

Tso would unconsciously shake his long mane-of-hair around as if he were a darker, thinner version of Brigitte Bardot, totally and absolutely unaware of the effect this had on both men and women. He reminded me of early Cher. My brother was a pouty looker even if he himself was not really aware of it. What thirteen-year-old is aware of himself? I'm here to tell you, people *turned around* and looked. He was very dark and skinny. But he had a gazelle's elegance. With his shirt off, he still looked like a shirtless girl; she might be twelve, and it sometimes stopped the freight trains, it did. My brother needed me to think for him.

"California," I said. Like I was pulling places out of the woodwork. Daddy had always done that and mostly on a dime. Pulling places from the woodwork. Lick your finger. Put it to the wind. You had to remember what grew and when. And where.

I knew where we were going and why. I was fourteen. A man. I could think. I could drive (not backward). I could read and write. I had to make the big decisions. I had learned how to drive as a migrant worker. I had driven trucks filled with watermelons, and tractors that pulled trailers piled with bales of hay.

A mythology has been constructed about the nineteen fifties and the nineteen sixties in America. It is the mythology of conformity and abundance. Apparently, America was a pretty conforming place, and abundance was everywhere. I wouldn't know. We were a little out of this white loop. We did not have the white Colonial home with the white picket fence. We did not ride bikes to the 7-Eleven. We were not on the baseball team. We were not anchored to a place. We did not own no goddamn TV. We were lucky to have teeth. We were hungry in the early years. Sometimes we were desperately hungry. We learned how to steal, and what we frequently stole was food. We loved sausages. We were not educated. We were in the fields.

It was that long, sad migrant bondage to the earth.

We had stolen food so many times, why not a fucking car?

You had to be there or you had to be fourteen.

Lights out. That's all there is.

Mama had been reduced to voices. But ironically, they were voices we could hear with more clarity than we could ever hear her voice when she was among the living.

When Mama died, we did what we always did. We moved on.

We knew something had ended but we were five and six. We kept thinking she would come back. We were like the shadows in the halls. Voices, sighs, lamentations, and strange tongues only we could hear. Sometimes Daddy would shake us to make us stop screaming. When he had gotten us good and drunk (and just about ready to keel over) we would piss all over everything including him. Everything just went from bad to worse. I would watch him go through this sickening tequila-shot repertoire of alcoholic-cowboy-bar routines with my baby brother, and wonder at the quickly swirling world around me.

Quickly swirling. I wanted o-u-t. The Corvette ripping up the landscape.

Throwing up stones and asphalt.

Mama leaving the house wrapped in her Navajo blanket.

The little wave she waved when she left.

I know she must have walked to town. The bars did not like serving Navajo dressed in their blankets. It gave the bar a bad image. The women who drank went from bar to bar until they found one that would serve them. Usually, the bartender just shook his head no and they left.

I remember a car pulling into the drive. My brother and I were by ourselves. The man in the car was not happy about a lot of things.

He came into the house. He opened the refrigerator (which was empty) and he wanted to know where the food was.

We pointed.

He thought we were pointing at a cupboard (which was empty, too) but we were pointing at the store down the road. We were not about to tell some stranger where we hid our food. Candy bars under the floorboard with our plastic soldiers and Apache warriors.

We went to stay with migrant neighbors.

The Mexican women, our mother's friends, dressed us in clothes that had belonged to dead boys. We had known them, too. Tuberculosis. Accidents. Testicular cancer in an eight-year-old. The funeral clothes were starched and stiff. Mama was in a box and she would not get up.

When Mama died, it was the Mexican women of the migrant camp who came to us, who embraced us, who fed us, who clucked over us, and held us together. I remember running around with actual tortillas in my pocket. Fresh ones. You could eat them whenever you wanted. It was more glorious than I could have imagined. I am still trying to understand her funeral. Everyone wore black like mascara. She tried to tell us so much before she went.

Mama, we had to live with it, you drunk fuck.

I am angry still. We wanted out.

The Mexicans moved to follow some other crop. We would not see them again. The tortillas in our pockets were gone. We started eating leaves.

Daddy was around at the edges.

His disintegration began. We lived in a school bus in the desert for a while. Daddy just stared out the window of the bus while we played with lizards in the sun.

Such a car—a red Corvette—to two boys who had never owned so much as new winter coats (our coats were from the Salvation Army FREE FOR YOU box) was not unlike a new and gleaming chariot made by gods.

It was a power we sought with our flesh and our souls. A power we could wield over our own pathetic lives. If we could just get our grimy hands on that car. We saw that car as the ultimate symbol of freedom.

With the top down, the road belonged to us.

Even in 1963, such a car cost fifty thousand dollars. Juvenile delinquents do not normally engage in grand larceny. Criminals do. We were criminals.

I am in blood. The car was red. The interior of the car was red. There were a few things like the glove compartment and the steering wheel and the stick that were either metallic black or chrome.

It seemed like Tso and I had been planning our escape since the space machine had dropped us off to roam among the dinosaurs. I had been studying that little piece of red juice for weeks, anyway. It was there when we arrived at the migrant camp. Daddy saw it, too, and said something surly about the dreams of boys and toys.

Like Daddy knew anything about what we dreamed.

I dreamed he died, and I prayed we could.

I saw this car, and I saw my brother and I riding it slow motion down some long Navajo cliff. *Freedom! Oh, freedom. Freedom for my soul. A band of angels coming after me. Coming for to carry me home.*

I wanted to be black and live like the black migrants on the other side of the migrant camp.

Of course, my fantasy about how they lived was about as rooted in reality as my fantasy that Gina Lollobrigida would fall in love with me and we would run away together and speak French.

I thought Gina Lollobrigida spoke French. I was truly pathetic.

Still (I refused to tell my brother this because it was *my* secret), *Solomon and Sheba* was my favorite movie. A migrant camp in Kewadin, Michigan, where we picked cherries, played the same movies over and over. The man who owned the cherry orchard understood that his migrants were not too welcome in town.

I wanted to be black and live like the black families lived in the migrant camp because quite simply—they had food. Good food, too. We weren't allowed down there, but I would wander around just to smell the bacon. Bacon! We *never* ate bacon. Not only did they have food (like corn bread, my favorite) but they seemed to keep track of each other.

You *knew* where your children were.

You *knew* where Grampa was.

We never knew where our dad was. Or if he might be coming back. The black families in the migrant camp always seemed to know where their family members were. I found this to be a breathtaking feat of bookkeeping.

The black families had fish.

We loved fish.

I had been fishing (because they asked me) with a couple of the black grandfathers in the migrant camp. I had had a blast fishing with a cane pole.

Fishing with my dad was another experience.

He did take us fishing. He did. But he never knew we were there beyond the competition he turned any fishing trip into. It always had to be us against him.

The red Corvette had an aura around it, and had been sitting next to a garage I was pretty sure was a New Jersey chop shop. The chop shop (every car in that lot was stolen) was quietly located down an old dirt road at the back end of a tomato field. The migrant shack we stayed in was back by the chop shop so we could see most of what went on in there. I could see the blue arc of welding going on with the spitting and the flying of the sparks inside the perpetual blackness and the shadows. Cars went in and came out as entirely different vehicles. It was an amazing assembly line of transformation. Sometimes men standing around with white Styrofoam coffee cups would smile and nod at us stupid migrant fucks on the other side of the electrified fence with our buckets and our hoes. Stepin'fetchit. The only thing that concerned me was the Dobermans they kept in the garage.

It was late summer in New Jersey. We were there picking tomatoes.

I'd wave to the chop shop guys, and they'd wave back hello, you.

The chop shop guys were armed. I had seen them put shotguns into car trunks. I liked looking at them to try to figure out where they hid their guns. Sometimes it was just in the pocket of a coat. The funny thing was, nobody came to claim that car. It belonged to no one. It needed me.

Like Solomon needed Sheba.

I wanted to have muscles like Solomon. All I was ever going to be was a tomato picker with a bucket. Again. Again and again. Pennsylvania, Ohio, Michigan, Florida, and New Jersey are all states you can get employment in picking tomatoes.

I did not understand what it was about tomatoes Daddy liked. We were always picking tomatoes, and I *hated* them.

It's tomatoes or cotton, boy, take your pick.

I had picked cotton in Alabama, Arkansas, Texas, and New Mexico.

I hated picking cotton a whole hell of a lot more than I hated picking tomatoes so I went with the tomatoes. Cucumbers were the worst, as they had these little barbs, but there were places like Eaton Rapids, Michigan, that would take every cuke we could pick. Huge vats of cucumbers being pickled.

The tomato field had long, long rows, but I could always see that sweet red car from the corners of my eyes. My brother would stand there with his hands on that fence for hours. I had to grab the back of his pants and drag him off that fence. Too many eyes. "If I could just drive it around the block one time," Tso told me. "Just one time."

"Put a plug in it, okay," I told my brother. I wanted more than a joyride from that car. "With what I have got in mind for us, we'll go more than just around some friggin' block, okay. Baby, *we* are going to California."

"Do you really think so?" he asked.

I could only sigh and count spiders on the ceiling of the migrant shack.

Spiders. Bullet holes. Wasp's nests. Cum stains.

There have been times, too, when I have dragged him out to see the stars at three a.m. in his underpants.

Pointing up: "Okay, Tso. Pick a star. Which one did we come from? Try to r-e-m-e-m-b-e-r."

He has slugged me a couple of times. In play.

I love him anyway. There isn't much Tso could do to dissuade me from it.

Our conflicts were actually pretend conflicts. Like my shoving him out of my space. This was our way of joking. My dragging him outside in his underpants to see the stars. The reality is that we simply didn't fight. Life was hard enough. Why make it any more miserable? We adored one another in different ways. I enjoyed holding hands, and sleeping next to him, and cutting his hair. He enjoyed not having to make the decisions.

Like going to school. Was this a migrant camp where we would enroll in school or not? I would usually check it all out, including whether there was any expectation that our father would be involved because he would not be involved in any way. Two weeks in school was usually not worth the effort. As we grew older, we would invent reasons why we had to stay another week, another month. But never longer than that. The migrant life was harder on Tso than me. Every single time Daddy pushed him into a bedroom and slammed the door and locked it, I felt so sorry for him I thought the two of us going off a cliff would be downright merciful. Tso would scream bloody hell. *Daddy, you're hurting me, please!*

Do you think it made anyone in a migrant camp come running?

When Daddy was through with him, he'd walk through the living room and say, "Your brother needs you."

I would sit there thinking: *I feel unqualified to address myself to my brother's abuse. I can only address him. There is a difference.*

I would have to go in there and clean him up while he shook and cried. Shit, blood, and cum. I was the one who did things like laundry, and I always had to remember that the Salvation Army had washrags and towels, too. I would clean him up and talk to him while his legs trembled.

People in a migrant camp do not go out looking for more troubles than they already have. The migrant life had been the bane of our existence forever. At least New Jersey was one of the few places where there weren't too many signs with the words: NO MIGRANTS.

One of my favorite places to migrate was northern Michigan. Lake Michigan was beautiful, and picking cherries with the Chippewa could even be fun. We would pick in places like Kewadin and Traverse City. But all up and down the lake the stores had signs: NO MIGRANTS. You saw these signs and every single time you did it took another fragment of you, it would eventually—in time—have your pound of flesh. There were worse places than New Jersey. Discrimination in New Jersey was more subtle than that. You would walk into a place and everyone there would pretend you did not exist. They could look right through you.

The West was different. Waitresses, doormen, cabdrivers, busboys, and people who made less money than you did all ignored you as if you weren't there. We existed. We existed with a vengeance.

I was not sure why.

Every time I closed my eyes I wished Tso and I were dead. Sometimes we would cuddle close at night and pray. I am not sure, even now, to whom.

"We want to die tonight, please," Tso would say. "Please, we are begging you to not let us wake up in the morning. It is all we want, to just go, please. We do not want our lives, please. Could we just die together? I am begging and asking you to not let us be alive in the morning."

There would be a long silence in the night.

I love my brother. I love my brother's sensuality because he got it from my mom. I was all he had. I allowed him to touch me. Hug me. Sometimes kiss me. Crawl all over me as a baby. Now, on these dark suicidal nights of shadows, I allow him to hold me in a grief he has. I do not even have to understand as long as I honor it as being real. It was very real. He was grieving for us. For a life we never had and never could have. I have to give him that. It was his prayer. It was not something you could attach a grade to.

"Is my prayer okay, Nasdijj?"

"Yaaa. It's okay. If I have to die, then this would be the best way, Tso. Here. With you. If I am going to die tonight then let me be with you."

When the dreams come, he shakes so hard I sometimes wonder if he is having a seizure.

By the time we were thirteen, we were ready (in our dumb heads anyway) to challenge the man who was our father.

He had been waiting. Sort of with a smirky smile on his face. Chewing toothpicks and cigarettes. You would need more than the ability to wear his boots to challenge him. It was not a good idea and we knew that, too.

As a teenager, I would put his boots on when he was asleep. I would walk around in them for a minute thinking: *So this is what it feels like to be you.* Daddy was no thief. He looked down on it. I think the idea of it scared him some. He was already in debt to so many white men he could never measure up against. Stealing from them would have been more than he could do. I do not know that he had a moral code of conduct. You did what you thought you could get away with. Daddy preferred to work in the back-breaking sun all afternoon. Tso and I hated our migrant worker lives. We would have turned to thievery in a minute, and Daddy knew it, too. He watched us hard.

He hit us hard.

He fucked us hard.

He hated hard. Bend over, boy. Daddy undoes the belt. The night before we stole that car, he had *ordered* Tso to fuck me. We refused this. He found his gun. It was always loaded. He was always drunk.

Daddy believed that his children existed to serve him. It is so easy for other people to say we should have told someone. An authority figure. They do not understand. Authority figures were the people we were attempting to deceive, go around, and we only confronted them when we were ready for a fight. You had better be prepared to lose.

~~~~~

I heard voices. I wonder if there was ever a time when I was not hearing voices. I do not recall it.

I was beginning to understand something my brother might never understand, having not had the opportunity to know our mother as well as I did.

I know that when my mother held me, it quelled the voices in me. They became less distinct, almost as if they had started to hum some sad song versus competing with each other in a shrill acceleration. If she were able to have that kind of internalized effect on me she was probably able to have some of the same calming qualities on my father. What he was doing in demanding our sexual performance had less to do with sex than it had to do with calming his own inner demons through the voyeuristic experience of seeing, and touching. Through seeing, he was touching something of the tenderness that existed between us as brothers.

Looking for a piece of her in us. In what we had together.

Knowing he could never have it.

The tenderness belonged to us, but it had all her fundamental human qualities.

Through us, he was touching her.

"I didn't mean to."

I knew that. For Christ's sake he was performing at the insistence of a loaded gun. I do not know if our father would have shot us if we refused him his performances. I did not want to test him. I did know that someday my brother was going to make some lucky woman a very gentle lover. I had to get my brother away from our father before the man destroyed the boy. I was in my way already destroyed. But my brother still had time on his side.

"Someday the day is going to come, Tso, when someone—you, me, Daddy—is going to be holding that gun and it *will* go off. It will. It's just a matter of time. We have *got* to go."

California loomed. "It's tomorrow night."

Tso looked at me with a trust that ran deeper than the planet's crust.

If we had waited one more day, someone was going to die, and it just didn't have to be. Daddy's gun was going to go off and it would get a mention in the paper as an accident.

"I want to be with you on the beach in California, okay? We will find us some girls and some jobs and our lives will become infinitely better than they are right now. Are you with me?"

I am not sure in retrospect I used the term *infinitely* but I am *sure* my brother connected to what I was saying.

There was only one thing we liked about the migrant life.

California.

California had girls and waves. Nice girls. Girls who did not have to know about us. We knew how to get there, too. We had driven it a thousand times.

In 1963, a perfect year, a year nothing happened, and in the beginning, anyway, it looked like nothing ever would—happen—a slow-motion year, everyone going about their business in slow motion, all you needed to hot-wire a car was a pair of needle-nose pliers, and half the time you didn't even need them.

A pair of nail clippers would work just fine. All you had to do was strip a few wires, and connect them to the starter. Really, Mafia chop shops should be more careful of their stolen property.

"We will be *killed*," my brother whispered.

We were already dead and he knew it. A migrant camp is a graveyard. Just look around at the walking dead. They're everywhere in a migrant camp. Skinwalkers.

I said nothing for a long while as we tried to sleep in that Toms River, New Jersey, migrant shack with our migrant daddy in the room next to us making noise with his New Jersey tomato-whore-of-the-night.

Counting bullet holes.

"We leave tomorrow night," I said. I did not want Tso to forget. And he might.

Every now and then—it was impossible to predict—my brother gave in to his fears. He surrendered to them. Bowing like a supplicant. Diving under beds. Crying and begging me to not make him come out.

He tells me he dreams of being buried in a coffin with our mother.

Although it was dark, I could feel my brother next to me in his under-pants in the darkness and the shadows caressing him and his Indian hair.

It was then that I remembered *she had cut his hair* once. Just before she died. She had taken an entire afternoon to do it. Daddy had bitched at her to get her fat ass back into the fields, but she had ignored him, touching, and touching, and cutting her youngest son's hair. Her eyes darted to me and she smiled. We both did.

Another of her lessons that I am to care for Tso gently.

And I have, Mama, I have.

Before he falls asleep, he turns to me, and hugs me, and on the hot nights Tso sucks his thumb.

I still sleepwalk.

One night, I found the "family" gun.

A .45, and always loaded. *What good is a gun that isn't loaded? Daddy would say. Daddy was always, always right.* I was aiming that gun at Daddy.

Who was asleep in his bed.

Or I thought he was asleep. I was.

"You going to just stand there all night, Nasdijj? Or are you going to shoot me and be done with it? Isn't this what you always wanted? Go for it, boy. You always were nothing but talk, talk, talk."

It was in that moment that I realized that Daddy was addicted to the violence of his life. I woke up quickly, which is the worst possible way to wake up.

Holding a gun.

Pointed directly at that fuck.

I wanted to shoot it more than I have ever wanted anything. I started to hyperventilate. I was afraid.

I dropped the gun on the floor with a thud and went to bed.

The next day, he beat me so badly, I spent the whole morning throwing my guts up.

I'm vomiting blood and my brother is getting very scared.

Okay. We couldn't kill him, but we could leave him.

That whole next dull and aching day hung like stones in my eyes and moved about as fast. We tried to pick tomatoes like nothing was up. Just another day.

But our dad kept giving us funny looks. Daddy was mean as a basketful of snakes but he wasn't stupid.

"Whatever it is, Nasdijj," he said, "you best think twice about it, boy."

The coyote in him was suspicious.

He would shake his head, and muttering about migrant brats and how he had never wanted one. Now he had two. I was only then beginning to understand that what came out of his mouth was fragments of the poisonous slur that churned in him.

I'm thinking: *I am fourteen and not a brat, you scumbag.*

Daddy did not use the word *boy* lightly. It meant you were walking too close to some edge he would rather not have to pull you out of.

I took my New York Yankees baseball cap off. I scratched my head. "Whatever *what* is, Daddy?"

Daddy looked over at Tso, who was peeing on a tree. Tso only peed when he was nervous.

Mainly he never peed.

I shrugged like I had no fucking idea what he was talking about, and went back to work filling my bucket with green tomatoes.

Daddy just chewed on his dumb toothpick like a hayseed and scratched his balls.

That night, the chop shop was closed. It was dark as Bibles and there was fog in the heavy air. We crawled over the barbed-wire fence. It virtually hummed but we could avoid the higher part of it that was electrified but not barbed. Toasted migrant was not our idea of breakfast. That car just glowed red in the night. Take me. We heard barking.

Dobermans. Shit.

We knew no one ever went back there at night. I eventually opened the door with a whore's hairpin. The old-fashioned kind. Very sturdy. You could hear the hairpin clicks like crickets in the moonlight. I could hear my brother's thirteen-year-old heart banging away like a gong in his adolescent chest. The Corvette started like a charm. I'm trying to quietly steal this fifty-thousand-dollar vehicle, and I hear the sound of water. My brother (*not* in the car *yet*) is peeing in the parking lot. Jesus. *Get in the fucking CAR.* Like an idiot, I stalled the thing. My brother was a little nervous. "Did you wreck it?" he asked, jumping into the passenger's seat.

"Yaaaaa, Tso, I wrecked it."

Tso was holding our journals. They were all we had.

"You need to hold it lightly. You're forcing it, and it's not a car that can be forced."

My little brother the car mechanic.

He was right. I relaxed. The car started up again, and we burned rubber all the way out of that fuck bucket they call New Jersey.

Those journals were vast symbolic monuments. At least to us. That there could even be a life outside the context of picking cabbages. I just aimed that pretty piece of juice west for California.

I was in blood. And more trouble than I knew. The last battle between good and evil before the day of judgment had not arrived.

<center>~~~~~~</center>

In the bad dream *Ra tu tsa kntesa tu* has infected me with snakes. They slither out from every hole. The eyes. The nose.

Biting.

I wake up. Soaked. Exhausted. Shivering and shakes.

The blackness comforts me. I hope I am dead.

Then, something will stir.

The dream and the hope fades away. I am a tiny man who does tiny things. Only tiny things.

Add it all up. My life isn't worth the pain it rode in on.

I would do anything not to have the dream. I see myself back there holding my head in my hands and screaming in the middle of a thousand nights. I have had that dream every night for more than forty years.

Then you must kill your father. Finally.

I know that, too. Come, pony-warriors. We must make a circle of the past, and with our magic hoops, we must take back the world we live on for the people still walk upright in this place. Come, pony-warriors, bring me heroes in your dreams.

Geronimo.

Who despises snakes. My plastic play men. Armies and armies.

But you know that, he says.

It's true. I do. I will have to kill my father. I will find some way.
To bury the whirlwind.

~~~~~

There is an old farmhouse in Colorado that no one has lived in for a long,
long time. Ruins and the wind sings songs in sand.

Just another of our rented houses. Whirlywinds kick about as if they in
their constant flirtations had missed the dance.

I, too, am wreckage here. My bitterness is a thousand of my plastic
armies. My legs barely carry the rest of me around. Now the wind laughs
here and sings its songs in longitude across the land. Sings time. Sings
wars. Sings what silence brings. The long, twisting drive is crowded with
tall pines. They were shorter once. I was a child and they were little like
me. I drive here in my jeep with my dog, Navajo.

Whose old spirit goes back. Way back.

From this dry spot of dust where the whirlywinds play (the Navajo call
them *yiyols*) I could see far across the mesa to the mountains. It was here
that I saw the first of the vast migrations. I was just a child. Maybe four or
five. Who heard voices. Who had dreams. Who saw them coming—the
migrants coming and coming—across that vast expanse where the snow on
the peaks touches the babyblue of the big sky. I thought if I ever saw
them—knowing in my heart, and in that place behind my eyes where my
dreams live, that I would live to see them—they would all be riding horses,
but it was not to be.

They arrived long before the horse.

They walked and they carried things and they had dogs that pulled
things. Their blackblue hair blew in the wind. They wore the skins of animals. The dogs that were not pulling things barked and barked to see the
vision of me in front of them fluttering.

As a child, I would stand on this dust bowl spot and see the coming of
the nomads. Even then, I knew I would die in pain.

The great migrant tribes in their traveling weariness put down all things
here. Looking about for water. The dogs would find it first. The running
and the laughing of barefoot children.

Then I would run to tell my mother.

"Mother, Mother! I have seen people coming."

She was in the farmhouse kitchen drying dishes. "What people? Go
play. Do not disturb your father. He doesn't feel well today."

"They were coming, and they were carrying things. Dogs were pulling
long poles. I saw them coming."

My mother, Shima, would just stand there for a long time, wiping some already dry dish, looking at me, and she was not amused.

"If I listen correctly," I told her, "I can hear their moccasins."

I could.

"Nasdijj," she would ask, "what are moccasins?" I did not know. I shrugged.

She never said she did not believe me, and she never dismissed me lightly, but she would bend down to my height, and she would take her fingers, and she would close my eyes gently with her fingers, and she would say, "Nasdijj, you are not to see these things. You are not to see these people. You are not to hear them or see them, do you understand me?"

I would shake my head agreeably. But she knew. It seemed as if she were speaking to the voices, and not really to me.

And I would run and play.

It is so cold, the jeep's brakes squeak as we turn a corner. We drive by the small family graveyard. No one I know is buried there. Perhaps these are the people who built this place. I wonder why everyplace my father ever found for us to live always had to be haunted. They, whoever they are, have been forgotten. You live out your days, and they will forget you. There is a small black fence that outlines the graves. Lined with old weeds like an old man's craggy face. As a little boy, I played here. Pretending to be sad.

Just an old rented family farmhouse. The family forgotten.

We would try to make a go of it here. My mad, sad, cold family.

Failing again and again. My mad, sad, cold parents.

Their dreams are buried here. I can only remember one winter in this place.

Every time we moved, we would be leaving behind one more set of failures. It was *the failures* that *followed us*.

Always from the land behind us. Chasing crops. Chasing history. Chasing the image of strange men who arrived at night and they wanted money. My dad would run out the back. The screen door slamming. The sounds of heavy men running and breathing that hard way only heavy men breathe. I would run out in the crunchy snow holding my little brother's hand. Tso did not have his coat on. Tso did not want to be dragged out into the snow. We would get to where the whirlywinds came in the summer, a soft, bowl-like indentation in the even softer earth, and I would instruct my brother to be quiet.

Why?

Because they won't come if you don't make noise.

But I don't see anything. I don't hear anything. There is NOTHING OUT HERE!

My younger brother would trudge back into the house. I do not know why but the house seemed colder than being in the snow.

I did not care if men arrived looking for my father. Let them find him. Out here in the blue-snow.

I could see them and I could hear them as clearly as the back stream ran with trout.

The nomadic migrants in their buffalo robes covered in powder. Pulling their stuff. Pulling babies.

The children and the dogs would run to me. The image of me fluttering.

Come! Let us play with the boy who comes through time to see us! The boys would push the girls into the snow and everyone would laugh. Walking and walking and finally losing their color and disappearing into the snow.

Leaving me to my winter and my own mystery of a graveyard.

The same people are buried here as when I lived in this sad failed place as a cowboy pipsqueak with my caps and guns. No one has moved. Maybe no one is buried here. I thought they were all gunslingers once.

Draw, Cowboy.

The gas station down at the four corners is gone, too. The old man who had owned that place once told me about the gunslingers. My dark eyes wide as saucers. He had grape pop. All lies. But fun ones. Percy Simonton is buried here. If you brush away the leaves and the weeds, you will see his name engraved on a small stone grave. PERCY SIMONTON 1847–1900.

No one around here ever heard of him.

Perhaps he never left this house. Stumble up the porch steps with my crutches. In places holes. This place is getting dangerous. You wouldn't want to live here with children now.

My crutches sink into the wood. Small wonder the place has been condemned. The windows are broken here and there. Kick the door open.

Dust and time.

Rust and sun.

Emptiness and your voice echoes. *Mama! Daddy, Daddieeedaddieee . . .*

I pound my gloved hands together.

You can see your breath inside, too, like frost. Navajo thinks it's a great adventure. She explores every room like we might move in. Her dog feet clicking.

I laugh softly at the notion.

"No, girl. Not this lifetime." I pet her.

She barks at something she thinks she sees outside. Probably a snow gopher. My mom and dad slept in one room. Upstairs. I can hear them moving about. Light laughter. I can still smell them. Liquor and sex. Cards. Same curtains. Now dull.

We never did make it in this house. We were hungry. We walked slowly here. Eating ham the neighbors brought over. We were someone's charity and it broke my father's back.

He would not eat that ham but we would.

It was the best ham ever. And lima beans. The old water pump doesn't work.

Someone has written graffiti on the walls. How sad. My brother's car pulls up. He's late.

We hug. He walks around like I did.

My brother has just been released from a psychiatric hospital. He seems fine. He takes his meds. We have agreed to meet in this place. To see it one more time.

This time I do not pull him outside. I simply stare out the window.

They are still arriving, the nomads.

"You still see them, don't you, Nasdijj?"

"Yes."

His fingers are touching my shoulders.

At first it made me weep to hear these strange tongues of wind that come in through the uneven windows. The house sags with age like an old man's chest rasps sick with pneumonia. A fox lives in the root cellar. In August, there would be tall sunflowers over by the clothesline.

No clothesline. Just dead weeds.

Ra tu tsa kntesa tu had lived out here in these weeds. Pulling his slow reptilian length along. My brother and I kick up frozen weeds. No snakes in winter. *Ra tu tsa kntesa tu* sleeps and dreams of me.

"Them big old snakes lived out here," my brother said.

Yes. I used to talk to them.

My brother smiles and remembers.

He does not trust me not to talk with them now. And I might, too.

My brother's hand touches my shoulder.

The sound of some boy screaming.

Some boy being beaten. Whipped. Some boy being raped. I put my hands to my ears. I do not care to hear this boy. I do not want to know him.

My brother speaks very softly now. "We were just kids who had dug this deep emotional pit and we could not find our way out of it."

Perhaps.

"Let me show you something," my brother says. My brother is forty-nine. A man. A man who struggles like any other man. I have always regretted our shared history. As if it were this poisonous basement with corpses and secrets in the wet dirt. I look over at my brother and I understand for the first time that we have shouldered this huge, huge thing; it has been a horrible burden. For all of its rough edges and bloody stranglings, nevertheless, it is what we have had to share.

I love him but I cannot tell him. I hope he knows. We go up to the sounds of those same nails in the stairs squeaking. It had been a warning then. The Cowboy in his underpants was coming up the stairs. He would sit on our beds and cry softly while his hands roamed about our bodies. First mine. Then, my brother's. Touching. Then, hurting us. We pretended not to even be alive through this. Horror. Our old room. The floorboard comes up. I had forgotten. They are still there.

Plastic men. Some soldiers. A few Indians.

~~~~~~

7

The First Car I Ever Stole

Changing Woman looked out at the many things her sons had done. At the many dragons they had slain. They were both covered in the thick, burning blood of dragons.

Changing Woman dipped her finger into the blood on their naked skin and drew symbols on the rocks.

Using blood as paint. It was a good paint, and all of the people who would see it would pray to all the gods and all the holy people. Those symbols burned into the stone forever. They will always be there. They are the symbols of the People going up.

Into the fifth world where no one is sure if there is another world of going up. Many of the People have said no, and they have claimed: the fifth and FINAL world. But the People have said that before when they were insects going up the reed of life.

Changing Woman took a piece of lung from Deelgeed, the slain horned monster, now hard and defeated, and he would always be known as the mountain of the southeast corner of Dinetah, and Changing placed this piece of lung in her mouth. Then she began singing and dancing all around the rocks where she had drawn her symbols in the blood of dragons.

"Naayee neizghani *brings for me:*
A piece of lung he brings for me.

Deelgeed's *lung he brings for me.*
Our people are restored.

"To bajish chini *brings for me:*
A piece of wing he brings for me.
Ninahaleeh *he brings for me.*
My people are restored.

"Enemy Slayer brings for me:
A lock of monster hair he brings for me.
Monster of the cliffs he brings for me.
His people are restored.

"Monster Slayer brings for me:
Monster eyes he brings for me.
Binaa' yee aghanii *he brings for me.*
Our people are restored."

The first car I ever stole.

Was like the first ship ever made by man. It floated perfectly.

The first car I ever stole (by myself) was a dark blue 1955 Pontiac Star Chief whose glistening chrome hood ornament reminded me of the spirit of Geronimo.

This was the early sixties. Daddy had moved Tso and I to New Orleans directly after he had been fired from working Ferris wheels at Louisiana carnivals.

The carnival fired Daddy because he gave free rides to whores.

The carvival people said no free rides for anyone. Tattoos and all and rubbed in grease. I can't say it was better than living and working in the migrant fields. What I can say is that my brother and I lived on a diet of hot dogs in buns and mustard, and pink and purple cotton candy. Living on hot dogs and cotton candy was better than living on nothing at all. When Daddy was fired we moped for a week because we were sure we were headed back to starving in the fields. But Daddy took us to New Orleans, where some folks were so stupid they left the keys in their dark blue Pontiac Star Chief.

Walking down the street, I never saw just cars. I saw cars whose owners had either taken the keys with them or not.

Or not was good.

Getting caught was bad.

I never did get caught. In my own defense, it was more a joyriding thing than a stealing thing, although I did like stealing cars. People ask me *why* I stole cars.

To drive them, of course. What else can a car do?

I loved to drive, and since I could not afford gas or even as much as a hot dog, I used someone else's gas, and I simply drove around until I had had enough of it, and then I always returned the car exactly where I had stolen it. I was lucky. I pushed it and wondered if my luck would run out like Daddy's had but mine never did, and I just kept on stealing cars and taking them for rides around the block. I had learned to drive trucks and tractors in those migrant fields we hated. I had also driven trucks (usually with sheep) around the Navajo reservation.

I saw women looking at me when I was stealing cars. Stealing glances. Sideways stares. Look at me, I'm the driver. Me and Geronimo. Driving that chrome and glistening boat into the night, down St. Charles like I owned it. I could barely see over the steering wheel.

I was Dionysus on his way to lay waste to both Troy and Helen. Once she got a look at my new car, she would melt into my arms like heaven.

I was a jackass.

I think Daddy knew. He'd watch me in that calculating way he had. He would tell Sugar, his whore, I was an arrogant little shit today.

"Don't mess with him." Sugar would always rush to defend my honor. "He likes how the ladies look at him."

New Orleans was wet and brick and Metairie Cemetery and alligator sauce piquant, and they made gumbo where we lived in Gumbotown. That was what Daddy called it. Not too many people, but a few, left their car keys right there in the goddamn car. It always ended much too soon. The gas would go to empty. The whore would bake Daddy boudin balls and pack his bags. We always had to pack our own, but the whore made sure to pack his bags because she had to know that he was really gone.

The writing on the walls.

Was done by July and I.

I knew what we were doing. We were spray-painting walls with our *art*. If you could call it *art*. July did. She called herself an artist, too. July was a fast woman and a fisherwoman and an alligator-wrestling-woman and one of my father's better whores. She referred to herself as a whore, too. It was at least honest. She had flaming red hair and green Irish eyes. She wore lipstick and drank whiskey. It hurt me to see her with my dad. I would try to look the other way, and, forgiving her, I would attempt to see her as separate from the Cowboy. I liked her well enough. She lived with us for a while or we lived with July—I am not sure which one it was. I know we moved in at her kind if naïve invitation. We were tramps and always guests in someone else's house. In no time, it would smell like us.

July was from Florida but had migrated north to pick apples in Washington State. Somewhere in there there was a divorce and a very bad man. July always joked that she could take her life to Nashville and put it on the stage. Then she would have to buy a bus, and she didn't have that kind of driver's license.

"We lived on a bus one time," Tso chimed in. "It was fun. But Daddy never left the bus."

"No, honey," July said. Putting on her maternal face. "That was a mental health bus. I would need a broken-down, old Greyhound bus. Where hope lives eternal."

She was dirt-rag poor. We were down to our last bag of Fig Newtons. We had arrived to pick apples, too. Nevertheless, I was always reading. Seattle was a great place to do it. It was me, the rain, a book, and all the places books took me to.

I had remembered July before she came to pick us up in Walla Walla because July and Daddy had had some of the better fireworks in Florida. Tso and I always thought they should put it on the road, set up a stand somewhere in the South. South Carolina would do. *Free fireworks! Watch us explode some big ol' crackers, you crackers!*

And then we'd laugh because we had to.

Before July arrived to pick us up (there we were dripping wet with our bags and smelling like soaked dog), we made Daddy promise no fireworks.

Or we would ship the two of them to Crackerville.

Daddy's eye to the sky.

Apple-picking season ends as winter finds her wet and rainy way to Seattle. July picked us up in Walla Walla and drove with us back to her place in the bigger city. When the rain comes to Seattle people hunker down and paint their skin in shades of gray. They walk around the city as if their bones grind at them.

July and Daddy would get along famously for a while, and then the peace would clear like fog to be replaced by the smoke and smell of war. Dead bodies in the sun. The smell of rot. July had once wrestled alligators at a tourist clip joint outside of Port Mayaca country in the Florida swamps. Moms and dads and all the little children dressed in shorts and peddle pushers would stand behind the fence and watch July and several other of the Seminole Indian wrestlers wrestle and hog-tie a poor old gator who had been wrestled and hog-tied so many times, he really did not care about it anymore, and I always thought that gator would rather have been chewing gum. July was from Okeechobee, where she had learned to wrestle gators from her mama who was an artist, too. Not the spray-paint kind of artists we were, but the kind of artist who painted pictures of alligators in the swamps. July had tons of these paintings decorating her Seattle apartment walls. Gators everywhere you looked. I did not care for them.

July referred to my father as *that gator*, too. Other women had called him other things. July was the only one I knew who saw him as a reptile.

I have this twisted thing about referring to the women in my father's life as *whores*. If the woman-of-the-moment wasn't my mother, then she had to be a whore. I often feel as if I am a haunted tool my mother uses from beyond the grave to redeem herself or to extract revenge in a thousand ways. Some of the women my father brought into the house *were* whores. More than a few. More than most men would introduce into the family fold. Most men do not live with the whores they frequent. Not like Daddy did. It is as difficult for me now as it was back then to regard any of these so-called loose women as Daddy's lover. But if I want to be honest with myself that is what they were. They were whores who took my father, and his bags, sons, dogs, sorries, fishin' gear, drinkin', card games, dreams of being the Las Vegas King of the Desert Trash *in*. Into *their* apartments, trailers, lives, kitchens, strip-joint dressing rooms, and into *their* Las Vegas Queen of the Motel Dreams and Donought-Holes-of-the-Heart. *In* and *in* again.

Sometimes I feel as if my mother speaks to me in odd ways, like in the kind of writing you find on walls. Flames. And dissolves in mist.

"Tell July with her red frizzie hair and her green eyes to beware of YOU KNOW WHO," my dead mother warned.

But, Mama, it's not up to me.

July would have to deal with Daddy on her own terms.

She was the only one I told about my stealing cars. It was safe to tell July. Or rather she squeezed it outta me. She liked me and she was wise as they come. That does not mean she was the proverbial hooker with the heart of gold. No. July's heart was a doughnut hole heart. Sweet but bad for you.

"But I always bring them back to where I ripped them off," I told her. "I can't back up too good, but I'm okay at it if I just go slow."

"Nasdijj, yer such a goody two-shoes—I just can't *imagine* it!" July laughed somewhat hysterically.

Then she paused.

"Well, there is a gloomy part to you, boy. Let's go stealing cars together."

I had never once considered stealing cars with anyone other than myself. I just looked at her with my mouth open.

She was an adult. The enemy.

"We could spray-paint Seattle."

Spray-paint Seattle? Now I knew July was crazy.

"Are you nuts?" I asked her. "Seattle will not appreciate the thought."

"They got some fancy cars up there on the hill," July contended.

I had no idea what hill she might mean.

"But they got some meanshit cops around here, too, July."

"Aww, come on. Or are you just pulling my leg?" She laughed again. The thought of me as a car thief was too much funny bone for July to hang with.

She claimed she could hot-wire a vehicle as well as anyone. My eyes to the sky.

Daddy was knocked out beer-cold one night, and July said it would be *the* night. Car thieving. Tso did not want to know about it. "Don't tell me where you are going, what you are doing, or when you might be back," he said. "I *do not want to know*."

Fine with me. Fine with July. It would be our secret. July seemed more my age than Daddy's age.

All the way to Riverton Heights in her gator truck, July went on and on about how that scofflaw daddy of mine would never marry her, fish, or cut bait.

July had seen the wedding in her dreams in a downtown department store window. Big church. Tons of people dressed in their Sunday-go-to-meeting clothes. Daddy at a wedding? When elephants roost in trees.

We drove around and around until we came to a pink church big as broad daylight with nice big cars parked all around it.

Pink. I thought for a moment I was back in Florida. "How's this?" July asked.

"Church is good," I said. "I like to look for the latecomers. The latecomers will be flustered some, and one is likely to leave the keys right there in the car."

I had not developed my hot-wiring technique yet to the point where it was quick and slick. It took me about a month to get a car started that way. Eventually I would work the kinks out of it. But for now, I looked for flustered folks late to church.

There was an evening church servive going on inside. We were on the opposite side of the church when we saw the car. It was not a car I would usually take.

It was a Volvo. I would never steal a Volvo. I would rather shoplift a vibrator than steal a Volvo. The keys were in the car.

"Is this the one?" July asked. "It's a vulva."

"No. V-o-l-v-o—look, something's in the car."

A dog.

We both sort of stepped involuntarily back. The dog seemed to be driving the car.

The inside of the Volvo was a mess of broken liquor bottles. All over the seats and floor. It looked like an argument had turned vicious. The dog's feet were cut and there were bloodstains of paw prints everywhere in that car. "Oh, I have to get a picture of this," July said. She made a mad dash back to her alligator-toting truck to get her camera.

We were artists, thieves, photographers, and we loved dogs.

"What kind of mean old ugly person would drive a Vulva and keep their dog penned up in it? Oh, *look*. Poochie is wagging his tail."

"Poochie?" I had had a stuffed dog named Poochie. July was thieving again.

"I'm stealing him. He needs a mom and he loves me."

"He has never met you, July." The dog barked.

We took him home. Poochie would live happily with her for the next ten years. Our father did not marry her.

She was lucky. I could hear my mother sigh. "Okay, Nasdijj. Honey, you did good this time."

8

We Were There

The crows set the boys down where the spider trails ended.
There was an old kiva here.
But the crows flew away. Saying nothing.
Inside the kiva, they could hear the music from a single flute.

We were there.

The migrant boys talked among themselves about how cold the winter was. The migrant boys did not wear socks.

I knew all their secrets.

Some did not have blankets. They slept in their clothes and at night they were cold. Their beds were wooden slats. Being wary with their quick mean eyes. They were uncomfortable around white people. Even the white ones were uncomfortable around white people. The pretty white girls liked boys with moms and dads and houses. All migrants ever had was a vehicle. It might or it might not start. They never started in the cold. We called them vehicles, then. I do not know why.

I always wanted socks. Socks were a big, big deal. I never had any.

I liked cowboy boots because if you did not have socks, no one knew.

Being adolescent was the worst.

"Are you okay," I asked my brother. We had both driven hours and hours to get here. The sun was far away.

"You mean, *Am I okay now that I am not locked up on the loony ward?*"

"Yaaaa. Something like that. The light here in this place at this time of year in Colorado is always cold as toes."

"You used to make me kiss your toes."

"I certainly did not."

My brother laughed. Outrageously.

"Take me home," he said.

This place had once been that to us. It had kept our secrets safe all these years. We had hidden Geronimo away.

Men would say: *Because their father was a lunatic.*

That, too.

But no. We had not really hidden Geronimo because our father would hurt us if he caught us playing with toys. Oh, he would, but we had learned how to soak his abuses in. Like Noxzema. No. We had hidden Geronimo because Geronimo's voice haunted us.

~~~~~~

Sometimes we moved away quick in the middle of the night. We would drag our feet about it. Wondering why.

Quick, boy. We have got to go.

My brother would ask me with his eyes. There were so many times we had no use for words.

Yes. Yes. Yes. I have Geronimo in one pocket. Our book in the other.
Move!

They did not explain much. Move meant move. We moved so often that there were times when we did not bother to unpack until the sixth or seventh day. Just in case.

A man's gambling debts were serious. Men would show up at the migrant shacks and they would throw the migrant men who owed money into the darkness and the parkingt lot. The migrants all too aware of what is coming next.

The crunching of the baseball bats.

The screaming.

The migrant men begging.

But our daddy never did. Beg. They just beat him up.

They set them up. The traveling gambling games were often owned by the ranchers who also charged them rent. And then they beat them. It was about keeping a man in his place.

And connected to the migrant life.

You wanted him in debt to you. You did not want him in a place where he could make independent decisions. My father's mad chasing from camp to camp was designed as chaos to beat the gambling debts that followed him everywhere. Gambling was just another way to bend the world of chaos into a less turbulent place that gave you what sustenance you needed. Leaving one migrant camp for the anonymity in another, all the while thinking you could beat this rap when, in fact, it just followed you like a virus that attached itself to you in a hundred thousand places. Do not tell me that the ranchers never did this—had these ongoing poker games—because you weren't there. We were there. Don't tell me that the ranchers and the farm bosses would have treated their workers better than that so their migrants could pick and work. No. You could pick and you could work even if half of you was swollen black and blue. If his place was broken then you broke the man. It kept the man in debt. You were never able to pay the migrant rent (on those broken, broken shacks). You were never able to pay your gambling debts, either. It kept men in the fields. Always hustling to be one step ahead of the men they called *collectors*.

If you did not speak English, the *collectors* simply shoved you around, picking up objects you treasured, a toy ballerina belonging to one of your girls. By ruining a few symbolic things, he made sure you got the point.

Collectors were never above hurting migrant children. The interest on a man's debts compounded daily. Owing someone a dollar quickly turned into owing them a hundred dollars. We saw them grab a little Mexican girl once, she was playing barefoot in the dirt under the porch of the migrant shack next to us, and they picked her up like they were going to hug her, and then they smashed her hand with a hammer, breaking all the bones. It was almost impossible to get out of this kind of debt, and we saw people who owed their lives to gambling debts, then turned around and had to borrow money to pay the rent from the very same people they owed all the money to in the first place.

You are running in circles so fast you can't tell the beginning from the middle or the end. Always working to pay off the dog that bit them.

Only they never could. Because it was impossible. Do the math.

It was years before we finally figured out that our father could neither read nor write and he could not add or subtract, either.

Yet he drove (he never had a license) and he could move from one ocean to the other and never once be lost. His sense of place was awesome.

He sat us down once, and in his own hand-wringing way attempted to explain (one of his life's-lessons speeches) that a man was better off paying for everything he needed up front in cash, and never borrowing a single penny. Pay in cash as you go. We'd nod, and wonder what his problem was. He'd sigh. "Go play," he'd say.

When you talk about *place* with most children, they will envision a *place* or a *house* where they have lived.

My brother and I would envision a *rug*. I swear.

When we were little migrant boys we collected plastic Indian men on horses (you could buy a whole plastic bag of them at the Dollar Store), and we would hide these in the Navajo rug (we always had at least a dozen hiding places where we'd stash our treasures) we slept rolled up in. That rug was our safe world. Even if some of the bad things he did were done here (we would and did block that out). Still. That was the world we could hide under in the blackness. We would dive down into our rug and hope he could not find us.

Even if he always did.

Still. You hoped.

He wouldn't.

Hope is a big, big thing to ask any boy to give up. Sometimes (not often) we lived in a real house. With bedrooms. Like the house in Colorado. But then, we always had to move. When our daddy wasn't looking, we would play with these plastic toy-men, and we named one: *Geronimo*.

We were careful not to let Daddy see us having fun. Having fun meant you had not done your work. Having fun meant you needed a kick in your butt. Our butts were black, blue, green, and yellow.

Geronimo sat on a fierce-looking steed. His arms raised holding a war ax. Geronimo would save us.

From our cold mad migrant father.

Who could not make up his mind if he loved us or hated us. Until we just didn't care anymore which way he went.

Someone had to save us. We were dying by inches.

I was just thirteen. We were on our way to New Jersey. I looked up at the blue sky, and saw a jet, turning, glinting silver in the sun, and I wondered what it might be like to be the kind of person who could outrun his life by flying as fast as a jet could go. The night would arrive, and Tso found me sitting on a fence in the parking lot of the motel in which we'd rented a room for the night. Looking up to see if I could find the same jet. My remembering is like the universe of stars and they simply spread themselves out in a rich tapestry before you. Pick and choose. The good ones. The bad ones. All of them are here in the shadows tumbling.

My brother's arms around me. I point out the stars, and constellations.

There are the stars that make the bear.

There are the stars that make the hunter with his bow.

There is the dog star.

There are stars that make the snake.

We should have run. We should have started running from the snakes then and there. We should have run and kept running and never looked back.

But how many times can you run?

Mainly children do as they're told. They do not want to upset the family applecart. By rights, we should have been stretching our arms to the skies, but we weren't stretching, we were mending, seeking complex alibis.

I heard voices so I did not have to listen to the single solitary howling of one particular voice. A voice in big trouble. A voice holding on by its fingernails.

Mine.

I heard voices so I did not have to listen to my own agony.

There must have been a time when I loved my father. There must have been a time when things were good and he did not hurt us and humiliate us. There must have been a time when things were okay. I just could not remember it. But if this time had never existed then why did I love my dad?

I loved my dad.

I was so afraid to see it.

To hear it.

To whisper it.

"Nasdijj, you love me?" my brother would ask. Maybe he was three or four when he asked it. He needed to know I loved him.

I was in *high protector* mode. I had convinced myself someone had to protect him. I would pick him up and hug him like a five-pound bag of potatoes. It gave me a purpose.

"I love you. Now, go to sleep."

Our *togetherness* was a survival strategy.

We had made it our rule to bathe together. We took turns standing guard by the door. If there was a door he hadn't ripped off the hinges. That was the thing. He could not bear it if you could open and close nicely. Keeping him out. The way you were made to do. No. He had to rip you from your hinges and make you question why you had ever been born. To not *be* in that small, migrant shack bathroom alone. Or any of the bathrooms of any of the places where we lived. They did not all come with bathrooms. Many only came with an outhouse that had to accommodate fifty people, five of whom would be over eighty. This together stuff was a safety precaution. Neither one of us saw this as an imposition on our privacy. (Or erotic.) We had no privacy. (We did not know what erotic was.) We had simply agreed that we would never go in there *alone* because *alone* was when he came for you.

He saw his chance, and he took it.

Our lives were totally devoted to one thing: *surviving him.*

The world had gone mad.

I had to stay after school (he would beat me for not making it back to the migrant camp in time to help him in the field) for punishment. The world had not gone mad. Just the people in it.

I was called inappropriate. One of those stupid migrant kids who did not have all their papers or their shots. I remember a school nurse giving us polio vaccinations on a sugar cube once. School vaccination papers were always an issue because we did not have any. We would typically be given two weeks to get our health papers on file, and then we would be kicked out of school because we did not have them. At the end of those two weeks, we would probably be gone anyway.

We tried going to school on the reservation once, where our mother had lived, but when we got caught speaking Navajo, they would wash our mouths out with soap, and we found this so vile, we were always running away, and schools hated that. Rules were always there for a reason.

We'd nod. Then we'd run away again.

I had not followed directions. It was important to follow directions. This went double for the migrants. Migrants were just plain stupid. If you were someone who could not follow directions then you would live all the rest of your days picking up pop bottles at the sides of the road. In the ditches. Two-cents-on-the-bottle.

It was all my fault. Daddy made that very, very clear.

We really did think that someday Daddy would kill us. *"I will kill you, boy,"* was something he said two, three times a day.

Death has been my steady companion. But I do not speak to it; nor does it speak to me. Geronimo and I speak *of it* as if it were not there. I have touched it and like a rope the thing has knots.

We were not men quite yet. That was coming. That, too, would be something we would share.

Between the two of us.

As brothers. The thrill. The mystery.

The *warriorness.*

The *waiting* until the day arrived we were big enough and strong enough to stand up to him and come out of the confrontation alive.

The pumping of your muscles in front of the bathroom mirror. Our dream that someday we would be strong enough to fend him off.

Our visions. Our fantasies. *Geronimo! With knives!*

You! Daddy! You! WE will HURT you!

Geronimo! Will hurt you.

We wanted him to be afraid.

Just once. Let *Ra tu tsa kntesa tu* come out of *his* mouth. Not mine.

We wanted him to *fear us.*

He had humiliated us. He had mutilated us.

He had raped us, and gone with his hard body inside of us, and he had torn us, and he had made us bleed so that blood dripped from our rectums down our legs onto the old wood floor.

There were small puddles of it wherever we sat.

It soaked our clothes and marked us for who we were.

Our underpants were brown.

You didn't want anyone at school to see *that.*

I had to show my handsome little brother how to wear a rolled-up wash-cloth in his butt.

So the leaking didn't come through your pants.

You could spend another entire lifetime attempting to fathom the *why* to any of it. There is no sane understanding. Jumping into that particular swirling water hole, that liquid vortex of questions without answers, was one *b-i-g* unfathomable *suck.* We were his. Like a possession. And not even that. Lower. Go lower. People show their possessions more respect than he showed us. We were his animals.

That is all we were.

He would kick me, and I would hear the bone snap. Breaking joints was the worst. You didn't want to let him kick an ankle or a knee. Even if we were filled with a deep and silently running rage (and we were), the fact remained that what we were (to the man who was our mad father) was tempting.

Even if we were filled with a deep and silently running rage, the fact remains that what we were (to the man who was our cold, mad father) was empty.

We were slow and sad and broken. A vacuum. Our shoulders sagged. We were always limping. No one cared. No one! What he took from us was any enjoyment or delight we might have had at any time in our lives upon this earth—but most especially during childhood—in being touched, in being open to being touched, by the nurturing, tender touch of any other man.

We were boys. We could still love. We could still be loved.

There was no grace to it. No joy. No direction. No road. No map.

No man could touch us—or even get that close to us—or we would tremble like cowering animals caught solidly in a trap.

People ask me what saved us. Or what gave us hope?

The stories the old people told gave us hope. In those myths, the War Twins always persevered. It wasn't an abstraction.

You could see the mountains that were the fallen bodies of the dragons. You could touch and stand on the lava flows that were the monster's blood. These things were real. I had seen Spider Woman's rock. It was a real place as real as my grandmother's sheep.

Even today I am asked how we taught ourselves to read. People do not believe it. But it's true.

Reading was a going inside of yourself where you controlled things, and things were safe.

I remember our fingers lingering over letters. I remember watching the mouths of the people who read to us move as they made sounds. I was more determined to read than I was determined to learn how to drive.

Reading was something white people did. If I could read, I could have something they had, and I wanted that very much.

To my surprise and complete delight, I found reading to be one-more-time a matter of interpretation. I did not understand I was seeing words and letters upside down until I started reproducing reading as writing.

Everything I wrote was upside down, and not in the temporary way most preliterate preschoolers read, but more for the long haul. Teachers saw it as being almost shameful, but I saw it as just one more thing to slow me down. I saw words upside down. So what! It was no different than learning to read French. You read it and then you take the time to interpret what it is you have read.

Learning how to read saved our lives. I learned to write my secrets down. In such a way as to keep the secret of them being secret, secret.

Even though they called us stupid, we were trilingual. But we did not necessarily share this with you. Easily. We read, too, from the corners of our eyes. We were infinitely suspicious and infinitely spontaneous.

Especially if you were an adult. Or a white person (they all wanted to know who your mother was and where she was from). Our reading (our real reading) and our writing (our real writing) were secrets.

We owned one (stolen) very small, very ragged play by Shakespeare.

We *fell* into Shakespeare as if he had been sitting in some chair at a family function, and he had tripped us as we were attempting to walk by him. Everyone else was outside on the patio eating barbecue. But we were inside with Shakespeare.

"Oh, let me help you up. Did you fall?"

Nod in silence. After all, you are the family retard. He sets you on his lap. You're five.

"Let us see if there are any stories around here we might read. I wonder if they have anything of mine."

They do.

Our one printed book could fit in my pocket so it was mainly safe. Daddy wouldn't readily find it. We were simply attempting to connect the events in our lives to the mythologies that had preceded us. The mythologies that had obviously been written down. And the ones our grandparents told. From remembering. We really did think our grandmother Sa *was* Spider Woman.

All mythologies were essentially the same to us. We did not separate the Navajo ones from the Greek ones. All stories were from the same kingdom.

The past.

Geronimo's bones were the solid things that held him up.

Geronimo's bones are the past.

Geronimo is his bones.

You are your history.

We saw the Athabascan mythologies as one great and glorious adventure.

People ask me why. Why would our father destroy the writing of a child?

At first, I was surprised people didn't get it right away. And then I realized again just how far our experiences were from people who had never been migrants.

Most fathers like our father wanted their children to be focused on picking and the work of a migrant camp.

The more you could focus on this work, the more valuable you were.

As a family member.

As a migrant.

As someone who made money from what you picked.

The more you picked, the more valued you were by the person who collected the money from the farm boss.

Daddy was afraid that this writing stuff would become more important to us than the work we did around the migrant camp. And it did. Daddy was afraid we might write his crimes down. And we did. What he didn't know, of course, was that he had lost that battle some years ago. In fact, Daddy had lost the war, and he didn't even know there had been a conflict.

My brother and I would write vast epic poems and clip them into our *Vast Epic Poem Book*.

We would hide these things and clutch them to our chests. Sometimes we would show this particular book to the other migrant children who *could not believe* we had written a whole book, but we had.

Words saved us.

Mythology saved us.

Our mother's people taught us the value of stories. They kept their stories in their heads.

We tried. But our heads were never big enough.

I remember a county librarian who came to the migrant camp in the Bookmobile. It amused us to no end that the librarian (a woman, no less) could actually drive the Bookmobile. She gave us *Macbeth*. Telling us it was for adults. Which made us want to read it very much. We were of the opinion it could exist side by side any Indian myth we had ever heard.

We stole that book.

We didn't understand it. We were far too young. But what it represented was hope because *maybe someday* we would understand it.

Looking back, I see she saw her chance to light some already smoldering tin of tinder. Driving her great Bookmobile in the hope it could compete with the music from the ice cream truck. The plays were small. They could be hidden. That librarian looked the other way. I could tell from the look in her sad eyes, she suspected something. About us.

She whispered to me. No adult had ever done that. "I would take you home in my pocket," she said.

She did not know that we were thieves. Or that our sky was breaking again and again.

She smiled. But she did not really know me or my dreams of *Ra tu tsa kntesa tu*, and how he came out from all my holes. Snakes everywhere.

Macbeth made it to the next migrant camp and the next migrant camp and then Daddy found it.

We had pawed through it and had tried to sound out the words. We liked the end where it looked like the king got his head cut off. That play was too written for children. Like us.

In my dream, Mama said it was her book.

No, no, Mama, but I will read you some pages. You, Geronimo, you're in here, too.

She tried to save us. In dreams anyway. In my dreams, I still hear her whiskey laugh, and her squeezing laughter from the rocks. Then *Ra tu tsa kntesa tu* would come. In life, Mama was not too good at saving us. She would cringe, and cower, and look the other way when he went off and after us. And then he beat her, too.

Power. Sex. Greed. Love. Sex.

Are all universal.

After he beat us, we typically slept for a long, long time. We lived in our heads. We lived in stories. But adults did not. Nor could they see any Shakespearean analogy to Geronimo. It was too big a stretch. We learned not to talk about where we had been or what we had seen or what we knew. Or why the world was nothing less than fantastic. We learned more than anything to keep our mouths shut. Most Indian children learn to do this, too. Shakespeare would have *loved* Geronimo. The two of them would have stayed up talking and writing and drinking until the cows came home. Even if they faced the hurdle of speaking vastly different languages, Shakespeare and Geronimo would have stretched the cultural limits of the icon into something far more useful.

Daddy might burn our writing, the stapled-together books we made, and the smoke would drift like some heavy ghost was now leaving the hogan. Daddy was the kind of man who squeezed the life from you and never blinked. What Mama squeezed was laughter, and your ability to share it. The migrant men our father worked with (and sometimes they worked *for* him when he was the camp foreman, which was an easy job to get if you were the only white migrant in the county, and Daddy was often that) eyed him from the Spanish corners of their black eyes where their suspicions lived.

Rolled cigarettes stuck in wet lips.

They did not like him or the dragon on his biceps.

He knew it.

But they would pretend.

He knew that, too.

Most men would have hidden this. They would have given the Hispanic migrant the dignity of pretense. He could have pretended that he did not know they despised him. No. He let them know he knew. Oh, they would laugh with him. They would play pool with him in the back of cool desert Tucson bars. He almost always drank tequila. Warm. Up in a shot glass. He almost always had something of a beard, and the tequila would stick to him like glaze. Sometimes he drank vodka shots. But only when something was deeply wrong. Murderously wrong. Usually it was tequila. We were there. He could and usually did consume a gallon of tequila in a night. Every night. It was not unlike running warm water through his blue-and-thirsty veins. And when they slapped him on his back like *compadres*, he peered around as if some slime had been wiped there on him.

We noticed, too, that every time we stayed in a migrant camp that was anywhere near the carnie life, his tattoo became deeper, more and more detailed, and darker where the dark things were, and lighter where the light things were. He was slipping into the carnival and getting work done on the tattoo. He would never tell us anything about this, of course, because the tattoo was expensive. The reds were redder. The tongue a tongue. The flames were livid now. The tattoo was alive. The eyes of the dragon were brilliant.

When we were little, but old enough to hold a shot glass (we were delighted with any new, shiny toy), he would half fill the shot glass with tequila, and admonish us—like we understood this—not to spill any if we wanted to *be big like Daddy*.

We were scared to death of Daddy.

He didn't get that.

We would spill most of the tequila, the clear, warm liquor leaking down both sides of our mouth, but he would hold the bottom of the shot glass precariously up with his finger, as we tasted this bitter stuff, frowned, and cried. I remember this because I saw my baby brother go through the same insane torture. The adults all around would laugh—alcoholics-in-training—although Mama was not too thrilled with this stupid game. If Daddy was tired-drunk, field-drunk, out-in-the-mud-all-day-drunk, he would slap the sides of our heads with the palm of his hand if we spilled the tequila, which was just about a sure bet. The shot glass would go flying, which never failed to startle us. We would wail and he would roughly hand us to Mama, who was as terrorized by him as we were. Maybe more.

Mama had an out. She could kill herself.

We could not kill ourselves. Our voices and our vices could grind us down. But for the big one, we could not be depended on to do it. We still had to live with him.

In time. In time, everyone left him. Even us.

Particularly us.

"I should like to paint portraits," Van Gogh said, "which would appear after a century to people living then as apparitions."

Daddy was an apparition. A bitterness of endings older than the elms. Dark hawks could hear his thoughts. Night! Night! Always slipping away, my cold father, my cold, mad migrant father of the barren thorns. My cold, mad father of the churchyard morns. His fog. His soul swooning through the universe of Texas bars and parking lots. Bored housewives in their pink Chihuahua boots. Mexican cantinas. Runts-and-cunts (his term). Tecate. Arizona bars. New Mexican bars. Bars that ringed the reservation like a night-electric string of lighthouses. Ensenada bars. Tijuana hookers.

We did not have shoes. Mama would ask him nicely for food for us.

"Food! Fucking cunt! You want food!" He would rip the house apart.

She tried to hide her precious photographs.

Him off in dust and gravel.

Comes back with eggs he throws at her.

She tries to scoop up the yolks off the wall with a bowl and a spoon.

The dog licking the floor.

Snow was dusted over all the desert.

He started picking us up from our bed and putting us in his bed not too long after she died. At first, we thought it was nice. And then, the hurt was like the voices loud and hoarse. He seems to be dead but is spread out on his bed reeking like a pickled corpse. Naked and his left hand holding the twisted sheet as if he had twisted someone softer than he was. His body repulsive. The door from his bedroom to the bathroom had been ripped off in some satanic rage. One of a million. All forgotten. Mama had been dead for six years or so. We were soaking wet and trying to tiptoe through this cage. Of rage. If we looked at the gruesome body on the bed it might stir. *Ra tu tsa kntesa tu.* Snake eyes.

I looked at him. Being all of thirteen. And realized for the first time how *gone* she was for him.

Gone.

His was an estrangement from the world. His bed an exile, too. His skin the dragon's scales. *Ra tu tsa kntesa tu.*

I would hold my head in my hands and it hurt so much.

Cold, mad migrant father.

Who would pick me up from my window perch as if I were a bird. His lips to mine. His tongue in my mouth. His words: "Nasdijj, please, please love me."

Like I was his last hope.

I was not his last hope.

His last hope would be his death. But I knew him. I knew him better than anyone, and I am sad to say it. I knew him better than Tso, and I knew him better than Mama. I knew he would hang on to life like the grasping, essential hand of a skeleton. As if this entering of my soul could bring me into contact with the earth. It couldn't. It was the world that could not be heard. The world was mainly silent.

We would wear our long white sleeping shirts and fall from some roof-top to swim like angels through the air.

The rain would wash us of the smell.

Of him.

Sometimes I would scrub my brother's back with a brush. We wanted him *off* us. His smells and the sweat like a cigar. In that winter window of our long shirts where even now nothing grows and the wind comes in to dance with ghosts and crows. The road crunches whenever a vehicle drives upon this Colorado snow. The headlights of our father home from bars. I would escape from his morning arms in my slipping nakedness and I would run outside nude-in-the-winter to my now half-dead summer forts, where I would scream and scream to get the voices out. Out! Out of me, damn you, voices! The sun's rim dips into the black like ink. The stars rush out for they are certain of their secrets.

9

I Had Grown Scattered Like a Scarecrow

"We have no boys left here," Changing Woman said. "All of our boys are gone. All of our boys have disappeared into your gullet. Or they have disappeared into the gizzards of your giant people. You have long since eaten our children, which you very well know."

"No boys left here?" mocked Ye'iitsoh. "No more children?"

He did not believe it. He lived on the blood and the bones of children.

The human woman was lying. He would pull the truth from her belly if he had to. He noticed that there were many tracks, small tracks everywhere in the sand. "If there are no children here then who made these tracks, Changing Woman of the humans!"

"Oh, those," replied Asdzqq nadleehe. "I have made them all."

"And why would you make the tracks of children?"

"I grow so lonely with all the children eaten and gone. I make these tracks so I can pretend there are children here. I do it with my hand like this."

She showed the giant how she had made the tracks of children in the sand with the sides of her hands.

He examined them closely. He walked away from her house very slowly. Looking back from time to time.

I had grown scattered like a scarecrow. Parts of me were everywhere. In time, I would come to myself again. Becalmed. We were in a pancake place. The parking lot was almost full. We parked in a spot where we could keep an eye on our new car from the booth we were having breakfast in. A Toms River pancake house house-of-pancakes. A very busy morning place.

People were reading the paper at the counter. Tso bought five packs of gum, which was odd. I let it go. I was anxious to hit the road. The wide-open spaces.

Cigarette smoke like lead. Truckers drinking coffee and just about ready to drive into the city. Bread trucks. Older guys with wives and kids at home. Dads gone to work. A small group of people waiting to be seated.

We were going *the other way.*

Not east.

Waitresses laughing. No one waited on us for a long while.

We were sitting in the back in a booth. A little out of place as always. We tried to cover it up with a bad attitude. The waitress thought she was our mother.

We actually drank the water. Our breakfast had not arrived. I was having toast and coffee. I remember this clear as day. I thought my brother was being a little lavish. He was having strawberry pancakes with whipped cream. Then I thought, *Oh, let him have some fun.*

In time, the money would run out and Tso would have to deal with it like anyone else.

Money.

I knew a farm in Half-Moon Bay where they will pay you to pick pumpkins. Or you can sit by the side of this road, and carloads of little kids come by, and everyone buys a pumpkin.

Pumpkins were a cash crop. They grow millions and millions of pumpkins in Half-Moon Bay.

It would be money. We would go there.

We would make our fortune in pumpkins.

Our breakfast still had not arrived and Tso had to go pee. He returns and pulls out a wad of cash from his pocket, and he starts counting it.

I knew he might have a couple hundred dollars. Maybe as much as three hundred. His tomato money. But surely not more than that.

When he reached five thousand and was still counting, I became a little concerned.

"Where . . ."

"Daddy owes me," Tso said. His eyes got real small and pinched.

Like *do not fuck with me on this one, Nasdijj, and do n-o-t take away this money as it is mine.*

Okay.

Almost six thousand dollars.

"I took it from his pants when he got home late just before we left."

We had waited for Daddy to get home. After his poker game. A game Daddy almost never won. Almost.

"I think you should put all that money away."

It did occur to me that all that cash might be Daddy doing something stupid like running numbers.

It was possible that the money next to my brother's butt had only been entrusted to Daddy. Tso put his wallet back in his pants. He was lifting his little butt up when a table of high school girls across the restaurant noticed him.

They giggled.

They were older girls. They had to be sixteen. Older girls did not normally look twice at us.

Had to be the car.

Or they were looking at my brother's butt. Had to be the car.

This was 1963. That meant the long, ironed hair hairsprayed to happy-glue. Disco boots had been invented but nobody had been to a disco yet. Thick makeup. White lipstick that made most girls look like ghosts. Beehives. Mascara. Slit skirts.

Nylons. Black flats. In 1963, when girls got runs in their nylons, they'd crack out the fingernail polish from the purse. They all start applying fingernail polish to their legs. This stops the run. They are painting their legs with fingernail polish. We were speechless.

"I swear," I told my brother, "if you so much as even head in the direction of a cigarette, I will grab it and I will break it in two."

"You would."

"You bet I would. Now, are you telling me that last night you stole six thousand dollars from Daddy's pants? This is fucking serious."

"Well, *you* just stole fifty thousand in wheels from someone you don't even know!"

I was growing grim. "Daddy will track you down to the ends of the earth."

But Tso knew that. He knew what the consequences were going to be if we so much as put one scratch on that car.

There are times when it's impossible to argue with him. I had been up all night and more than a few of the previous nights walking my scheme through its paces. There were gaps but I knew one thing. It was now or never.

The girls were leaving. They were walking by us. As they walked by us, they brushed up against us.

That soft push of tits and sweaters and perfume.

My brother would have to get up to go pee again.

One of the girls slid like a roller skater into our booth. She was wearing a pink angora sweater. She had a gold chain with a tiny heart that she fingered. She had a huge purse and a black leather jacket. She was sitting next to my brother. Who said nothing.

I know my brother.

No one loved him more than I do.

Right away, I saw she could see it. His fragility.

Right away, I saw her experience with men. She removed the red Tootsie Pop she had in her mouth. "Has your food arrived yet?" she asked.

Blink. Gulp. No.

Beehive.

Mascara.

Slit blue skirt.

Fingernail polish nylons.

She raised her finger in the air and snapped it.

Waitress with coffeepot hanging on finger: *Yaaaaa.*

"My friends have not been served."

We were served and quickly.

"My uncle Paulie owns this place. Uncle Paulie would shit mud bricks if he even knew I was in here."

She did not know us, but that was half the fun. Bad girl grins like a light had gone on in her head and it was telling her to skip school. We were going to *have to make some serious miles today. There was no time for this.*

Flirtation.

She took the gum Tso offered her. Purple.

"Oh, no, I can't but I love grape."

But she did.

She had *stuff,* and she was pawing through the *stuff* like there was something in there she needed. She was supposed to be in school.

School where she was bored.

School where she was failing.

School where she had no excuse for failing.

School where she had discovered her talent for drama, singing, dancing, acting.

She had to have a mother and a father and a sister and a brother and a dog and a cat *somewhere. And I wanted her to have these things. Please, have these things.*

She looks around. No Uncle Paulie yet.

It hit me. She did not have these things.

She had a father. That was it.

We can always tell.

The ones with just a dad. I am never sure how we can tell. But kids raised by their father see something in children raised by one man. It's like you have this sore in your mouth and it hurts.

It had never entered our minds that this could be the situation of *a girl.* We always sort of claimed ownership to being children raised by their father. All we could do was stare. It was a real girl. We had never really talked to one before. Not one like this.

Her purse had cigarettes. There was a lot of pulling and holding and burning and clicking and lighting. I said nothing. I hated them. They reminded me of the smell of the Gallup, New Mexico, bars we always had to drag his carcass out of.

Suddenly she hauls out a huge can of hairspray and she sprays everything within a twenty-foot-radius. "Daddy hates it when I smoke," she said. "He thinks he is the fucking mayor of New York."

"What does your dad do?" she asked. It hung there.

It was just a question. However, it was a question we weren't going to be answering until we knew her a little better. That rarely ever happened and we did not think it would happen now.

More lipstick to the lips. There was enough *stuff* in that bag to resupply a Woolworth's.

"I'm not supposed to be over here in New Jersey," she lied. "But I took the subway. Then the bus. I just thought I would see how far west I could get in one day. I did pretty good, too. It's not even lunch. Daddy will lose his dentures down the toilet when Uncle Paulie tells him I was in here."

The truth lay dormant somewhere behind her eyes. Her eyes were hurt. Her daddy didn't really care, and he had grown tired of fighting with her. She was from an upper-middle-class family that had done well. Now her. No one in her family thought for a moment she would do well. She had been spoiled. She was from the suburbs and Manhattan was another dream. One of many. Her family had worked hard for several generations to get the fuck *out* of the Lower East Side. Now they didn't ever mention that place. For her to pretend that she was *from* there was a sacrilege. They had once been from Puerto Rico themselves. But now they were white as cream soda pop.

"That big-mouth cow bitch will tell Uncle Paulie I was in here, too. Every waitress in here is on probation for murder." Her eyes locked with a waitress. "F-o-o-d D-o-g E-v-i-l B-i-t-c-h," she mouthed silently with her lips. The waitress smiled.

We looked furtively around the restaurant. No one looked like she was on probation for anything other than rather bad coffee. "Now Daddy's sending me to study in London just so I can't be around Angel. Me, study in London? God, he *really hates* Angel."

More gum. More cracking. She draws you into her secrets where she is her own expert at everything. "I do my own hair."

We nodded. She was so proud. The hair was a work of art.

"Angel's from Puerto Rico. I don't think where a person is *from* should even really matter, now, do you?"

No. Her father was from Puerto Rico. The old and the new clashed in their holds on memory. Both men had obviously held her, her father, and whoever Angel was, and it would not be enough, not for her.

She would invent new things. New names. New places she could be from. New talents. New stages to perform on. She, too, would get behind the mirror time was, and move the thing around to reflect a newer, better her. Maybe a tattoo somewhere. Something that would make her father stop dead in his tracks. We did not laugh when she said: *Stop dead in his tracks*. Men and stopping in their tracks and death were not abstractions to us. She asked us what we thought of tattoos. But we just looked away. Far away. Not every dragon was worth its wrath.

She was going to go a lot farther west than New Jersey. She had just had breakfast with her cousins. A few of them had been as far away as California.

"The goody-goodies," was how she referred to them. Her disdain could be seen, too, at the corners of her mouth where scorn had found itself a home. Her scorn like most scorn was more playful than destructive. *"They went to some fancy-schmancy Catholic girls' school where everyone thinks the virgins go but the last untouched princess to attend Mother Mary's Mount of Olives was none other than Marianne Faithfull herself, and* she got a recording contract the very day *she got to California so-why-not-me cuz I really can sing and dance, too, because God knows I've been taking lessons all my life, but at some point the lessons have to turn into the real thing or what is the* point! *Fuck Marianne Faithfull."*

She posed crude questions with the elegance of an atom bomb.

My brother's head was nodding up and down like the bouncing head of that fake dog he wanted me to buy whose head nodded up and down and whose beady pink eyes blinked like a traffic light at Christmas—boiiing, boiiing—instead of the plastic Saint Christopher I *was* going to buy for the front dash no matter what he said because there was no goddamn room for the dog to be mounted in the rear window nodding like an idiot on thalidomide.

This was not a car for dogs, artificial or otherwise.

My brother was lost in some convoluted psychic maze. I had to touch him to break his trance. He would have nodded yes to anything she said. This was dangerous.

"What, huh?"

"You are sooooo cute," she said. She touched his nose with her finger. She could squeeze her butt cheeks together and this propelled her up like a Mexican jumping bean. "And I think the long hair is so cool it would drive my dad to sending me to Rome, probably."

Probably. She was touching his hair.

"Most of the cute ones, they already got a girlfriend. I suppose you already got a girlfriend, huh?" The haves and the have-nots. The world is always divided into two groups. The have-a-girlfriend group and the have-not-a-girlfriend group. She herself belonged to the always-looking group.

"Yes. He does," I said. "He's getting married to his girlfriend this Sunday. Big wedding. Big church. Big hair."

"Huh?"

"Yes. You *do* have a girlfriend. You have ten girlfriends. You are *taken*."

"I do? By who? You mean those funny-looking dogs where the head bobs and the little pink eyes blink?"

"Yeah."

"I want one."

I shook my head. "No. We need something religious so when the cops see us they will think we're on our way to church. To your wedding."

"What wedding?" he asked.

I figured marrying him off was about the only way to discourage her.

"Your marriage to Audrey Hepburn, you idiot." I laughed but only to my evil self.

They both just looked at me. But I *was* going to *get* that Saint Christopher. It was good luck for driving and when you crashed your dick didn't get cut off. I had heard this from older men. The fifteen-year-olds.

This was worth the lighting of another cigarette. She regarded me carefully. She left traces of red lipstick on her cigarettes. I hated cigarettes. I could see a conversation of great religious significance coming on. She fingered the black leather jacket lightly.

We knew how much those jackets cost. We had never even touched one in a store. They were way above our station. We had been told that Elvis had at least a dozen. The sky was breaking blue again. There was always light behind her. Even now coming through the restaurant windows in a yellow slant and opaque dust, it made her seem holy. Like a nun in an Italian villa. I at least knew where Rome was.

"They say Elvis has a dozen," she said. "I'd bet you'd look so sexy in this jacket." She did not mean me. They never mean me. They always mean him. I am never more than anything but the older brother. He is always beautiful. I am told that men are handsome, not beautiful. But he was beautiful. His virginity (a complete fabrication) appeals to women. He had worked shirtless in the tomato fields and was as brown-and-red as the red-ribbed sand. Him shirtless in a black leather jacket. She could see it, too. Only she was playing with his nipple. She batted her fake eyelashes and mascara around. Reminding me of a crow bathing in a mud puddle. "This one is Angel's only he let me borrow it cuz it was that or a ring. I'm sure he wouldn't mind if you wanted to wear it. Well, of course, it's much too big for me. Now, a *ring* will give my old man a coronary as big as Brooklyn. But the jacket just made him want to send me to London, England. To study. Something. Hair maybe. You know, they got a bunch of great groups over there? Maybe I could even see the Beatles cuz I'm really a good singer and a dancer, too. My drama teacher said I ought to be in show business."

She glowed in this self-revelation.

So much for Angel whoever he was.

This girl did not need to take drama.

She was a dancer, too. Drama was her second skin. Drama was her life.

"But we never did *it*. *Yet*. Ya know." This is where the eyes go down, lowered into her soft bed of nocturnal secrets, a pressure cooker where his nipple is about to pop and bleed. Her eyes look back up again, scanning his frame from his crotch to the top of his head. "The dirty anyways. Today, well, today, we were supposed to get together over at his apartment over on Dee, you know, Avenue Dee, it's got that zebra shag, the apartment, well, it's really his cousin's, and they gotta stereo, but, I was thinking, you know, a girl goes to a guy's place down there, and I'm thinking he's going to want to, you know, do it, Angel, if I show'd up which I'm not, but I'm *thinking* the first time, you know, *the dirty deed*, and you've always thought it would be somewhere like the Plaza with a doorman and there's a cake—with the guy and the girl on the cake, and maybe a ring, you gotta have a ring, a nice one, like with diamonds, *but fucking Avenue* Dee? *So what kind of girl does he takes me for anyways?*"

Pop! goes the bubble gum. The eyes tense. Squeeze. When she popped her gum like that my brother's body jerked, and sparks flew from his toes.

And then his toes curled.

For a brief minute there, she lets you in. It is rare when people let that wall crumble, and you see into them, or into what is behind the wall, with some electric snapping-of-the-moment where their vulnerability shows, their mistakes in thinking thrown all around the room not unlike some soft bedroom that has not been picked up, the shades are drawn, and her panties are everywhere, and then you note she wears boys briefs, and the moment ends.

The lids with the pitchblack lashes thick as a paintbrush close slowly like the door to that messy bedroom. You can see her breathe. Her breasts heaving at every profound epiphany.

Click. The lips purse.

The nose exhales smoke like a dragon.

I'm wondering: *How can anyone chew purple bubble gum and smoke cigarettes at the same time? She was exhausting.* She *inhales* on her cigarette. She has gone inside herself. *What kind of girl does he take her for anyway?*

You can almost see him, Angel Perez, in his T-shirt, plowing through the crowded sidewalks of the Lower East Side, the Puerto Rican music on the balconies, the fire escapes, the babies, the sound of Mama deep inside the apartment, his midnight eyes hooded, the black hair slicked back, the thin beginning of a mustache, and she's ten paces behind him, tripping in her high heels, wondering what happened, trying to keep up, but she cannot. "Angel, wait," she says. Over and over. "Angel, wait for me!" She needs an unobstructed path. *"Trocha!"* The other boys and men on the sidewalk look at her and smile and wink and laugh that low-belly laugh where you know Angel is way over his head, but if you were him, you would treat her so well she would love you and make babies for you and you could take her back to Puerto Rico like a prize.

Turning around. Watching her stumble. Imagining.

At her kind.

The kind that smokes four cigarettes before the guts of her story come spilling forth.

The kind bees think is a real beehive because it is a real beehive.

The kind whose jewelry jangles jingles.

That all your spook is, honey? Rings-and-things?

The kind whose nylons are repaired repeatedly and erotically whenever she sits down with pink fingernail polish from her repair kit for F-14 fighter jets. The kind whose black leather jacket is far too big for her. It isn't hers anyway, but she'll definitely keep it.

The kind who wears your gold class ring with purple strands of angora thread woven around and around the gold so the thing fits, and the angora flies around her always gesticulating fingers like purple butterflies.

The kind whose eyeliner has swabbed the decks of aircraft carriers and now hangs like lint in mops. My brother cannot take his eyes off her.

He blinks, but she has hit him with her stunozinger ray gun. One blast from that and his eyeballs will melt into white goo. She is an alien who landed on the wrong planet.

She understands (at some painful level) that we are staring at her.

"Have I, uh, landed on the wrong planet?"

Or is it the image of her? The Gina Lollobrigida her. The Lana Turner her. The Ava Gardner her. The Liz Taylor her. The Rita Hayworth her. The Debbie Reynolds her. The Loretta Young her. The Marilyn her. The Judy Garland her. The Sandra Dee her. The older hers and the younger hers desperate to catch the train and the hooking up. Is this what we are staring at? The gathering of hers, all the women who now make her up, shoving and pushing and interrupting all her selves.

The darker hers. The hers that make her a woman. The kind of woman who will not have any of this removed from her person because it *is* who she is.

She was looking at my brother, Tso, when I got it. It almost knocked me out of the booth. Stunned.

It was the mother her. We shared something, her and I.

There was something deep within her that wanted to mother him.

That was my job. Nevertheless, she had a rhythm. A good one. I am not always what he needs. I am aware of that even if sometimes it eats at me, and it does. It hurts. Even her gum cracked with drama. If anyone knew where the real her was, would she, please, stand up. And point *her* out. Who can tell underneath all of that—stuff. The masquerade her. The hairspray her. The lipstick her.

"A girl's lips can't be red enough." Everything is said while applying makeup. Applying makeup is a full-time job. In time, she will collect Social Security for years and years of applying makeup. The "powder mirror" never being too far away, and usually opened for some official inspection. The mirror seemed to be a microphone, and she was always talking into it. Tuned to Alien Central, her superiors were worried. Over.

Come in. Come in. This is Makeup Central to Makeup Forever. Was she real? Or the creation of a magazine's Creative Girl Department?

Or good God all of the above.

I am not sure it really mattered.

She was a *her*. Alien or not. If it turned out later on that she had a reptilian tail (well concealed), it mattered not. We were thirteen- and fourteen-years-old, and she was sixteen. The *reason* anyone steals a car like that, and assumes those enormous risks—like going to jail for the rest of your life— *is to attract attention* so *girls* will notice you. Guys just want to lock you up or beat you up. This was an *older girl*. In our strange book, this was the equivalent of: *the older woman*. She even had tits. The real kind. Not the kind girls my brother's age had. The tissue paper kind. This was the real thing. No one needs more than two hundred and fifty cubic Corvette centimeters of highly engineered compressed obsessed beautious *car* to go to the store for a loaf of bread. No one. You drive more than two hundred and fifty cubic Corvette centimeters of highly engineered compressed obsessed beauteous *car* to go to the store for a loaf of bread in the sublime hope that a *girl* will notice you.

Come in. Come in. This is Makeup Central to Makeup Forever. There is a thirteen-year-old boy staring at you. Shall we vaporize him?

Please. Vaporize him.

Everyone in the world knew what a Corvette was.

Do you think for one silly, solitary moment that had we arrived at the Toms River House of Pancakes in a 1955 four-door Ford station wagon with a plain, unadorned, flat, unaffected, inornate, common-mongrel-rut-of-a-steering-wheel, the kind you haul at, fight with, cursing, and pro-pelled by a Russian engine your grandmother-from-Prague would have approved of as levelheaded, that *one girl*, name me one girl, *ONE girl with a beehive and nylons and lipstick and eyelashes and all the things that make girls girls*, would have looked at us for five seconds?

It would never happen. And there we'd be.

In a tomato field.

If we wanted to attract levelheaded girls, we would not be stealing cars and hoping to hell we could make it to California.

Little did we know that a chunk of the money we were stealing from our dad had been honestly earned in those tomato fields, and that it was sup-posed to pay the property taxes on a postage-stamp-sized piece of property in the New Mexico desert that had a two-bedroom trailer on it. Running-water-and-electric.

Two acres of bristle, gristle, and cow thistle.

Little did we know that our dad had purchased this place years and years ago—this was the place where we had lived when Daddy had worked at the *horse slaughterhouse.*

We loved the place and longed in our hearts and spirits to go back. We had dreamed about going back for years. It was only a dream.

Little did we know of the few opportunities for employment that would

be offered there. Little did we know that he hated it—the butchering of innocent animals—far, far more than we did, and he hated himself, too, far,
far more than we ever could go.

Down that eternal road of screams.

*We hated all of that horror. But we never hated that little scrub patch of land.
In fact, we ached to see that place again.*

I could never in a million years explain it.

Some places you do not pick. You stumble into them. They find you.
This scrubby place was like that. Hard and dry. I do not think I would have
survived my father's involvement with the horse slaughterhouse and the
many dull uses of the baseball bat if it hadn't been for the poetry of this an-
nihilated place of crows among the scraggled pines.

As a fifty-year-old adult, I have taken many of my cityslicker friends *and*
my Davey-Crockett-King-of-the-Wild-Frontier friends *and* my Let's-Go-
Climb-the-Himalaya-Mountain friends to this thorny, clunker-ridden,
rust-eating, improvident, back-in-the-bushwhacked-bucket-of-bulldog-
bristle, trailer-brambled piece of real estate epidermis, and they *all* have the
same comment.

I time them. I look at my watch, and I time them. Thirty seconds.

The only person on the planet who has taken longer than thirty seconds
to comment was my daughter, Kree.

Kree, horsewoman that she is, actually got out of the truck I had driven
us all the way out here in the dust with.

She turns all the way around very, very slowly.

She kicks up some rock with her cowboy boot just like she would have
kicked the used tires on a used truck I wanted her to purchase. The rock
rolled some. She went and kicked it again. Then she went and kicked the
piñon pine the rock had landed next to.

"There ain't nothing here," she said. A glint in her eye. She could not
hold it in another second longer.

She bursts-out-*laughing.* Holding herself and her boots and her bowie
knife and her bloomers all together-as-together-can-get. "Dad, I'll bet you
a thousand bucks"—she *has* a thousand bucks, I do not—"every single person you bring out here to see this place says exactly the same thing."

I did not take that bet.

No. Every goddamn cowboy who has laid eyes on the ranch-of-my-
dreams says *exactly* the same thing. Same words. Same sentiment.

There ain't nothing here.

Or sometimes . . .

There is nothing here.

It isn't true.

The trailer is just fine. I like it. It's small, but who wants to live in a place the size of France that takes a month of Sundays to clean?

There's an outhouse that no one uses.

There are my *other friends*: skunks, rabbit brush, the pine, the juniper, cottonwoods, grama grass, mourning doves, rock wrens, sparrow hawks, red-shafted flickers, piñon jays, rattlesnakes, bluebirds, ravens, robins, bobcats, starlings, house sparrows, gopher snakes, lizards, coyotes, red foxes, cottontails, wild horses, and prairie dogs.

There are, of course, ghosts, too.

I have gone through the county library and the county clerk's office and I have made a list of all the various cowboys who have lived here and have paid taxes (the trailer is from 1957).

They liked it, too. It grabs you, or it doesn't.

It grabbed Daddy. I deplore saying that something (anything) grabbed me that grabbed him, but it did. It grabbed my brother, too.

Elijah Buck. Arapaho Bob. The Red Jack Gang. Donaciano Aguilar. Bad Nell. Mose Beard. Lucky July. Guadalupe Caballero (aka the Owl). Ben Cravens. Zacariah Crane. Dodds Hogg. Boone Hicks. Smoker Rigs. Christobel Romero. Anastacio Sandoval. Sage Selman. Bud Snow. Jack Bone. Dutch Heshotauthla.

All lived here. Like scarecrows.

The land has been divided up. The ranch house gone. Or rather *houses*. The land has seen drought, snow, and poker games all gone bad.

But my father wanted to hang on to it.

I know why, too.

I loved this place with all my heart.

10

There Were No Roads
on the Way to Sa's Hogan

There were no roads. There were no hogans. There was hardly the suggestion of a cloud. There was not even so much as the slight smell of smoke that might have drifted up from someone's smoke hole. Every time they took a step toward what they thought they had seen, everything changed. The only thing that never changed seemed to be the stars that floated overhead. Even during the apex of the day, they could see the stars above them. The War Twins stood together staring off into the far distance of what appeared to be another vast desert of sand.

They had seen desert after desert. They had walked across desert after desert. "We will find our father now," *Monster Slayer said.*

Child Born for Water agreed. They would search this place for the sun god, Begochiddy, for they had many questions they wanted answers to.

Like why had he cast them out. That especially.

"Have you ever considered the possibility that your father, this sun god, this Begochiddy, *might simply be old and arrogant?*" *Coyote asked them.*

Out of nowhere.

At first they were startled, as there had been no other creatures there when they had arrived. They thought they were alone. But there he was. Reclining on a rock and drinking Teezwin, an alcoholic drink made from the giant cactus that had arms and heads and legs like men. Coyote seemed quite comfortable while they were hot and sweat dripped from their legs.

"And who might you be? For we are War Twins who search for their father so we might defeat the monsters who are eating our people."

"I know who you are, silly boys. Always monsters. Always war. Always lost."

Whoever he was, the animal was mocking them.

"Our mother is Changing Woman who is the sister of White Shell Woman."

Their pedigree.

Coyote had considered this. "I am the dog who sleeps with your sisters and who sticks it in them when they spread their legs. I give them babies with ten heads whom your fathers have to bash against the rocks but the babies never die. They just grow up to become the monsters who would devour you. I have played tricks upon the travelers of time, and I have tricked time itself into telling half the universe that half the stars must go out. Would you like to see this?"

The War Twins were just about to tell him no. They had other more important quests and did not care to follow this Trickster into the stars for they did not trust him far beyond where they could see him and even then they did not trust him.

But it was too late. Just at that point where they would assert themselves, they had been plunged into the vortex of an utter blackness punctuated by blue points of effervescent light.

"But how do we know these are only half the stars?" Monster Slayer asked Coyote, who had brought his Teezwin with him.

"Oh, you can never know that," Coyote said. "You either believe me or you don't. Have faith. But look at earth, boy, slayer of the powerful and the ugly. Where there is summer, winter will arrive in time. Where there is winter, it's the memory of summer that helps keep the people warm. When it is cold outside the door, the girls like to stay warm inside their rugs, which is when I go to them in my disguise as a warrior in desperate need of a wife."

This tale did not impress the War Twins, who demanded to be taken back. Coyote pleaded with them to look upon the horror of the sun and to know that when winter came he would be there to keep the glow among the girls whose brothers were away, having slipped down into the pathway of adventures, killing monsters who would dare to show their ugliness.

Child Born for Water was just about to grab hold of the tail of this wicked animal who would taunt them so. But even as he reached out, the brothers landed back in the sand again where no dog goes.

There were no roads on the way to Sa's hogan. This made it hard to find for outsiders.

The Navajo in this dusty corner of the universe where volcanoes had lived but were extinct had generation after generation and hundreds of years of making themselves hard to find. There were some who even had a talent for it. There were boulders at the base of mountains where you could walk right by and never know a hogan was there and people lived in the hogan. You had to leave Pinedale and take the trail up. You had to find the fence post with the boot on it. Cross the cattle guard and follow the creekbed to where the big rock juts out of the side of the volcano. Turn around, walk through the juniper, and listen for the sheep. You will hear them before you see them. The big goat will have a bell around her neck. Follow the bell. The hogan behind the boulder where the sheep gather once belonged to Sa.

Our grandmother of the ages. For all that I loved her, I wonder if we or anyone knew her? I know we needed her. But I wonder at who knew her well?

As with most Athabascan-speaking peoples, property belongs to the females.

Divorce is handled easily.

She sets your saddle on the ground outside the hogan. End of ceremony.

When a Navajo dies, the body is removed through the smoke hole and not the door. To tell the lingering ghost that it cannot come back. The door itself is nailed shut forever. No one is to enter this hogan again.

All of this was explained to us as children. Matter-of-factly. In that death, too, was a part of life.

As Sa was explaining about how ghosts come from the north, Tso let out a holler that could be heard down into the canyon.

"But I don't want you to die, Grandmother." He could not be consoled. When told that everyone dies, Tso just kicked at rocks. He was four and innocent. And mad.

Now he was thirteen, and just about as innocent. Was she going to be worth it? This new girl with the huge handbag and the mascara of a thousand colors? Never in a million years; but what boy ever stopped at the things that caught him in his throat? She was the kind of girl who knew when angels passed her by like whispers. She was psychic. "Oh there goes one," she would say. She would look their way. Askance. Tso touched her with his finger to see if she was real. More electric sparks. She stared at her almost cold shoulder for a brief moment where she had been touched. She touched where she had been touched and knew that place was warm.

First it was strawberry red, then turned pale white.

"I saw your car. And I was wondering . . ."

By this time, the waitress at the House of Pancakes was standing near her sta-

tion by the coffee machine, holding a steaming, round pot of coffee, filled to the rim, and steam, too, was blowing silently out her nose, her foot tapping in slight impatience seeing as how we had arrived some hours previously when it had still been quite dark.

We were now approaching the afternoon menu: steaks, burgers, salads. And there we three were. Screaming, laughing, having the time of our lives, eating when it pleased us to eat, falling under the table, doing makeup, writing songs, reading poetry, telling scandalous stories, and generally being annoying adolescents. Two of us had arrived in a car that would have cost some poor waitress three years of salary. Our waitress hoped fervently that we were either going to leave her with a very, very nice tip, or that we were going to leave.

Period.

Having worked these kinds of jobs ourselves, we knew how hard it was, you're sixty-five years old, and your legs scream at the end of every fucking day, and in 1963, you were bringing home ten bucks in tips a day. If that. If things did not improve, and there was no evidence that they would, you would be slinging pots of coffee for the next thirty years after which time they would put you into the House of Pancakes Home for the Impoverished Who Might, They Just Might, Forget to Put Out Their Ciggies at Night and They Would Burn Down the House to the Very Last Pancake.

We would go with the tip. In 1963, a dollar was a big, big deal. No one tipped a dollar. A quarter was more like it.

"We're on our way to California," I said. Only men lie in their throat. I would have told the Greeks that half of Troy was burned. I regretted having said it the instant I was done saying it. *On our way to California?* It was as if a kangaroo had jumped from my mouth and was jumping all around the house of eggs. *Boiiing!* It was *so* stupid. I am the kind of person who can be depended upon to say the wrong thing at the wrong time to the wrong people. *Boiiing!* Then, I wondered . . .

If she could drive.

Perhaps.

There should be car keys in that purse. Jingle jangle car keys like her silver bracelets.

I at least looked sixteen. If the light was right. But who was kidding whom? Our chances were not good. Somewhere they were going to pick us out and pick us up and pick the meat from us in prisons and we knew it. We wondered if we would even make it out of New Jersey. We just didn't want to look at the alternatives because the alternatives meant living with our father.

What we were was between flophouses.

"We're going to Half-Moon Bay to pick pumpkins," my brother told her.
"Pumpkins?"

It had sounded like a good idea when we had thought of it.

In our book, picking pumpkins in California by the beach was a lot more
fun than scooping up chicken guts with shovels in the heat of the Everglades. Another one of our more elaborate skills. The chicken processing
plant.

Suddenly, she felt a need to do her eyebrows. No one—no one—drives
to Half-Moon Bay to pick pumpkins. She did her eyebrows. Regarding us
suspiciously. You slip inside yourself when you do your eyebrows. Inside
yourself where no one sees you. The two very strange boys were beginning
to scare her. They were so odd.

Throwing social caution to the wind.

A mirror appears from the bag. She paws. Frowning. The bag filled with
girl things and surgical instruments.

For nails. For eyebrows. For lips. For pancakes.

My brother nodded. "Yeah, we like pumpkins," he said.

I saw that his smile was a beautiful thing of some desolation and I
knew how badly he wanted to be happy. It was a dumb and simple thing—
wanting to be happy—but my brother had yet to reach the stage of life
where you understood that *happiness* was an absurdity and most people as
they aged just wanted to be effective, and maybe if they were lucky contribute something to the world. My brother never saw himself as being
strong enough or effective enough to contribute something back, so what
you do is settle for the compromise of happiness. Tso and the girl just
looked at each other and they collapsed laughing onto each other and she
tasted his whipped cream on the pancake with her finger and fed it to him.

They knew this: Life and everything in it was ridiculous. The moments
we arrive upon. The trips we do not take. The damsels-in-distress we do
not ensconce in nice motels. The next thing I knew his arm was quietly
arranged over her girl shoulders. Soft shoulders like Helen of Troy. I could
not believe this was happening. I had had him in the palm of my sweaty
hand all his life. I had been his mother and his father. I had been the
brother who did nothing himself, and yet was his own executioner. I had
led him back through deserts. This was the soft moment I knew I would
lose him forever, too. But she was a nice forever.

This *stuff* never happened to us.

She was a singer like Marianne Faithfull on her way to Hollywood to
make a record. Or they would sign her to a recording contract. Wishful
junkie thinking.

When she got there. Or something.

Shit. It was my turn.

Eyes to the sky.

Rivers of eternity. *So—that all your spook is, baby? Fucking music?*
Rock.

And.

ROLL 'em.

Angel knew a record producer somewhere. Never mind the books (hers)
on social studies for high school juniors. Well, they were going to start the
band but no one wanted a girl in a band because men are such pigs.

I found myself daydreaming in her accent. I was chewing on a pencil.
Sometimes I ate the entire pencil. For reasons I could not articulate even
to myself without getting tangled up like kite string I felt as though it was
important we make some kind of effort to understand her.

She Too Could Join the Man-Trap Set.

The *New York Times* said so.

She could walk the walk, and talk the talk. But first, she had to get there.
It was 1963, and California called to a lot of people back then. A lot of people had to get there. We would crawl it on our knees if we had to.

Some siren song and all girl grief melts away in California. Everything
was clean and new in California. Kim Novak lived there in a place called
Big Sur and she had coffee tables made from trees. Kim Novak was blond
and naked and lived in mink.

California was calling to us, too.

You and all the divorcées from International Falls to Mobile could
chuck-it-all, throwing their guitars into the backseat with their records,
and drive straight through the blinding night and the rain that would come
at them and come at them *like lead*, and voilà! They found themselves
on the corner of Haight and Ashbury and *the world* would never be the
same.

Yet *the problem* lay buried in the eyes of sixteen-year-old females who
dared to think. *The problem* lay buried deeper than their Boston grandmother's mother's grave. *The problem* was a whisper in the throats of American women everywhere. *Forget-the-men (for however briefly)*. Every suburban
woman wrestled with it in her own unique way. Every waitress who knew
she could do more than stand there looking maternal with her round black
pots of coffee. *Some* engine had to run America! Even as the aloneness of
it strangled them surrounded by creatures of their kind. She made the
beds. She shopped for groceries. She made the meals. She washed the
dishes. She drove the kids to soccer, to ballet, to piano. She lay in perfect

silence at night beside her husband who had reduced himself, too, to a series of grunts that were issued in lieu of communication. She was terrified. Terrified that this was all there was.

There had to be *more* in California. Just more and more. *That was what people were looking for in their quests for cosmic revelation. More and more! More subdivisions that would snake around the mountaintops. More cars! More highways! More pools. More garages. More surfboards. Computers for everyone! In 1963, our dreams may have been elusive, and that waitress from Chicago who was driving her Corvair to San Jose in search of a bigger and brighter future may have not really known too concretely what it was she wanted, but no matter what it was she wanted, it could not itself be divorced from more and more.*

We would buy surfboards and go on television. Everyone had their own show in California. She kept feeding the machine in the booth that played music from a menu. Of course, every teenage hoodlum with a new Corvette Roadster was going to Los Angeles.

The shift changed at the House of Pancakes, and the lunch waitresses came on.

She was doing her legs (or her nylons, rather) with fingernail polish (stops all runs in their tracks, just goop it on) while my loquacious brother said things like: *umm* and *duhhhh* and *umm* and *duhhhhhhhh*.

Somewhere it was decided.

Time would find the three of us in cheap Louisiana motels—I could see it in my head—where the grass outside had been burned by the sun brown and brittle. The pool was closed and empty. We sat in old chairs in rooms in nothing but our T-shirts, watching *Perry Mason* in black and white. Tso and I both touched her but in different ways, and what she in turn gave back to us was a kind of inner balance. All the while the three of us knowing that outside our dump of a room the world was on fire.

I knew why she had eyes for him, but I think she liked me because he did, too, and it gave her this extraordinary access to his perfect skin.

"If they arrest us," he asked, "will they put us in a cell together?"

We told him *no*. He was silent and sad for a long time, and went and put our only pair of underpants on.

Somewhere in Texas she needed stamps. She was driving and explaining to Tso that she was going to need some stamps for the postcards she had purchased in a gas station outside Telegraph Junction. Tso frowned when he saw the pictures of cows in Telegraph Junction and he asked her why she needed stamps.

We exchanged glances, the girl and I. "I never taught him about stamps," I said. I never had.

He did not know what stamps were for. He had no reason to send a letter let alone write one.

Time fades most everything, including human beings. A preliminary analysis of data, background stars, and particles postulating the existense of other particles, *all* short-lived. In light. Everything becomes indistinct. Like an old photograph of your mother on her honeymoon. If the universe is at critical density, ninety percent of the matter in the universe cannot be ascertained by the mind of man. Here, all luminosity is negligible, as were we, and as was California. There is now incontrovertible evidence that dark matter not only exists but that it exists inside us.

Noon approached in New Jersey. Out there on the gray ocean like windjammers, they could sail through rocks. I fully expected to look at one of the daily papers like the *New York Post* and see tabloid pictures of ourselves featured there as AX MURDERERS STEAL CAR NOW BOUND FOR CALIFORNIA. Over by the cash register with the toothpicks and the mints.

Bad things happen. Always to us. Always to us.

We were on our way to California with a girl. Two adolescent boys and a girl. All three of us struggling with *the problem* alone, and yet we had ourselves. It counted. It had to count. There were no other options. Going back for us, for her, was no longer a reality by the second cup of coffee. It was too late for that. Not one of us considered going back any more than one of us had considered the possibility of running for public office. *As we made the beds, shopped for groceries, cut out recipes from the pages of* Better Homes and Gardens, *matched slipcover material, and chauffeured Cub Scouts, we, too, knew even then that no life in the suburban dust was going to cut it for us. Not us. But no. We were stealing cars and heading west. Yes west! Just west! And there would be no married spouse beside us breathing in contentment as we lay there in silence beside them wondering between the sheets if this was it. Just it!*

Even then, sitting in that booth at the House of Pancakes in Toms River, New Jersey, we knew if we even once made such delicious love as this, the stars themselves would pour from our six eyes, in full nakedness, her breasts would be some new firmament, everything we knew would crumble, and we would know the world again and again. Even then as adolescents we knew that if we did this thing, slipping from the virginity of love, never having made love, but having had all our softer, swollen parts taken from us, we would set our flesh upright here again, and again, and we would redefine ourselves. We had been waiting all our lives for her and she

(she admitted later) had been to the limitations of herself and back again, only to start the process of giving up. She was almost ready to give up on us, that we would ever arrive, and that when we did, she would see that spring and summer's beauty had such a face.

Every time she touched one of us, hot swords like pain ran through our bowels and unlocked us from our slaveries as gravitationally bound objects.

Bound to ourselves, we were bound to California. The romance was in the getting there. The Corvette could barely handle three. It was a tight fit in the spaceship.

I let her drive. It helped she had a driver's license and had taken driver's education. She could back up, too. My brother was between us. His was the smaller butt.

I could smell the gum on his breath.

Her gum. Her breath.

Like they shared the same pink Woolworth's tongue. All our old books had either been destroyed by our father or gone into the trash except one by Jack Kerouac. We had memorized the books we owned anyway. We could tell you what Lady Macbeth said, but she was a queen, we were only serfs, and we could not necessarily tell you what the queen *meant* by what she said. It was gray as sadness in Toms River. Like Pompeii but without the ash. Or one whit of history. We were on our way to California and maybe that would mean we would not go insane after all. After all, California had no history. Even if we were coming there like Roman legions, to write her history speechless. We were the beginning of the barefoot armies, and the beads falling around our necks, and the Jefferson Airplane would never land, having filed her flight plan over golden sands and crystal brooks and silken lines and silver hooks.

Because that is what we had been doing all our picking-pumpkin lives. Going insane and more insane and more insane. I had conversations with Shakespeare and Geronimo. More Geronimo than Shakespeare, who seemed distant and untouchable. The man of words versus the man of action on his charging horse.

That is the only word for it. *Insanity.* To see your very own father rip the clothes off your very own brother who is screaming no no no and to see it all and all and all and he is fucking your very own brother who is bent over a kitchen table like an animal and even the dishes on the table fell and broke and there was food all over the floor and I had to clean it up. Like some pathetic cur who had been kicked and only looked at anything sideways. Because I had been cleaning it up all our lives.

The problem was.

"He's not an animal," I told her.

"What?"

"I said, my brother's not an animal."

"Well, he looks like a big old animal to me."

And she squealed and she tickled him and all he could do was shy away from me.

She was from Manhattan (liar) and her name was Ronnie Spectacular. Eyes to the sky.

"Everyone should have a new name every other year," she said.

I wondered about how many selves she had. In another life, she would have been a warrior, too. Like us. *She Who Rides with Warriors.*

I knew just the warrior. I knew who she had been. There was a female warrior who rode with Ju. Another one rode with Nana. The Apaches and many of the people who are allowed to get close to Apaches knew of them. I do not know that she—the one who rode with Ju—had a name. That way, it would have been more difficult to trace her, to track her down. *Who are you looking for* could not be clearly ascertained. A female warrior could blend back into the static background of the women. Simply put a blanket around her head and have her grinding corn. She killed more Mexican and American soldiers than twenty men combined.

I knew something of who she had been, this Ronnie Spectacular.

There was the hurt her.

There was the giggle her.

There was the sensual her.

There was the pretentious her. It went on and on like this.

My hunch was that she had only just now renamed herself. She was having a fight with her dad. We did not tell her much about our dad.

We did not have to. It wasn't necessary. Maybe we could forget him. Forever.

People could do that in California in 1963. They could forget everything behind them. She would forget her mother and her father and her Angel and her high school choir practice where she was the featured queen.

Her music instructor said she had incredible talent.

She shrugged. She was compelled to take her soul *and* her talent all the way to California where the braver poets had lost themselves. To rage. To write. To lust. To commend. To the flower shop down the street on Haight where she worked from noon to eight.

In her dreams anyway.

She *had* something.

All we had was what we had stolen, and were running from.

The haunting vision of our father.

She could not know anything of this. Because we did not want her to.

Maybe we could forgive him someday although I seriously doubted it. Maybe we could forgive him for hurting us when we were finally, at long last, rich and had more and more. I had forgiven him and unforgiven him and forgiven him so many times I did not know where either one of us stood in relation to the other. The entire notion of forgiveness was now like some subtle knot around my neck. I could not remove the knot. The rope was wet and swollen.

We would die. In pain. We would become the pain, and the sword the pain rides in on.

That all your spook is, honey, pain?

This girl was going to hurt everyone and we would both love her and it would be everything I could do not to cut her throat. She wanted the other girls to see her in the car so we took a loop around the Toms River High School where her poorer cousins attended school, and another one around the Reverend Mother's Mount Mary Olive of the Virgins where the richer snots (all relatives) were educated.

She waved good-bye to her cousins in their uniforms.

"Come, girls, get away from the windows."

And the sight of freedom unwrapping itself like so much smoke ascends.

"So, when were you planning on telling us you were really from the sub-urbs," I would ask later (much later in the motel that night).

She laughed. "What suburbs?"

"I am sure Angel is as real as Avenue D," I said. "But where you're from has to be the 'burbs, honey. I will bet that right around the age of nine, they painted your bedroom pink." At fourteen, my cynicism was ocean-deep, and my sarcasm was as heated as a lava flow.

Her ears turned volcanic red.

"Ever hear of a town called Cranbury? It's not too far from Princeton."

In fact, we had. Migrants picked there. Not that she would know any-thing about that.

"Nice houses with nice people who own nice lawns."

"Perfect lawns. No weeds, please."

And that was what we were.

Weeds.

California would be bleached clear by the weather and we would all be blond except those of us who could not be blond no matter what we did.

It was only the beginning of the school year, and entire floors of windows would be flung open, and Ronnie Spectacular would stand up in the convertible driving and wave good-bye to all that like the homecoming queen had just up and flown the coop and her beehive became undone as my brother pressed the accelerator to the floor. We would disappear from the radar screens of high schools everywhere and pop up again wherever dark halo matter is detected.

I have always wondered why the cops never stopped us that day in New Jersey. Maybe—if they had been doing their job—none of the things that happened would have happened.

My whole life is one slow motion up the horse ramp.

It was as if the daylight around us were a safe cocoon. I looked over at my beloved brother who was sitting in the middle. His plump and hairless testicles pressed up against the stick although he denied it. I laughed so hard I thought we might go off the road and I wasn't even driving. His balls were going to be pressed purple if we didn't stop and stop often to stretch our legs. I suppose she should have sat between us but I was kind of glad she didn't. I had never seen my brother smile this much. She grew on you like mold.

We aimed the Corvette west and never looked back. My brother put his arm around Ronnie Spectacular and grinned like he had just won the New Jersey State Lottery.

My children, I had grown scattered like a scarecrow. There is another me that does not move. It does not rave. They stuck me out here by this Rez Road. The Wizard of Odd.

A reservation highway. Restrain in me the cursed thoughts that nature gives way to in repose. The selfsame winds she breathes in husky whispers.

The me that does not move. Of all the things I am. This is the *stuck* me. Passing boys in rez cars would throw beer bottles at me. I was a tattered scarecrow who was standing in the middle of a hopeful dry Navajo cornfield with his arms spread wide. Geronimo in bondage.

Gagged and tied.

Bad clothes. Bad shoes. Another roadside suicide.

Hanging, flapping in the winter winds. Gloves for hands. A broomstick for my arms. A poet with his guts split open. An *idiot*. Standing in the wetness of his mortal sins.

The past.

Geronimo's bones means the past. Mine. Means my brother's, too. I cannot write the story of it without pieces, fragments of us thrown skyward.

I am told that the Chiricahua Apaches returned to the Fort Sill cemetery where Geronimo was buried and I am told they dug up his bones.

To make the desert a home for bones.

I am told things. Just things.

How are you going to find the bones of Geronimo? You won't. They will find you and it will be the end of you. How are you going to find anything like that in the vastness of the Gila Wilderness? The cow ranchers who surround the wilderness itself have been very nervous these past few years. Shooting at big cats and wolves. They say that the big cats and the wolves pull down their cattle, and some of that is true. Some of it is not true, as no wolf alone could do it. The cows are just too big. The lone wolf just slinks away. But the big cat—a cougar or a puma, both being home out here—could do it. So the wolves and the cats get shot even in the face of federal and foundation programs that reimburse ranchers for their losses.

Geronimo now rides the storms of legend. The warriors of the desert are the bones of heaven.

The past was a horse of eyes and time. The desert was a sea of waves and brine.

The creatures came from below to slither. Some flew up. Some into the river. Geronimo came to plunder and steal.

Some say Geronimo touched to heal.

We were there. In the rivers.

I am told that the river that has played such an important and essential part in the flowing story of my life, and thus the life of my brother—the Rio Grande—has, too, been viciously assaulted by the gold mines, the uranium mines, the molybdenum mines. Molybdenum is a mineral that is used in the making of radio tubes, auto and plane parts, chemical compounds, and dyes. The mining of molybdenum on the banks of the Red River near Questa, New Mexico, has produced a bluish green slime that has flowed through the tailing ponds of the Red River into the drainage of the Rio Grande.

The scarecrow sees.

Knows.

Too much.

More than he wants to.

That river was my life, and I made love to her. The ancient dusky Rio Grande. The scarecrow reeling, turning, *time* slips like water through my hand. Fingers. Increments and fragments and scarecrow stardust. We are all of us nothing more than collections of subatomic grains of sand.

Our daddy drove a truck for the uranium mining company. For a while any-way. I do not know how long.

What I remember is how he came home.

Covered in that dust they called Yellowcake.

It was in his eyes. In his mouth. In his kisses. In his clothes. In his nose. It was everywhere when he got down and played with us.

He kissed us back then. It was spectacular.

He was happy or as happy as he could be anyway. He was making money. It was a job. A real job. You drove the truck with the tailings to the millpond.

I was empty and alone. The wind sang through me. Cold and snowflakes were like tiny stones that cut into my eyes like bullets.

But it was the loneliness that was the worst. The sun came out and warmed my nose. And crows came by and pecked my toes.

I wondered if they would leave. I wanted to die. Alone. I did not want anyone to see me do this private and dull thing.

Dying.

Go away. Shooo. Be gone with you.

Crows!

But they would not. Leave me to my misery.

I knew then they were my children.

They cawed and flopped about.

I do things with them. I do things with each one of them that I do not do with the others.

Each child is unique. He is neither his mother nor his father nor the milkman.

He is not his brother.

He or she is his or her own *self.*

I did call them here. Children gather round!

\\\\\\\

The crows wouldn't have it any other way.

Gathering the children.

Geronimo had been out with the other warriors who had been fighting the Mexicans. The Mexican army particularly hated the Apaches. He had left Alope, his wife, with the baby.

When the warriors returned to the Apache camp in the Sonoran Desert, indi-vidual wigwams were burning, and a black smoke billowed up and blanketed the sky.

Geronimo found his young wife and baby butchered. Their intestines on the ground. Everything was burned.

Geronimo fell to his knees and wept.

It would be the one defining moment of his life.

After that, nothing seemed right.

Geronimo described his life back then as the Chiricahua-in-Wigwams.

It was Alope's wigwam (or tepee) that had been burned with Alope and the children in it. The only time the Chiricahua were that far south in the part of the Sonoran Desert patrolled by Spanish (Mexican) soldiers was 1800 through 1815. After 1815, *there were* no *Chiricahua wigwams in the southern Sonoran Desert. It would have been much too dangerous to have entire tribes pull wigwams. There* was *the horse. But horses were valued instruments of the warrior, not the squaw. Apache horses were sacred and NEVER, EVER P-U-L-L-E-D anything. Horses existed for speed and war.*

Not pulling.

Dogs pulled.

If you were stupid enough to eat all your dogs, you were relieved of all of your possessions. Because you would have slowed down the group. If you ate all your dogs—there was enough food, root and cactus, at this time to feed the people of the desert—you were shunned, and put at the back of the line.

The wigwam in Sonora as Geronimo described it places him at the age of fifteen in 1815.

Clearly, Geronimo was not *born in 1830, and was far, far older than any American military historian wants to make him. If Geronimo was born in or around 1800, and died in 1909, not only does that make him old, but consider this: Geronimo was also the last of the Bedonkohe. The last of his tribe. The last of his ancestors. Many of whom lived more than a century. Consider the Apache chief: Nana. Both Geronimo and Nana had seen into the life of two very different centuries. Perhaps Geronimo's "powers" were rooted not so much in mysticism as they were in experience.*

I have lost children, but I cannot imagine finding one butchered. Geronimo himself would say years later that finding his children like that changed everything about him. I gather my children like small stars I might hold in my palm. At least when they died, I was holding them.

With Kree, my precious daughter, whom I almost never write about, we do her horse's hair. We wash it. We comb it. We gossip. We brush it. We put conditioner on it. We put ribbons in Blaze's hair so the horse is pretty. My shy, pretty Kree.

With Tom, we go to art museums. We stomp about. We are the critics. Why?

Because it's not fishing.

We go to art museums and we look at pictures. At first, he thought this was the stupidest idea he had ever heard. Here: paper, Crayola (Tom limited his colors to red and black), *zip-zaaaaaap*, presto/chango—instant art.

Now, let's go fishing, Dad.

I wanted Tom to be more than just a critic.

I wanted him to know the *joy* of making art. A putting together not taking apart.

Here: paper, Crayola (red, black), *zip-zaaaaaaap*, presto/chango—Tom was done. Tom was busy. And on-the-run. Instant art.

Tommy Nothing Fancy, like Picasso, just had no goddamn time to suffer fools.

But by the third or fourth art museum, he sort of started to enjoy himself.

He had to hold my finger. So as to not get lost. *And if he ran away from me in* any *art museum, I would spank him.*

Fortunately, Tom never put me to that test.

Tommy Nothing Fancy had huge black eyes. Black like liquid. He was beautiful, and I was afraid someone would snatch him.

It took a while to get Tom dressed in the morning. He wiggled. We would finally get to the shoes.

"Uncle Tso showed me how to do tie."

"He taught you to tie your shoes?"

"I can."

And he could.

He had his favorite artists. Gorman, of course; the Navajo painters. "But," he said, "just because I'm a Navajo doesn't mean I can't like Van Gogh." (The kid was six and had severe learning disabilities.)

Tommy was an odd little goat.

For all his behavioral deficiencies over here, he made up for them with talent over there.

Starry Night was his favorite painting and he had a poster of it in his room. Tom liked the swirls of yellows that were the stars and the dust from stars. He insisted that *that black thing* that had thrust itself up and out of the ground was, in fact, a monster coyote.

He showed me the coyote ears.

Sometimes we had to take the poster down.

Those nights when the picture moved. Tommy screaming. Pointing. Burying his head into the muscles of my shoulder.

We are often scared to death by the things we want.

Crowdogboy was easy.

We sat in rain.

What are you doing!?
We are feeling rain.
With our tongues out. And tasting it.
Awee liked making things. He collected old cigar boxes. He made them into coffins. Then, he stopped making coffins. We started fixing up the cigar boxes together. We made them nice. We glued pieces of fabric in the box. Silk. Woven wool. Glued pictures. Awee explained that our boxes were places in which you could keep your treasures. Like a medicine pouch. A leather jish. He painted his boxes, too. They were in a way a living wish.
All my crows are artistic.
They liked things that sparkle. Precious stones. Glittery things crows collect to jazz up their nests.

I drown in them. That deep breath and to let it *go*. Gently, Nasdijj, gently. Write gently as if your journals would be open for inspection.
Water. Waves.
I have this dream from time to time. In my dream I go outside to find them. I call them by their names. Crows take note, but they do not necessarily respond.
Might I find them? In that far beyond? My children.
It is more difficult than you might *think*.
I use my nose—I suppose—they're the ones whose feet do *stink*.
Now they're laughing, and rolling on the floor. My children have arrived to dream, and dream forevermore.
Awee is in his tree house. Built far up and off the ground. I hear him hiding up there.
Being a *girl* one might assume my Kree would be in her room trying her dresses on or *doing* makeup, mirrors (her room being filled with them) everywhere, and twenty tubes of lipstick, eye shadow, and tutus from her ballerina daze. But Kree is riding horses. She is dust and racing Blaze. No perfume for her I'm thinking: Where can there be harm? My daughter is the one who smells not too unlike the barn.
I have this rule that says Tommy may not fish alone. I see his tackle's gone. My heart sinks like it's a stone.
I am angry he makes me do this.
This constant *finding* him.
I can feel the blue veins at the side of my head bulging. I yell his name!
Like I don't know where this child is.

No, your *dog* is *not not* alone!

I don't care if you can swim.

Because it's *dangerous—that's why*!

Because I said so.

Because I cannot bear the thought of losing him. When, in fact, I lost Tommy *how many years ago?*

I do *not* count the years. I measure time now in increments. In images of summers and of tears. I bring him back to me. His cold, mad father.

Tom cries as we walk back to the house. No, I will not help him carry his fishing tackle. Yes, I am acutely aware that he's mad at me. Yes. I do make the rules, I do. That flash. That look I get. That light that flames from the pinched corner of his eyes. Tommy stomping home. Navajo the dog bounding ahead of us along the path. I just can't bear to lose him and lose him and lose him. I cannot.

Do you have any idea how difficult it is to get them all into the same room so we might function *as a family?*

The cathedral of my skull.

I wish they could have had what I had. A bondage to a brotherhood where the world was changed and nothing was changed when we fell together in the grass. I do not wish that they might have what I had. My intense connection to Tso was forced upon the two of us by madness. Contradiction is ironic but it isn't madness.

Crow is in the barn. Fixing his jeep, which has no tires (today anyway) and is up on cinder blocks. His three-hundred-dollar jeep. His butt is bent over the jeep and his head is stuck inside the jeep engine. Tools everywhere. The Greasemonkey from Hell.

I dote on every illness. Nagging at him to take his vitamins and pills. When he is away at school, I do not want him to even know what any of my problems are. They are my problems. Crow spills into my mind every waking moment. Me: wondering what he is doing. Maybe I can *help!* Maybe not. He stands up. I just know he's going to put that greasyblack finger with the greasyblack hangnail caked with greasyblack jeep engine grime into his mouth. He does not disappoint me.

Lollipop! Lollipop! Lollilollilollipop!

That is the mouth he likes to kiss girls with. I make a mental note to never allow him to kiss me ever again. Sucking his middle finger (now glowing quite purple). Makes the Indian sign for the word: *fuck*.

Never do this within sight of an Indian grandmother. When you see her making this sign, politely look away.

O! My children. Go putcher story jammies on, and come sit by me tonight. The fire is gone to ashes cold. Daddy's got some stories of unfolding and unfolding rivers might.

Unfold. Unfold. Unfold.

Untold. Untold. Untold.

I gather up my children like the sweeping of the sawdust workshop floor.

To tell. My job. The reason for my being. I am learning how not to scold. And in that telling of the river the bottom glitters golden cold.

Until such time as some new dad wants his babes to sit with him and hold. Their hands to dance the story's chance it will not freeze to death in cold.

Oh! Silly daddy! A river does not unfold!

Ha! Ha! What does Daddy know—he's nuts!

His sanity now a thing in cups.

A silly daddy whose words and poems fly and jump about like birds and bats that tumble into the night. So the swollen bellies of the boys and girls might learn in spite of stretching yawns and almost bursting appetite. Of a world that spins and spawns and gives like torrents of the river. Where boys and girls who have swum all day are shakes in shadow's shiver.

A silly daddy who holds his boys and girls so close to his breathing chest and breast. To keep his babies safe and warm and freed of emptiness. Those who see my daddiness as basically insane. Must live their lives within their hives of business and shame.

I became a father. I was by myself in it.

But not so nuts his children do not sit around his chair. Their sleepy eyes and tired butts pretend they're far too old to care.

My oldest son who does not hear yet holds my hand in love. People ask where my children come from, and I am shocked to learn. They know nothing of Coyote who gives birth to babes in Navajo-snow. And grabbing babies one by one, he bites them around the neck. To swim them downstream from the sun, who threatens storm and wreck. The sun has said they are not his, and they will not live to see the day. Where rivers suck and gravel sieves and water knows the way. But armed with bolts of thunder, the children rose to slay. Everything but wonder. Let it die another day.

Let us cut the roof off the house tonight so we might see the stars.

Yes! Yes! Our stories will unfold and fold their miseries and ours.

I *do* do magic.

Try as I might (and I have *tried and failed*) you will always *be my babies*. I can't help it. Even when you grow up. You are *still my babies*. I will take attendance. One by one. My Tommy. My Awee. My Kree. And my Crow-dogboy. Three boys and a girl. No man on this earth has been so blessed as I. I must be as happy as the sun.

Who has just learned how to come when called. Out of breath and on the run.

~~~~~~

My dead babies call to me. Daddy. So soft. They bring me to my knees.

What could I have done? The rivers run. The emptiness.

Say *please?*

They did not deserve to die. Time held me. Pale and alive.

I am finished with my ranting. I only wish I knew why.

It helps me to bring them all into the same room. To tell our stories set against the thunder and the gloom.

The scarecrow.

Writing is all I have today. My *last* connection to the wild.

Some men are empty.

I was. I do not know why. I was absurd and ridiculous. I had poems and scraps of paper and the sky. Another storm and another storm and another storm came and ripped my house of cards to shreds. The babies and the stories were tucked safely in their beds. I would have slit my wrists with a razor blade but I knew something of the pain it would bring to the boy who was my brother. He would have been all alone and I do not know that he could have coped with the constant assaults from the man who was our father. Someone had to stay alive to protect my brother. I am probably still quite ridiculous. I was tired. I wanted the agony to end.

At some point, it isn't the hunger that gets to you. It's the *Being Tired of Always Being Hungry* that gets to you. And the holding on by the edges of your broken fingernails. And the darkness of the down and down. I would have sold my soul for a speck of light. I had always been able to push the nocturnal edges of the shadows away. But I was losing the ability to do this. I would push, but when I pushed at the shadows, my fist and my arms just went through them.

The shadows remained. Unmoved.

I did not like this magic. I did not own socks.

I do not know why this bothered me. But it did. For some reason, this was enormous symbolism. No socks again.

I kept giving my fucking socks to my brother.

So he could make it through school. And not be laughed at by those white children I hated.

I would beat up any kid who looked at my brother the wrong way. They all had homes and a mom and a dad. They all had rooms and they were never sad.

This was my *take* on the kids our age. My ideas around how Other People lived were like some lone basketball that, popping up, could see inside the bedrooms, the stairways, the kitchens, the closets, and the bathrooms of the kids who would never in a million years invite no heathen migrant up to play checkers (I loved checkers).

But I never had no (shirtless migrant boy alone in alley hangs head) checkers game. The streets of America were paved with gold. I very much wanted to *be* that basketball as it bounced up by their kitchen windows, too, so you could see what was cooking on the stove for their dinner.

When our mama was alive, it would likely be beans and rice, and we liked it. After Mama died, the only thing around was beer. Oh, we'd drink it if we thought we could get away with it. Like that sad old man who lived in our house did not count 'em. One bottle each (neither of us weighed more than fifty pounds through childhood) and we'd pass out where we stood. I would wake up in bed. Daddy must have put us there. Tso would have likely wet the bed. I always had to make sure he did not drink anything in the evening or I'd find myself drowning in it.

Daddy never mentioned it.

He knew.

He knew the hunger that ran through us.

It wasn't that Daddy could not make money. He could. It was the series of steps that followed he could not take.

The I-will-cook-this-tonight.

The I-will-shop-for-this-today.

The I-will-turn-a-paycheck-into-steaming-mashed-potatoes-for-my-boys-tonight.

I do not know with any accuracy where or when the break came. The break where Daddy had no more light in him to offer us. After he died, I was told by a public health nurse that the old man had had liver cancer for some time before he kicked off. His liver had been turned into a prune pit the consistency of pumice.

Of all the weird sisters that haunted him through life's uncertain voyage—alcoholism, violence, gambling—it was the sisterhood of gambling, the agreement that on this bet the man who could not afford to bet anything was not only betting everything, but he was being egged on to bet the house, the car, the family business, and his son's college education. He could be a high roller with the best of them. Just like any other addiction, the addiction to making that bet one more time can and will destroy you, and as it takes you down, it takes everyone connected to you with it.

What I mourned wasn't him. What I mourned was everything he lost and when the dust settled what we had left standing was him. Such men are masters of themselves and take forever to die, and all their livers are the consistency of stones.

We would hide in dusty attics and sometimes under the house where the spiders were while the men who arrived in the migrant camp for him came and yanked him from the house. Daddy in his underwear being beaten by men with fists and clubs. If such was justice then why were we boys crying? It, too, was an addiction. The *Being Beaten Up* like that. A public humiliation that knew no limits. They were beating him up one night after a whole week of reminding him to pay them what he owed from a weekend he had spent with them playing poker. I could hear his flesh hitting the ground, and his grunts like an animal as they kicked him. When he was playing cards with them he was their brother in the brotherhood of thieves, but when they were kicking him and beating him up, he was nothing more than a termite they would exterminate. That was when I knew beyond the shadow of a doubt—and no matter what he said—he was certifiably insane.

There was a point at which our roaming ended. I was never really sure it would. I would pray night after night for a home. Just once. A place for us that would last longer than a week. Tso and I had grown weary and exhausted with never knowing where we might be next. We, of course, blamed our dad for that and for everything.

The neon lights outside the window and the neon motels had to end. The migrant shacks and Quonset huts and trailers where the rain came in had to end. The half sleep we could fall into lightly as we waited for the rodents to arrive as they skittishly crossed the floor and the barriers of our bodies had to end. The setting of the mousetraps up in circles all around us had to end. What food we had being invaded by the spiders and the worms had to end. The snakes dropping from the ceiling had to end. Often, when these things happened, Tso and I would grab a blanket, remove our cowboy boots, and stretch out in the bed of the pickup. But often the things that came into the house from holes or underneath the trailers were coming in because of cold or rain, and that meant we couldn't use the bed of the back of the pickup. We had to use the front seat. The front seats of trucks do not usually have a whole lot of room.

Sleeping with your brother and a blanket in the front seat of a pickup truck, knees everywhere, elbows pushed into someone's chest, and your brother's breath in your mouth adds yet another layer to the frost that forms on windshields in the deep freeze, and was, too, another layer and another layer of our shared history.

Sometimes you had to laugh.

"Why are you laughing? I am fucking *miserable*," Tso would say. He would take out his long shopping list of miseries but I had one of my own and it was a lot more miserable than his.

"I am laughing because this one blanket is a joke," I complained. Still laughing. "It doesn't even hide your early-morning hard-on."

"*Don't look at it,*" Tso would almost yell.

"I'm *not* looking at it, but it's pressed into my bad knee."

So we tried sleeping with my head against the passenger's door and his head the other way and pressed against the driver's door.

It didn't work. In two minutes, I was laughing again.

"Nasdijj, I swear, I'm so tired."

His feet smelled, too. "You need to cut your toenails," I told him.

He frowned. "What do you mean *cut my toenails?*"

He didn't know.

"People cut their toenails the same way they cut the nails on their hand. What a mess you have made of your feet."

"I just rip the nail off."

"I see that. *How* do you rip the nails off?"

"With pliers. You grab the nail with pliers and then you rip it off."

"Doesn't it *hurt?*"

"Yeah, but the bleeding usually stops the next day."

That was why his socks were bloody. I had solved a great mystery.

He did the same thing to the nails on his hand. He ripped them off with pliers. I had always thought of them as simply being short. They were very short. They were nonexistent. I would buy him nail clippers. I had yet to teach him that you had to lick the stamps.

~~~~~

Finding sleep was often a haunted search for temporary sanity. Tso was just coming down from a rotten case of mononucleosis, and the free clinic doctor I made him go to grabbed *me* and impressed upon me the very real need for my brother to find some *rest*. "If your brother doesn't get some consistent sleep and soon, what is now a case of mono can quickly start going south, and that's going to be a very serious pain in the ass not only for your family, but for all of the migrant families you are living with. I will be required to inform the county health department, and they will take a good long look at the family arrangements involved."

This was code for *county foster care social worker*.

My dad wanted Tso in the fields, but I locked Tso in the truck so he could sleep in there undisturbed. Using duct tape to secure aluminum foil all around the windows of the truck solved the light problem. "But I'm afraid of the dark!" my brother joked. No one in the migrant life can afford to be afraid of the dark, and if you are, you put a lid on it.

Tso recovered, and *while* he was recovering I'd look back at the truck with the aluminum foil covering the windows, and worry because I did not know what I would do without him. I did not know if I could even *be* without him. I would go check on him and bring him water. "You're not picking too much cotton today, Nasdijj."

"Shut up and drink."

He had soaked the blanket in sweat. I would find him another.

We only picked cotton on the places where they couldn't afford the machines that can do that kind of work. On payday Daddy went to collect our money but there wasn't any.

His eyes were furious and his face was lined and his jaw was set.

"They took off without paying anyone."

There was yelling going on up and down the row of migrant shacks. The Mexican women who had children to feed would track these characters who had ripped us off *down*, and they would shoot them. It was not a joke; they *would* shoot them.

Daddy and a few of the other male migrants went into town with their guns and rifles.

The man who had taken the cotton we had picked was set to pay the man who had run off with the cotton we had picked. But he had not paid him yet because the cotton—having been delivered in the middle of the night—had not been inspected. It was supposed to be inspected for things like parasites.

The parasites had delivered it.

It was a sure thing they were around somewhere.

Close by. And waiting.

The migrants convinced the man who was buying the cotton to pay the migrants for it. They returned the money that was not their fair share, and the lot of us got out of Dodge before all hell broke loose. This is where the sheriff usually arrives and they are never on the side of the migrants. Daddy always said that knowing when to leave the past behind was what had saved his skin many a time.

After our road trip to California had come to its inevitable conclusion and *it-had-to*, I went from job to job. I was a man now or so I thought. I had to think that. If I had still seen myself as a boy I could never have done half the things I did. Like lifting bales of hay and throwing them into truck beds. This was not the work of boys. This was the work of men. Finally taking responsibility for my life was not the work of a boy.

I liked where we were living (above a store at the edges of an ordinary town—close enough to the edges of the reservation I have always loved—and close enough to the volcano our grandmother had lived on so we could get in the truck and be there in thirty minutes) and I wanted to keep it. It wasn't a palace. But it was ours. It didn't have the smell of Daddy anywhere in it. I *liked* the Formica table. I *liked* the plastic kitchen chairs. I *liked* the plastic red and yellow containers for mustard and ketchup that sat in the kitchen window, my last attempt at interior design, and I *liked* the old wood floors that squeeked and creaked. The place was dry. The rain did not come in. There were no mice. No rats. No spiders in the food. It was quiet. It was clean. It was a palace *to me*. I vowed to work my butt off to keep it. *I* would pay the rent. *My* rolling stone ended here. I was staying. So was Tso. We would be on our own. We had been *that* for years. I *worked* and the money I made was money I made, and it did not go into my father's pocket.

- dishwasher
- barn cleaner
- calf roper
- cow milker
- collector of bull semen
- artificial inseminator
- grass cutter
- seed planter
- tractor driver
- tomato picker
- bean picker
- plum picker
- apple picker
- orange picker
- combine driver
- horse groomer
- horse trainer

- mare birthing midwife
- bartender
- waiter
- ambulance dispatcher
- truck mechanic
- scarecrow

Maybe with any luck my brother would be the only person in our illiterate family who had a high school education.

He wept when he found out.

That I had given him all the socks. Again.

I pinched every penny. I kept account of every single dime. I hid our money under a secret floorboard because if our father were to find it, he would spend the rent on a drunken binge.

Daddy had crossed that line. Now he was just killing himself slowly. The man had diabetes and was going blind.

I did not (have to) see him all that much. I saw him once coming out of a bar as I was walking by but he did not recognize me and I did not want to see him.

Ever again.

I didn't want things to be as bad as things were when we were around eight and nine. My brother and I would sit in our truck parked in a Jose Cantina's parking lot (Jose had a six-foot neon sombrero) freezing to death while our daddy was in the bar spending the rent money on tequila shots. Finally we would go in there to get him. Elbowing our way slowly through the dead wet coats, and the dead passageways through remorse, the dead and the deep damnations of the men who had taken off, leaving tiny noses pressed against the glass, tiny fingers hanging on, and elbowing our way through crowds of broken cowboys, the cowboy boots dripping mud, the blue air thick as seas, and knives in pockets or safely sheathed, and steer the carcass of our father to the truck (it was often more than the two of us could handle), and Daddy would vomit all over himself, and if-we-were-out-of-luck all over us, and all over the parking lot that is what his life was. A parking lot of vomit, ice, night, and endings. I did not care about any of this. I only cared that Tso not cry. Enough. Of this. My brother's whole world had been to fly or cry and I had had enough of it. If we had been a little older we would have left Daddy sitting in a snowbank. But we needed him.

We needed the image of him, or we'd be sent off to foster homes.

What the social workers seek are symbols.

We knew about the foster homes.

There is a pipeline between kids. Then. And now. They communicate. They find one another with their eyes. We knew kids who had been put in foster homes. It's real hard on the parents if they are migrant workers. If they leave the state, the consequences are forever.

Many, many children are abused in foster homes.

We did not think we could handle that. We did not think we could handle that and not end up killing someone. We would not be separated. They could try. But we would have run down to Mexico if they had pulled that cheap shit trick on us. We might have pigshit for a parent, but it was better than a foster home where the people who abuse you are strangers.

We had our *Mexico Map*: The map was filled with red lines and they all went to Mexico. A few of the red lines simply retraced the route the Mexicans took when they came to America to pick and make a few (very few) extra bucks. If push had ever come to shove, we would have made it to Mexico. I have no doubts about that. We had friends in Mexico. Other migrants. *People with families who would tell us at the end of a picking season that we could always come to Mexico and live with them and we knew they didn't mean it, they could not afford to mean it, but we wanted to pretend they did mean it.* All we would have had to do was put ourselves (and our thumbs) out on certain highways, and our chances of a migrant family coming along, or even a caravan of them, were pretty damn good.

How many families did we get so closely sucked into back in all the migrant camps? This intimacy was the real thing. Just to call someone *auntie*. We did it any number of times. Auntie Rosa. Auntie Maria. Uncle Raul. You felt vulnerable though, like you didn't have *anyone* who was *anyone*.

Geronimo turning the instrument around in the glinting of the moonlight. Admiration.

"This evenhanded justice, knives."

"But you do not apologize."

"Why would I do that? I am a ghost. You put me here. Dredging my bones up. Apologize, ha. They wanted me to apologize to the citizens of Tucson who took a vote to see if they would hang me. I was well over a hundred years old by then. Hang me for crimes I had committed before their grandfathers were infants. Their grandfathers were infants, and I was leading armies. Apologize? For what?"

We did not at that time see our father in the same context we saw Coyote or Mosika. The dog and the cat. In the stories, both Coyote and Mosika were far, far more benevolent than our father was. On the other hand, there was a very ribald aspect to the stories. Both Coyote and Mosika were *compelled* to stick it into anything that walked. Gender was almost irrelevant. This did not surprise us as children. As boys, we'd squint, shrug, and *get on with it.*

We had half brothers and half sisters in Mexico and "aunties" who were naive enough to believe Daddy was *coming back to rejoin them* as soon as he could get away.

From us.

Daddy always knew where the door was.

My brother was out of socks. Again. Where do all the socks go? I had not done the laundry. I was going to do that tomorrow. I was a day late because I had gone to his high school to attend the parent–teacher conferences. My brother's teachers thought it was extremely odd that I would even attempt to take the place of my father but I was better than nothing at all.

They all had students who had close to nothing at all and no one.

They pretended I was older and wiser than I was. And I pretended to understand what they were talking about.

I boiled it down to two things: time. He needed time to do the schoolwork. You could not do it without copious amounts of time. Otherwise, it wasn't possible. And things to write with. Paper. Pens.

Time and things.

Given that, a body could do anything.

Toward the end, I had a steel-rigid schedule so things got done and I could make it to my three jobs. Without falling apart. Sleep was something I just kept shoving away. Until it shoved back and hard. Tso quite appropriately looked into my sock box, which was an old shoe box (empty) I kept in the closet we shared.

He pounded his fist on the table and said something dumb about hating Daddy.

We *all* hated Daddy. It didn't solve anything, and it didn't *get* anyone anywhere.

My brother went out and stole a plastic bag of socks from Kmart.

My early birthday gift.

Tso had little experience at shoplifting.

Where did he t-h-i-n-k we got all that kielbasa from, anyway?

There were things you just learned to stuff, and there were things you just learned to stuff down your pants. Dinner.

The cops who brought him home were pissed off like this shit would stick to them.

Our lives were fragile contradictions that if challenged by a finger would fall down and come unraveled in the wind. It didn't take much. We slept in our coats so the heating bill didn't put us out on the street again.

I had to take time off from work. I had to speak to the manager at Kmart.

I even had to speak to my brother's counselor at school.

I had to work to get him off the hook. The manager at Kmart sent us a big box filled with socks.

I sat there and wept.

There are kind people in the world.

Some of them are ordinary.

Any number of people from probation officers to school counselors would sit down with you and throw lectures at you about how hard you were going to have to work to turn your life around. Any number of well-intentioned people can put their finger in your face and lecture. But how many of them will send you a birthday box of socks?

Ordinary men are often kind.

My brother's socks were also mine.

I made my brother promise to never steal from Kmart by himself again.

One of the jobs I was having difficulty holding (because I had this bad habit of passing out, as I was working twenty-four-hour days and running the waxing machine on the shiny floor of a small department store, which was downright dangerous) was as a restaurant dishwasher, and the *pain* when you had to slip the skin of your hands into that industrial-strength soap and that cold and horrid water was enough to make your eyeballs turn to black. The water should have been hot but there were cost-cutting measures put in place by management.

The butterflies that late summer were already yellow and dined on ditch-sunflowers that grew parched along the dirt roads of the arroyos time and time again. We could hear him coming down the hall. We could grab a baseball bat before he could get to our room. He tried stealth. It did not work.

"Did you ever think about having children," my brother asked.

Maybe we were ten. Then. Again. In Memphis. The mattress stunk like piss.

"Did you ever think maybe we could have been great baseball players?"

Maybe we were eleven.

Some other flophouse. Some other gin bottle left behind by Daddy. "Did you ever think maybe we could save enough money for a Cadillac?"

Maybe we were twelve.

"Do you think she loved us? I can't remember how she smelled."

She loved us, and she smelled like vanilla.

Maybe we were four.

Maybe we were crows.

Maybe the past is not where memory belongs. Perhaps memory belongs in the beauty of the moment.

It was hard to buy my younger brother things he needed like books. He was in school. He needed paper, pens, books. I was sixteen and my shoulders were broad. Strong. Tough as gristle. I was vibrant from a distance. But what you touched was thistle.

I had survived the canyons of Utah where Daddy had left us while he worked in Page. "No," I said. "I haven't thought about it. All I can think about is now." I was holding down three jobs. Which was ridiculous. One was going to have to go.

The very idea of children was not a good one.

Children need a mother and a father. This was not about having children.

This was about my brother—who had no father—thanking me for being there for him.

I was a year older than he was.

Or a decade. Take your pick.

Maybe I had done something right. I wanted him to make something of his life. My own was the hopeless mess it was. Nevertheless, we were alive, and not just taking up space upon the earth. We had minds and I saw us as using them. And there was this warm, enveloping silence between us. A good silence not unlike the dark spaces of the Navajo rug we used to sleep in. The memories of her.

Sometimes hath the brightest day a cloud, and after summer evermore succeeds barren winter, with his wrathful nipping cold. So care and joys abound as seasons fleet.

Sings warm songs of socks around my brother's pink and stupid feet.

Those small dark pockets where all communication ceased—no longer words—and we were our eyes. We were summer. We were winter. We were our joys. We were our clouds. We were our exhausted sighs.

Knowing how to do it.

The scarecrow tips his hat and sings.

Before my brother dashed to school in the morning, leaving me to my three jobs of earning us an income, he made sure there was food. He never once ate the very last one. Of anything.

~~~~~~~

The blood runs like rivers through the islands of our souls, for it is our souls who have connected, and that is *what* writing *is*, connecting souls, *my babies*, and the tale that so sublimely adjudicates, and unfolds, here, *my babies*.

My suicide.

Attempts.

You in your pajamas.

Your hair still soaking wet.

How could I?

Make such babies face.

Adult disparagement.

Let us speak openly of it like opening that box of secrets. I think we should.

SEE the members of our family units as the human beings they are. Fathers. Mothers. Brothers. Sisters. Forever piping songs. Forever new. They dwell with us in beauty's dust. Their sinking as the light wind lives. We must reach out to them with eternal trust. We must. For they, too, are the stuff of us.

They are not perfect.

It is okay for Grandma to put their pictures in frames and for her to hang those frames on any wall she wants to. But it is not okay for us to put them on some pedestal from which they cannot escape.

Yet I know my children. I know how deeply they love. I know how knowledge is accumulated by them and then, when the appropriate time comes—*used*. Put to a good and proper purpose.

They sit around me on the floor.

One on my lap. The girl. Miss Sleepy-eyes has gone and missed her nap.

One has his head resting on my knee. His hair is wet. You ache in bone-stillness for them. To not disturb. I thought someone had dashed into the bath. I do not care to move the knee. I run my fingers through their hair not unlike the way in which an old Spaniard tunes his classical guitar. I have their silence and their attention. And love them as they are.

They have been writers all their lives.

Writing to me.

Writing about me.

They put my bed by the window that time I came home from the hospital with the pulmonary embolisms sticking to my ribs.

It felt as if you had just inhaled an entire dictionary. What lungs? The lungs that have seen me through pneumonia after pneumonia? The lungs that have the TB scars? Oh, those lungs.

They're shot.

I work a bit. And then I go to bed.

My children arrive to sit beside me. Saying nothing.

My brother crawled into bed with me. I was naked. He was fully clothed.

I was drowning in my sweat.

"Remember that time we drove to California with Ronnie Spectacular?"

My children heard this.

Running to the bed. That faces the window and the woods.

"Of course, I remember," I said.

"You *knew* Ronnie Spectacular?" My children were incredulous.

My brother laughs. "Well," he said. "She was *our* Ronnie Spectacular. Not the one from Hollywood."

No. *Our* Ronnie was from New Jersey. Kids groan.

We are such vivid disappointments.

"No," I said. "She was not *my* Ronnie Spectacular. She was *your* Ronnie Spectacular. You married her. I didn't."

I would have said, "Oh, we fucked her in a motel room in Pecos, Texas," but I didn't have the heart. My children are truly over (a messenger arrived one night) my use of profanity. It just sneaks out like overflow.

Such confession would have implied an intimacy with my brother that is not really the kind of intimacy we share. Which is not about the skin but goes down into it.

We are blood brothers in more ways than one. My brother's bone marrow transplant being one *he* should tell. Not me.

"Don't," my brother said.

"Don't what?" I asked.

"Don't tell people about that trip. We agreed, remember? It was a trip just for us.

"They threw us out onto the sidewalk at CBS," Tso remembered.

My children laughed.

〜〜〜〜〜

My children, I want this book you are about to read *to unfold*. Like your brain must need.

Sustenance. My brother and I were there.

I know this, and I want you to know it, too. *Sustenance such as food, water, shelter, socks is not enough when winter knocks.*

~~~~~~

11

Traveling West Is Like
Following the Sun

That night as the boys were waiting to fall asleep, they talked between themselves even as their eyes grew heavy and the lids pulled them down into the soft center of dreams and volcanoes.

They were ashamed of many of the things they had done when they had been naughty boys and had cried.

They had been arrogant at times.

Their mother had only attempted to hide them from the monsters so the monsters, the Naayee, would not eat them.

In the morning, the sun would show them what to do.

Traveling west is like following the sun. I had always liked driving west. I felt free. I could point the Corvette in the right direction and the vehicle seemed to understand it belonged *in* and *to* California.

Direction is like sanity. My life has always been utterly directionless. How can I imbue with direction something that never had any? Chapter one should go right into chapter two.

Are you kidding? It might make lots more sense if chapter four leads flawlessly into chapter twenty-seven. My life did.

For the first time in our existence we were with someone who didn't see us as migrant workers, and she did not know our dad.

It was not unlike being shot out of a cannon. It was as if a tremendous freedom had been summarily handed to us, and like many people who have never in their lives handled freedom—not having the slightest experience at managing it—we rode it like a bull at the rodeo. It was finally not about Daddy. Or any of the things he did to us. We were not defined by him or by our proximity to him. Ronnie loved us for who we were.

Ronnie Spectacular was sixteen, and as such she was elected to be *the one who got the motel room.*

She drove. *She had been taught how.* She had that pass of passes, a driver's license.

What else could she do? She had more charm than we did. And in the right light, she might be eighteen.

"I wonder if I am doing the right thing?" she would say.

The right thing? What? You asking us? Then she would say, "They told me I had talent in high school. So you are either going to go out there and do something with that talent or you aren't, at least that's the way I see it."

She could sing, too.

She wrote music. She was famous (I jest).

She could get the motel room. It was worth something.

Whenever Tso or I tried to rent the motel room, we would get directions to the next motel. We had not really thought our battle plan entirely through.

Our battle plan consisted of driving west. Follow the horizon. *The sun.*

As far as we were concerned, we could sleep anywhere. The ground. But when you add the female element into the equation, everything changes. We would need motel rooms. Especially in light of all the glorious and pervervitated sex we might have with Ronnie Spectacular.

Might have. We wanted *everything* to be spectacular.

With our end to slavery (yaaaa, we had a lot to learn), we wanted fireworks.

There were a few occasions when the desk clerk craned his head around the corner to get a glimpse of Ronnie's two "cousins" sitting in the car.

You slink *down, down, down* into the car seats.

Tso throws a single piece of popcorn at me.

I ask him why he did that. He shrugs. I put him into a full nelson to remind him (he forgets) *who* the bigger brother is. We are laughing, and trying to stretch our legs, and I noted they were long, skinny legs that were growing about an inch a month.

Ronnie gets back into the car and sighs. We were an enormous pain in the ass. She smiles at her "two boys."

"No popcorn fights, no wrestling on the furniture—it's paid for, no stealing the TV, no cheese pizzas, no liquor, and no dogs at the Starlight Motel in Hemphill, Texas. And no rooms for *droonk dogs* comin' to Land of the Texas Rangers where they hang strangers eatin' cheeseballs."

There was a silence in Hemphill where no one had even seen a car built *after* 1957. We stood out like a meatball sandwich. An old dog walked to the middle of the road, lay down, and went to sleep. We just watched it.

There was not a single solitary soul or car parked at the Starlight Motel.

We were it, and they did not want us.

"Where to," my brother asked. "I'm tired."

Shoved under his feet was the stuffed panda bear he had only two days previously won at the Natchitoches, Louisiana, Fair and Rodeo Shivaree. One of my brother's more significant attributes is his twisted ability to take aim at ducks with a twisted rifle. One little old *ping*. That is it. *One little old* ping *and you get the panda bear.*

Of course, he gave it to her. Then she gave it to me. Then, we all shared.

We named it.

The Fish.

All three of us liked the name. The Fish.

The Fish had little button eyes.

Tso would sit on The Fish so his balls didn't get too squished when Ronnie hit fourth gear like it was Christmas. We had been up in Shreveport the week before Natchitoches at the Shreveport Rodeo.

No fair. It was purely rodeo and we liked that a lot.

I got a temporary job there working as a veterinary assistant to a veterinarian who can always be trusted to be worked to the bone at a rodeo. Especially a good rodeo like the rodeo in Shreveport.

We had ourselves a prize cow named Milly who was not supposed to do anything more active than throw a cowboy to the ground and stomp on him.

Milly had other ideas and to hell with cowboys.

Milly was with c-o-w and had been for some time.

Oh, no, I could tell right away from the way her belly poked that this calf was coming out more twisted than a carnival rifle at the duck shoot.

The vet was a nice young guy who had his reading materials all set up in the 4-H barn. He looked at me painfully. Sweat poured in rivulets.

"Relax," I said. "It happens. Not often. But it happens, and folks do not like having their cow die, and you begin to feel like all of Shreveport is looking at you." A guy shows up from the radio station, and another one from the paper in Shreveport, and it was time to lock the 4-H barn doors, which is what we did.

Both Tso and Ronnie gave me big hugs, and helped me wash my arms and hands.

The hand and arm should be warm. When it comes to the best *things*, they are never there when you need them. Tractor lube will not do.

But man has been birthing cows ever since the time man could herd them with dogs.

It is not too complicated. You wear clothes you will burn later. The hand goes in slowly because Milly is *very* uncomfortable. You do not want to be kicked. I saw a vet kicked once from behind; he was disemboweled.

You go slowly. As if you could squeeze the passing of the world down like Mama used to do when she held us in her rocker. You go only in pro-tracted inches. I remembered the night Mama gave birth to Tso. I cannot be convinced I was too young to possess this memory. Sneaking as I did into the closet of the migrant house. Mama on the bed propped up on pil-lows. The migrant midwives holding her steady. Mama pushing hard. Daddy drunk out on the front porch. Now, another one. Another mouth to feed. Another imtempestive kid!

The calf had been attempting to be born for a lot longer than we thought. *How* these people could have registered the animal at the rodeo is beyond me. Some people are just plain in too much of a hurry to make a dollar. They weren't *bad* people, but they were *not* observant.

Slowly.

Slowly.

Let the cow get used to the idea of it. She will. She will understand, too, that you are attempting to assist her. Cows are not that stupid. Ronnie pet-ted Milly and sang to her.

A few rodeo bums thought it a thing of extraordinary hilarity—singing to a cow—when Ronnie reminded them that Gene Autrey and Roy Himself Rogers *both* sang to cows, and Dale sang to Buttermilk. We kicked them out of there, and I don't much give a shit if they did know my Daddy.

I was in to the elbow, and I could feel hind legs. I had to flip her some so the legs would be pointed out, not in a supine manner, but definitely going in that direction. This is where the craft becomes art.

I am up to my shoulder, and I can feel both heartbeats. My own was in there somewhere. These girls are fighters and we were going to do this right. Ronnie smiles, and starts to sing again. It felt like we were standing next to an amazing waterfall, pristine, clear, my arm is in the waterfall of songs. A nice thundering. I stop thinking about what I am doing—I let the thing do itself. Simply guide the waterfall down the slope it wants to go. *Seeing* in the Navajo way. And tracing paths. Negotiating a soft place at the edge of the meadow is what I ought to know. I can hear my grandmother Sa asking me if I can *see* and, yes, yes, I am seeing with my hand, my arm, and inside my mind I can *see* why Little Cow is twisted. She is overdue, and in the excitement, and the noise (Big Cow hears quite well), and the in-transit of the rodeo, Mama had not found a dropping place where she felt safe enough to *do this here*. The birth mechanisms in animals have evolved, and without them, there would be no animals on the earth. What animal can say he has never needed help?

No animal is that self-sufficient.

The trick was to get my hand around the upper quadrant where the cow's *hips* would be. *Above the elbow of the hind legs.* I had to be sure of my-self and not be fooled into thinking I had her right, when, in fact, I could have her up by the belly. That would kill them both; I had to have the lit-tle guy around his upper hind legs.

Then pull slowly.

The big cow and the little cow will get the idea again, and the little cow's tiny wet rear hooves will begin to appear. And you have a brand-new baby calf.

Mama will *love* attention. Baby will be on his feet. Hooved animals are like that. They are bred to run from the beginning, but these two weren't going anywhere for a while.

We earned some fun money on that one and drove down to Natchi-toches, where we knew two whores from Daddy's old whoring days.

Still whores.

Still lesbians, too.

I could take a nice long hot bath there. They have pictures in the scrap-books. Tso was the only one who could shoot the ducks and win The Fish. When it came to motel rooms, we needed Ronnie to work her wonders. Sometimes, we'd pull into the parking lot for a good hour while Ronnie did and redid her makeup. Tso would talk to The Fish and all I had was Geronimo.

You could not stand there and sway back and forth (like my brother) and say *duhhhh* if what you needed was a motel room.

Tso let her read our journals.

I was unsure.

She was completely absorbed by them. "These are awesome," she'd say. "I can't believe you wrote this."

Meaning migrants wrote this. Or wrote anything.

Ignore it.

We kept them in the Corvette trunk. Other than that, we had very little *stuff*.

That book by Kerouac.

I would take it out in places like Zavalla, Texas, and wonder if he had ever been there. I had been there.

Picking cotton.

Ronnie and Tso entering the motel room as if this would be their honeymoon suite and I would have to open all the windows. If you have fingernail polish, you can fix runs. She curses runs. *Damn these runs*, she says. Ronnie fixed her runs sitting on the bed. Her toes just touching the floor.

I laugh. To migrants, runs are another thing entirely.

My brother's in the shower.

"You should tell her about his panic attacks."

"Why? Just let it go."

"No. If you do that she is going to be too shocked at the sight of it to cope with it. I remember. We had warriors. Brave men. Big men. They looked as if they could handle anything in battle and all the women spread their legs for these men. But I knew. When it came time for us to be in the thick of it—the middle of the battle and the blood—these men were afraid, they shook with fear, and they were of no value to anyone. And yet the smaller ones, the quicker ones, the ones you never noticed stayed to see the battle end."

"Are you saying my brother is a coward?"

"I'm saying your brother is thirteen and he has been abused. You only think he lives in light because that is what you want to think. Your brother lives in the darkness under the bed because it is safer there."

He comes out wet and naked and jumps up and down on the bed.

His cock flopping about his big balls. "Does he do this often?"

"Only when the multiple sclerosis twists his testicles and then you have to stick your arm in there and pull him out."

"Does it hurt?"

"Only in Texas."

"From the sound of things in these journals, you guys didn't much like Texas."

"Texas is a lot of work. One year, you pick all the cotton, and the next year, it just grows back again."

"I thought machines pick cotton?"

"They do. But in Texas you have a lot of tiny places. Too small to hire much beyond a few guys with hands, fingers. It's a dying thing, picking cotton. And torture in the heat. But most of migrant life is in the heat somewhere."

We put him to bed and let him sleep in shadows and we were not tired.

There was always *Perry Mason.* "I love the way Della does her mascara," Ronnie said. "Maybe I could work for Perry Mason or Paul Drake?"

But no.

Sometimes she would cry when she was reading. She would look at me with her black mascara running rivulets. She would look away. I had to look away from Ronnie Spectacular, too, and just drive. You do not really *drive* across Texas. It drives you. Ronnie took the wheel when it became apparent we were heading into more urban territory.

With the top down, the world is another place, entirely. You hear things. Battles. Tires. The world moving and shaking.

Cops seemed to pay no attention to us and we were glad for it. In those days, most highways were still two lanes. It was mostly dust, the motel. Neon blinking. Going *zzzztttt* about every other four seconds.

The motel gravel is dry and crunches under your tires. I remember there were people living here. Like those migrant eyes pulling the curtains quick. Red animal eyes. Everything closed. What if immigration came?

Texas is another country. People are afraid in Texas. I do not know why. In Texas they walk alone upon the road. Some road they have been walking all their lives. They know every flower. Every rock. Every Coca-Cola bottle, green like glass, and you have often wondered (to yourself) *who* threw that bottle there. It was a pornography. That one lone Coca-Cola bottle out by the ditch, and you knew, too, you would kick it, now, kick it hard and away from everything, maybe as far as the field, because you had to, you never wanted to see it again, it was just too all alone. The wind. It was a convertible. Your hair was born to it.

That all your spook is, honey? Texas and the dry emptiness hung so low to the nails of the horizon, you scratched red marks down your chest and wondered what woman you had been sleeping with.

No woman would have you.

Your head hung low walking down that long dirt road. Texas is oblivion, and love, and honor, and sacrifice, and pity, and judges, and whores, and cotton, and cows everywhere, cows all around the oil rigs, and wars some famous guys at the Alamo had, and more House of Pancakes strung out from one side of the Amarillo train tracks to the other than New Jersey has molecular particulates dispersed in fog.

~~~~~

The Plaquemine Motel. The legs of a woman out on the road light up in neon for about an hour, and then the left leg goes. Zzzzt. Flickers. Dies. One leg. The sheets were brown silk and felt as though they might crumble. I was going to sleep on the tiny couch but it had bugs.

I slept with them.

He was in the bathroom. Peeing.

"He pees when he's nervous," I explained. I needed to explain things. He needed me to explain things, too.

He hops into bed in his underpants like it's his honeymoon, again.

He looks at me and disapproves.

"The couch has bugs," I said.

I showed her his scars. The white popcorn ones where Daddy burned him with cigarettes. You had to make him remain still. She had touched his skin and both of us had even called it perfect. But to make him be still was another thing. He was always moving. When he moved you could not focus on his imperfections or magnify them.

The other ones.

She said nothing. I liked that about her. When she was in the presence of something where no words would really suffice, she gave herself to that moment, saying nothing. It hinted at a maturity she would have staunchly denied. He was beautiful and thirteen, almost fourteen, and dangerous, too.

"Look," she said. "Some of us don't got the scars, okay. But we got burned anyway, you get it?"

I got it.

"I know you do," she said. "I used to smash things. Sometimes I thought I would smash all of New Jersey."

Yaaa. New Jersey.

He cried that night. He was so ashamed. We both told him there was nothing to be ashamed of. He was sleeping next to the wall but I put him in the middle and made him sleep between us like he used to sleep when Mama was alive. No one is supposed to see his scars. I slept where he had been crying and the bed was wet with him all that night.

In the morning, the other migrants stayed behind their curtains.

～～～～

Do not ask me to write what other people have written. Let me go and fly. Like that sparrow my boys had who refused to die.

I owe that *to you*. My children. To make something never made before. Or what is the *point*? My voices to their wolves.

～～～～

We lived in migrant camps. I thought everyone lived in migrant camps.

I only saw houses when we went into town to buy groceries. I only saw houses when we were on the move to another migrant camp.

I thought everyone had an outhouse. I thought everyone got their water at a pump.

I thought water pumps were great places to play. They had nice grass and weeds and everything was usually wet around there.

Puddles to stomp around in. The water that came from the pump that you pumped or your brother pumped (and it was much better to have a brother pump) was always cold and crystal clear. You put your mouth up to the pump and the water came in great gulps of clarity. My shirt was always wet.

The first time I went into a *real* house I was shocked.

The toilet flushed and the water seemed to go down into the ground. I could watch toilets flush all day. I was a rude guest. I never came out of the bathroom.

We had a tin washtub that Mama filled with heated water. We took our baths with Mama and we crawled on her. I remember my brother nursing in the bath.

I spoke Apache once. And was possessed by it. The Apache came from the men who used to come in the spring to my mother's mother's hogan and sheep camp to help Grandma Sa shear her sheep. She paid them in wool. They were from Mescalero. They bounced me up high and told me scary stories about Coyote and Geronimo, whom they knew.

I had none then and I have none now.

Do the math. From the time of Geronimo's death to the time of my arrival at my grandmother's sheep camp on the slopes of Ak'i Dah Nast'ani, a grand total of forty-four years would have elapsed. Some of these men were well into their sixties, so the possibility that they could have known Geronimo did, indeed, exist. Do the social geography. Geronimo spent most of his life in intimate proximity to the Chiricahua, although he himself was a Bedonkohe.

My brother and I were there. We were there in the stories the Apaches would tell every night at the sheep camp.

In 1923, the Chiricahua, or what Chiricahua were left, and there were virtually *no one hundred percent Chiricahua* still alive, most having married Mescalero Apaches, were allowed to leave Fort Sill, Oklahoma, where they had been interred for almost fifty years, and return to Mescalero, New Mexico. Many people took this route, as many Apaches hated Fort Sill with their lives.

But there were a few who stayed at Fort Sill. Today they live in Lawton. We call them Fort Sill Apaches. But they are the descendants of the Chiricahua.

Geronimo was different.

Geronimo had always been different.

He was considered a *dangerous* prisoner of war.

White men see what they want to.

~~~~~~

Between 1816 and 1820, the Apache was becoming a more nomadic tribe (again). This was due to white pressure put on the Apache population, but it was also due to changes in the food supply and hunting patterns, especially around the Gila River in the Southwest.

They could not find Geronimo but they knew he was there.

Drinking Tzin and laughing at them, which is exactly what he was doing, although he was also raiding Mexican rancheros and burning them to the ground. He would hang American soldiers by their balls in trees.

He would laugh.

The warriors painted black and dancing all night down the mountain to the girls.

He loved women more than anything.

He was not a joke. Posses took him very, very seriously. As well they should have. He was a shaman (not a chief) who saw visions in his dreams—visions of what would happen to the People, and what he must do to aid them.

How do you divorce an Apache warrior? You gulp, and you gather his stuff, and you pile it *very neatly* outside the door.

With a Navajo, you simply put his saddle there. A saddle *is* his stuff.

Geronimo was never at a loss for words and they were usually as colorful as his life.

"How old are you, anyway?"

"I am not really sure in your years. We marked the intervals off differently.

There was your baby self and you had one name, but then they changed that name when you were older, and then if you were worthy, you were allowed to name yourself. You have years. We had names."

No one knows exactly how many children he really had. Historians account for at least ten, and there were probably double that. Many of them are now in graves scattered all around the Fort Sill Indian cemetery. The Geronimo family in Mescalero is alive, and well, and healthy, and justifiably proud of their heritage, although they are quiet about it, managing in this day and age to hold tightly to their dignity. They are dignified with their wisdom, they are smart in their ability to change, and they are tough as they are still alive upon the earth.

An accomplishment.

They know this: When the bigger boys find out whom you are related to, they will want to beat you up just to see if the rumors of the toughness are real. They are good people. White people are always shocked to know that any descendants of Geronimo live at all. My brother and I were thrilled to know men who had known him.

I usually got to *be* Geronimo (I learned very early on where the soft spots of the human animal lay around his body) when we played, although I could be bribed.

You could be Geronimo when we played but I got to keep your horse. I had a whole herd of ponies as the rich and just rewards of my authority over a bunch of five-year-olds (who all wanted to be Geronimo). Grandma Sa made me give all the horses back. I had a shit fit about it, and kicked the ground. She was bigger than I was, and if I wanted to kick the ground, then I could try to do so—having fits—while hanging upside down.

Which is how she held me. Sort of like a bat.

〰〰〰

The young woman was an Apache. We were adolescent friends. Her English was not good. Her Spanish was nonexistent. Her family had never migrated before. This was their first time. Learning the migrant ropes. People messed with them. This was Texas.

People loaned them money and then took the money.

They left them standing there wondering why they had just given someone all the money when they were only borrowing some.

There were a million and one ways to hoodwink the migrants. Who became gun-shy and angry.

She was an Apache with long, black hair, and she asked me if I could help her.

I could. At least I knew where the witches lived in Dog Town.

The migrant girls who needed abortions in Dog Town were never the girls who could afford abortions. I paid for one once. The Apache girl was shy and hurt. The fetus was not of my making. The problem was where to bury it. The old crone who did the abortion with, *yes*, the proverbial coat hanger handed me a shovel, and said in Apache *Bury it in the back*. And so I did. At night. Under a Mescalero moon and the wind singing the sad lone wailing songs of the Mescalero and the Chiricahua. The girl could hardly walk and I had to take her home. All romance ends here. Mine did.

With a bucket and a shovel and a hole dug into the earth at night. With the lights from cars passing in the distance. People who did not have to do this on their way to places that were far away. I was taking too long, and the girl who had just had the abortion found me out there in the night. She wanted to help me but I said no. I could dig a hole if I had to. I had dug them before with Daddy.

I was hunting in the fields with another boy. I knew he had fallen in love with me. He was not a migrant boy.

His daddy owned the fields and the melons in the fields we were there to pick. His daddy owned the migrant shacks where the migrant whores came at night to suck his daddy's dick.

The men always leaving late at night, loud, drunk, the truck door slams, kicking up a cloud of rocks and dust. Payments made for Rent and Lent. The better stuff of us. I worked for his father.

I did not share any of these feelings for this boy. He was white and my own inveterate racism ran deeper than my brain. I was not just an idiot (although that, too)—I am hopelessly insane. I did not think I could have those kinds of feelings for any other male. I was innately attracted to girls. No white girl (with brains) would have anything to do with me. Although I appear to be whiter than Euripides, and am the spitting cowboy image of the desert-wolf who was my dad, the fact remained—I was a *migrant*. I lived with the migrants. I ate with the migrants who did not wash their hands after they took a shit. I used the same outhouses the migrants used. I was not *clean*.

No. The girls who loved me were *migrants*.

Or very lost hippie-types from Boulder.

That black hag white people call their culture never once gave my kind so much as spit in our mouths for half a chance at seeing sunrise. No. While their sun is coming up our heads are bent. As we pick their food to try to pay our rent. We are not worthy of being educated. I come from the migrant camps.

I know.

I am an angry man. It has been something of a mystery to my children. One who has dragged his punishments about these small, small mud holes, these migrant camps, until his wings have worn themselves to sores.

School was a few weeks here, a few weeks there.

The migrant children took their shoes off at school. We did not have socks. In fact, we did not know what socks were. There was a huge pile of stinking shoes in the hall of the school. We smelled. We had lice. Worms. I saw a worm once come crawling up and out of Dionisio Aponte's pants, held up by suspenders and no shirt. Apparently the worm had had enough. Carmen Iguaran screamed when she saw the worm. The whole classroom imploded into screams and laughter. It became known as the Day of Dionisio Aponte's Worm.

Parasites were nothing. I remember coughing blood. They made you clean that up, too. Before we got on the bus to go back to the migrant camp, we'd dive into the mountain for our shoes. The hall smelled like a pig barn. Had we worn our shoes in class, the teachers would no doubt have found the smell to be intolerable.

You knew you were not like those nice white children you saw at school. The ones whose moms came to school with cakes and red punch when it was Little Patty's birthday. We let our eyes drink this in until we were inebriated. We began that long slow haul where what we learned to hate was our lives.

We came back to the migrant camp late one afternoon with cupcakes stuffed down into our pockets. Hide the cupcakes. The cupcakes had been reduced to mush.

Mush was just fucking fine. Daddy asked us what was in our pockets.

We were afraid of him. We had reason to be.

I *asked* you what was in your pocket, boy?

Nothing.

We were not shit as liars.

Daddy put his hand down into our pockets. He scooped the cupcake mush out of our pants and ate it—paper and pink candies and all—and we cried.

He kicked us into the migrant barn, pulled our pants down, and whipped us with willow sticks while we were bent over a bale of hay until he had made a hot red gash over our scrotums that threatened to allow our testicles to pop through. The beating was so severe we could not sit for days—our small balls turned black, then green—so Daddy put us to work in the fields, which is where we belonged and not in some school where we might eat cupcakes and learn how to spell our names.

We did not know he was jealous.

We did not know then he could not spell his name.

We lived our lives on the brink of mental illness.

We would build a time machine.

And the single flashing moment just before he fucked her (making us) we would pull him off.

So we would not be made. No us. How convenient. No struggles to have to endure. Sign me up for that life, please.

He would kill us. Of course. But there would be no us. Yet.

We did not see our imaginary time machine as a contraption of escape. No. We would build a time machine to rewrite history so we did not have to *be*.

We did not abuse our children. It was something.

We changed *time* without the *machine*.

We taught ourselves how to read and write.

In English. I am able to write some Navajo. Not much, and not well. I am not around it. There are eighty-some dialects of Navajo, and it has only been in the past twenty-five years that the language has even been written down. *Writing it down* will imbue you with power. Instead of *my speaking Navajo*, it is Navajo that *speaks to me*.

In truth, there is no beginning. There is no middle. And there is no end. There is only now. For me, childhood was like falling down into a dark black hole. The stream of time. You will hear the fear and the echoes. You will hear the falling and the wings into the down and down.

The down and down was the place my voices lived. The soul shrinks.

From the visions of remembering.

I told no one about my voices. Only my brother knew. He hated the voices. He wanted them to go away. I would read my poems in school and win awards that turned out not to be money but pieces of paper with the teacher's signature. The girls would clap. I was attracted to one. Considering that my other male friends got hard-ons every single time a female smiled at them, I knew I was a circus freak.

A freak in the freak show.

I was not attracted to every girl who walked by.

I was very much attracted to one specific girl whom I was convinced did not know I existed. I was wrong. In fact, she eventually became Kree's mother, and she knew I existed. But we were adolescents and as such were about as dumb as a barn door, which did not qualify us to be parents no matter how you looked at it.

I saw no hope for my being able to connect to this girl.

I was a migrant. You could count the holes in my head and in my shoes. *I love you* was not a phrase I heard much.

The one thing in my life I loved more than life itself was the fifteen-year-old boy who was my younger brother. My children. Your uncle, Tso.

I love you the boy I was hunting with said. The boy with the gun. This boy did not know who or what he loved any more than my father did. And I think perhaps, like some infection of the race, most men, too, are inarticulate. You know when someone says *I love you* if he means it.

And I suspected his life was not so much removed from the kind of abuse I tolerated every day. I know abuse when I look it in the eye. Abuse is the child who is waiting out his life in the prayer that he will die. He may have been attracted to me in the way electrons are pulled into and out of the electrical, subatomic spheres they create with their positive and negative subatomic charges. This is passionate and, indeed, charged, but it isn't love. It lasts about as long as a double-AA flashlight battery from Wal-Mart. It is interesting but it isn't love.

He came to me and put his hand on my penis. Pressing. A part of me, the part of me that my daddy hurt—putting his hot cigarettes on my penis and burning me—I froze solid not unlike the way in which the Great Slave Lake freezes over in the Canadian winters of my dreams.

Me. Alone. Walking. On the lake. White on white. And then a blizzard comes. You'd better hope for something magical to occur or you are going to freeze to death out here.

I did not hope for anything magical. Back then. Or have much hope for anything. Back then. Back then, my dreams were my voices, and they spoke to me in torrents of rushing horror every night. Every night that man came anywhere near my bed.

My brother and I had strategized that if we slept together it made it just that much harder for Daddy to do the things he did. I would soak the bed in sweat and then shiver in that wetness. As we got older, we could ward him off.

That poor boy's hand on my penis was my father's hand on my penis, too.

Something snapped. The twig had been on the tree all winter long. It had been valiant. It had survived.

Until the ice storm came and the twig snapped.

I snapped like ice itself.

I looked down into the hurt and the emptiness of this boy. Where he was some subzero paralysis, I was smoke and ash.

My eyes said: *Do it.*

I dare you to do it.

Shoot me.

And so he did.

12

~~~~~~

It Was a Pilgrimage

Asdzqq nadleehe, the Changing Woman, and Yooigaii asdzqq, the White Shell Woman, came to understand that the twin boys had gone away. They were deeply worried that the boys might have taken Atiin diyinii, the Holy Trail. The Holy Trail had been built by the Holy People and as such it was extremely dangerous. But they knew, too, in their hearts that the twins could not stay and do nothing about the monsters that had devoured almost all the people.

But the War Twins were so young.

The boys had, indeed, taken this path of gods. They did not do so by design but in their confusion and eagerness to get away from the devouring Naayee, they set upon this strange, illuminated road. It seemed to be a trail of many rainbows, sunbeams, bolts of male lightning, and flashes of female lightning. Now they were tired, cold, and hungry.

It was a pilgrimage. Tso and I had been to Geronimo's grave maybe a hundred times. If we were picking melons in Oklahoma, our mother would bring us here, and we would have a picnic.

A picnic would be a six-pack for our mother (Geronimo got his share), and some Tootsie Rolls for us to chew on. A picnic is a picnic. Geronimo's grave is a great place to have a picnic. The soft cemetery grass just rolls on down to the river in the woods. Hardly anyone is ever there. The place is not remote; it's simply in a spot no one would ever go. The ancient oak that towers above the grave is always filled with medicine bundles, gifts, and things that sparkle in the sun. People leave their eyeglasses in the tree.

The tree sings and tinkles. To symbolize the nothingness of seeing so one might see.

"So. You are back again."

"Yes. My brother has a girlfriend."

"Oh. So, she's not your girlfriend?"

"No. Not really."

"But you like her."

"She is a good person. Maybe she's a little confused. But so what. Her confusion is harmless. My brother is falling in love with her. You know what I like the most?"

"No, what?"

"She laughs and it's like this music in our lives. We have so been missing music. I am glad to have it back again. Yes. Yes. I like her very much, but you know my brother."

"He's in love and he will now hurt because he doesn't know how to manage it. I didn't."

"Yaaaaa. I'm glad for him. That there is still something in him that can reciprocate. It wasn't completely burned from him."

"They're whispering together."

"I see," I said.

"He's telling her you hear voices."

"He shouldn't do that." I started to walk over to them.

"Relax! So she knows? So what! I know."

"You are a ghost."

"And what is she?"

"A singer. We're driving to Los Angeles. They make love, you know."

"I see. And they allow you to watch."

"We are a family. The three of us. It's sad when he makes love to her because he's still such a boy himself. The youngest of us and the oldest. I like watching them. When he goes into her, it's like he is dipping down into the universe of stars."

"You've stolen a vehicle. A little loud."

"Yeah. It's hard to drive, too. The engine gets too hot. I still can't go backward, but I am getting better at parking. I don't need twenty spaces, now, to park."

"I see."

"What else do you see?" I asked.

"Is that why you are here? To ask a dead man what he sees? Ha!"

"Yes. I *need* you. I need to know. I need to know *what is happening to us?*"

"Yes. You should know this."

"Know what? Are we going insane again? I keep thinking we might be going insane. And if we are, then . . ."

". . . then you might just want to run that little car off the road and into a tree."

"Yes. Before things get bad. Things are so good for us. But it always has to end. We always have to go to some other migrant camp."

"But there's the girl."

"Tso loves her."

"When I was fourteen, I was married to Alope."

"I'm not suicidal."

"We are all suicidal."

"I don't want her to hurt him. He's been hurt enough."

"It's not up to you. If you really don't want him hurt then you should know your father is looking for you. And he's not too far behind you, either. I'm supposed to know the smoke."

He meant any messages our father might be sending. I ignored this.

"I was hoping . . ."

"Differently? You are always hoping the pain will go away, Nasdijj. Don't you understand? Don't you understand by now *l-i-f-e is pain?*"

"Yeah. I thought that was Daddy's line."

"But what have I always taught you about the pain, Mia?"

"Even now I know I will die in pain. You become the pain and the sword the pain rides in on."

"Nasdijj, you become this pain, and it becomes liquid dark like a horse's eyes, and the rest of you is perfect."

"You mean, let it go, and let the knots out."

"No. The knots will untie themselves or, better yet, they will just become irrelevant."

"It's just called dancing," I said. "Dancing in a graveyard."

〰〰〰〰

There are no words for the impact that a shotgun makes. This was a 12-gauge and what I remember is the sound the BBs make as they pepper themselves through the leaves and trees.

Having left the insides of my guts. They just kept travelin'.

You hear the BBs behind you and you think: *Fuck, they just went through me*. I know you have always wondered at my scars. There are a few. Awee asked if he could touch them. His soft and gentle touch on those hardened places where underneath the hard there's places that still bleed. Even after all these years, metal shot and lead still work their way out of me, and my X-rays give radiologists heart attacks.

MRIs are dangerous because they can just suck the metal in you out of you.

There are still well over a hundred pieces of junk buried in my flesh. Damn, that hurts! You will have to read the book to know the story.

Of this life. It's still kicking, and refusing to go softly into this too, too gentle night. I want my nights to be like waves.

Soft. Yes. Sometimes.

But still able to crash into things, too. And thunder is my heritage.

Please. Just put my bed over by the window so I might see into the woods. Today the body is twisted like a twisting vine of poison ivy. Man marks the earth with ruin. He wants to fathom his origins. The People are told stories to explain these things.

This work has to explain not why I am here. But why I am *still* here.

I have wanted to die, my babies, oh, many, many, many times. I have prayed at night, all night, to do it.

But I am still here. In pain. It only is.

⁓⁓⁓⁓

And two of you are still here. It *is* a victory. It is. My children.

And two of you are gone even as those of us who remain still hold the pieces of you in our hands like water. Death carries us off everywhere. Like my rivers carry us to the black streams time has made.

Each one of you has his own story. We are a *family* of storytellers. How rich we *are*! Not that we can even pay the rent this month! But the stories. Will take your breath away. The medicine people on the piñon-green slopes of the volcano, Ak'i Dah Nast'ani. The drops that are your blood have flowed here. In the veins and in the smoke the stories made. Under moons. Under stars. And under shade. We just go on.

We have needed family to do that.

Let these tales be like a snapshot that catches my brother smiling at his and our adventure's cardinal points.

Back to your beds. You. Soft fugitives. To your rivers and your homes.

You. My children. Will have your own children. Even I have heard you speak of it.

Some cool summer night when the sun has slipped behind the sleeping volcano and the sheep have been put away and watered. And the dogs are dog-tired and the children are rolled safely in their rugs and the smoke goes up into the smoke hole just so as to cause faces and warriors and armies and wars and monster slayers to be seen in those enigmatic shadows and the dancing songs of soothing hope. Give such countenance as to bring this book out so you might, too, sing of those dragons with which we are compelled to cope.

The adversity of our lives.

You, too, are responsible.

The reader is responsible.

For being able to recognize that all human endeavor should be known. This is education. It is *not* the writer's responsibility to always and always make it nice for him and certainly not necessarily nicer than it was when it happened.

We have climbed out of holes to discover something of the light.

That is what adulthood is. It is the living in that illumination.

I found a fire in the soul of the man who is my migrant brother. We are part and parcel of the same innate hereditary vital spark. It has been a long, long journey where we lost boys would climb down ladders to sit in kivas with Spider Woman.

13

A Dust Storm Blew
Through Texas

White Shell Woman went out of that hogan and walked up to the top of a very high hill. She often took these walks by herself where she worried. From here, she saw many, many giants. Naayee, all walking in the direction of her house.

"Sister! Sister!" she cried. "All the giants are coming this way! The giant Naayee. What shall we do?"

When Changing Woman heard this, she picked up four brightly colored hoops.

She cast a hoop in each of the four directions. To the east, she threw a white one. To the south, she threw a blue one. To the west, she threw a yellow one. And to the north, she threw a black one.

Immediately, a great gale gathered where she stood and encircled the dwellings. As it became more intense, it blew outward in all four directions. To the east it blew. To the south it blew. To the west it blew. To the north it blew. So strong did it blow all around the dwellings that none of the giant monsters could get through.

That much accomplished, Asdzqq nadleehe, Changing Woman, went inside.

"For the time being we will be safe," she told her sister, Yoolgaii asdzqq, White Shell Woman. "But by this time tomorrow, the wind will have stopped. And I have no more magic hoops."

They did not know if the giants would come to eat them. And they were afraid.

A dust storm blew through Texas. I like to leave the East behind in Texas where the wind sings high notes among the telephone wires.

The drier air pulls me to it. I feel like a man again. In the East, I feel emasculated. In the East, I am an ant who runs one way not to get stepped on only to find another boot. You hit Pecos, Texas, and you know you're in the West. We stopped at a Texas Western Wear Shop—the real kind where everything is covered in dust, and things sit untended to in boxes—and my spend-happy, spendthrift brother bought everyone jeans, cowboy boots, cowboy hats, underpants, and socks.

Socks.

Ronnie had never worn boy's underpants before and she liked it.

She said the hole was redundant.

Mr. Deep Pockets Big Time Thief wondered what *redundant* was.

Redundant is when the cops find you anywhere in Texas.

They were waiting for us in our motel room.

Chewing toothpicks. Watching TV. I remember. *Perry Mason.*

They had been smart enough to park on the side of the motel where we would not see cop cars.

Della Street was on the phone.

Word was, our father was looking for us. And he wanted us back. That and six thousand dollars.

Our caring father who loved us and who would hug us like the long-lost children of the wilderness had finally come home.

The police would take us to the jail where we would be put into cells with the molesters until our dads arrived.

Ronnie's dad was right behind our dad. The cops weren't sure about the specifics, but it seemed that our dad and Ronnie's dad had done what we had done—they had, for all of its surreal unlikeliness, teamed up.

I was not sure I believed it.

Not many men teamed up too long with the Cowboy.

Ronnie's dad had the bucks. Our dad had the history or at least he knew where we might be likely to show our faces. Wherever that six thousand had come from, Daddy wanted it back real, real bad. He was a bad man mixed up with bad money and I wished in my simpleton mind I had the number of that transvestite who had hog-tied that son-of-a-bitch so she could hog-tie him again and hang him on a hook like a dead cow in a slaughterhouse freezer and be done with it.

Ronnie was suspicious right from the beginning.

"The daddy *I* know does not want me back."

The cops thought they would be here tomorrow. They would be flying in to El Paso and then driving to Pecos. This was the plan or close to one anyway. It didn't really matter because we would be cooling our heels in the county jail and how our fathers got here was their business. There is never a way to beat the Cowboy. He is relentless. We had been to Pecos before. We had lived here for almost six weeks while Daddy had worked at a cattle slaughterhouse on the road to Midland. This was cattle country. Oil country. It was the kind of place where kids grew up fast. It would not have been all that unusual to find some sixteen-year-old girl married and living in a trailer and working in the Meteor Crater souvenir shop selling postcards and lip gloss.

It was not all that much different from the horse slaughterhouse. Except that we were older, and we did not ask questions about his work, and we did not want to see it.

Daddy would come home from work, sit, and stare at his food, and talk to our mother, who was definitely not there. Some days he went looking for work on oil rigs and always came home disappointed and empty-handed. He would sit in his chair and stare at his hands.

Then he would go wash them.

Repeating this process until it was dark when he would drive away in a cloud of dust and a mighty hi, ho, Silver.

We were in school. We came home one afternoon and Daddy had packed the truck. We got off the school bus, got into the truck, and waved good-bye to our dogs—or any dogs that might simply be around—because this was no goddamn life for a dog. Not even a dog.

We were going to drive by that place where we had lived that very afternoon. It was not the place. It was the man who could not make it in any place. But now there would be no time.

That was the thing about time in West Texas. The sky is always breaking.

The wind would come in tiny circles and time was a dizzying disorder that went one way and then the other. Time always came to Buzzard Town with little luggage and always from some bigger town with old hotels. Places where men tied their shoes and barbers shaved you. You would not find that here. Not in this town where the lights are dimmed. In this town, time passes judgment. Time in this town is silent and demonic. Eighty miles to the east, a giant ball of fire created a crater that still moves the imagination of a man. Time is apocalyptic, a prisoner of history, but not now, only later. Now time is just the ticking of your grandmother's clock and she has the window open, and you wonder what is real. Even then, you know you will die in pain, becoming the light that illuminates the pain even as the sword the pain rides in on rusts as metal must.

The cops were pretty matter-of-fact, and a little bored. They did not seem like cowboys but more like the pharmacist who owned the drugstore down the street. They looked at us sadly as if we could have been their children up and run away.

They would want their children back.

I chewed on the situation some. I asked them if they had ever seen the men who were asking for their children back.

"No." But a man's children were his children. It didn't matter if they had seen these men before. They were the fathers of runaways and they were coming for their children. That was that.

I had a picture of Daddy. In one of the journals. It was a little old. But it was Daddy in his cowboy boots and cowboy hat.

The cop with the toothpick in his mouth rolled the toothpick around in his mouth a bit faster, now. The longer he stared at the picture of Daddy as a younger man, the more that toothpick got mushed to spit.

"Seth, will you look at this man, please."

The oldest of the cops peered for the longest time at that photo taken at the Pecos County fair.

Seth frowned.

"Isn't that that rodeo boy we busted for . . ."

"Attempted rape," Seth said. "The girl was an officer's daughter from Fort Bliss. He did not want the publicity and we let the boy go."

"Cops have been letting him go all our sorry lives," I said. I did not feel like a man again, that way I felt when we hit West Texas, and the clean dry air. I felt like a kid whose father was a rapist. I felt like filth.

The kind of filth and the ache of it that shudders run up and down your spine like the wind changes round and round the one Texas telephone line.

Left out here in the dirt where everything is left out here in the dirt and you can taste the dirt when it gets inside your teeth like grinding grit.

"It was a call over at the fair. I remember. They were in an Airstream, if I reckon correctly. Playin' cards, and some cowboys ought not to. I do not think anything happened, but I do believe the girl got beat up and badly."

"Anyone you might know?" the cop who had not said much asked.

"Sounds like my dad," I said. "His demons grow a little thick at county fairs and rodeos."

My brother sighed. No one had said anything about the car. Ronnie seemed to almost disappear into a ball. "Can I at least change my shirt?" my brother asked.

The night before, his demons had gotten to him.

It had been one of those nights when we found my brother under the bed and shivering.

Afraid that Daddy was just around the corner.

"He's a long, long way from here," I had said, trying to soothe him. But only Ronnie could soothe him.

He had dive-bombed under beds before.

As if our rug were still his universe of safety. The darkness. The ironic thing about the darkness, though, is that the darkness is where Daddy had hurt him—Daddy had climbed into the rug. The darkness could not save him, and so he gave himself to the darkness in his strange way.

In one motel, we had had to lift the box spring up and take it off the frame. So there was no space to hide under.

I was looking out the window. Knowing he could not have been all that far behind us. Looking for black storm clouds roiling in the east. Knowing that when he found us we might not come out of it alive. I was lost in this cool deep place when Tso was changing his shirt—there was this pause—I did not notice it.

I heard one of the cops, the oldest one again, tell Tso to turn around.

My brother, shirtless, turned around. I have seen the scars on his back so many times, I don't see them anymore. He often asks me to rub them at night.

"I will be goddamned," one cop said.

"Did a belt do that?" another cop asked.

Yaaaaa.

There was a conference among the cops.

Time stopped for me then. I was watching the cops speak but no words came from their mouths. As if the three of us were left in empty hotel rooms we dare not die in. The three of us standing still and together in the middle of that room with the bed and the bathroom off to the side and the motel sign my brother always reads behind the door. Standing there naked in each other's lives. Like we had been burned alive and would be West Texas wreckage and lonely forever. They let us go. Just like that. They were almost embarrassed. They seemed to understand that the man who had made those scars was on his way.

No one in Pecos could afford a car like that. And we were never here.

Now, *go.*

Ronnie *got it.*

I threw her the keys. She threw everything we owned into the trunk. No time to pack it nice. Tso was still standing there with a blank expression on his face. *Still I wonder. How I wonder.*

"Honey, we're out of here. Get in the car," she said to my brother who got in the car. Wondering what had gone on. *Boy wrapped in golden chains.*

Like she had driven drunk and determined any number of times. Wringing the steering wheel and her knuckles white for speed. You know when you've hit New Mexico because the sky turns blue. *Still, the rain kept fallin'.*

~~~~~~

The old trailer was still there. "Do you make it a habit to always return to the places where you lived?" Ronnie asked.

We kicked up some rocks. I would let Tso tell her. Now that he was a *man* and mixed up in a sexual relationship with a *female* person.

You will have to tell her, my eyes told him.

I know.

We had always wanted Daddy to have a real job, too. One where you didn't have to move in two weeks.

We begged him to tell us what the job was.

He only smiled.

For some insane reason we thought he would have a nice job like school custodian. I do not know why we thought that would be a nice job for our dad to have but we did.

He was not the school custodian.

We would never be able to visit him in his office in the boiler room.

She cried when he told her.

I just walk around this place and marveled that I could (I could, too) live here again. I liked the dry mountain vistas and the air.

We wept. That night we had to walk home with the cars on the highway whizzing by us. The dreams came like horses on the wind.

~~~~~~

Who would hunt the Apache warrior down? The Apache with the rope around his precious larynx. His eyes leaden-black like starless nights with no moon to reflect mountain gods out here and on the run. Painted black from head to toe. Lean and lacerated was Apache-wise. Back when there were warriors still. Riding feathers to the sunset and beyond the red and haunted hill.

Warriors were everything to us. Back then.

All we had to do was wait.

Someday. Someday. Someday we would be warriors.

We would have picked the lock on the trailer but it broke in my hands.

We owned it. We just didn't know we owned it. We were breaking into our own house. All the places we have ever lived have been overrun with mice and dust.

We spent the night with Ronnie in our old trailer where no one lived. Playing house.

Sweeping rooms with some old broom.

Pretending that if we could do it all over again—just right this time—the pain would go away and the sword the pain came in with.

We were her boys there.

She tucked us in. We bought blankets. We were sleeping on the floor. Tso got up and in that fading sunlight she held him and ran her fingers through his hair.

〰〰〰

We once saw a migrant family leave Grandpa on the porch of a migrant shack.

He did not know they had gone.

He was just sitting there in his lawn chair like he had done every day they had gone to work in the fields picking.

He sat there in his red-and-black-checkered coat and smoked cigarettes until they burned his fingers yellow and cracked. His fingernails, too, were yellow and cracked like the cracked and yellow life of something old and put away into the closet where it sat in mustiness and smelled like every musty thing in there with the mouse droppings.

They cried as they packed their truck.

He watched them curiously.

Like he did not know who they were.

Papie, *they are YOUR family.* They love you.

The children were wailing when they left but the older wiser sister was very severe and yelled at them to be quiet until finally she said shut up shut up shut up and she hit them across the face with her hand slapping and slapping.

He watched them silently—just smiling—from his lawn chair.

It was cold.

It was an old lawn chair and some of the plastic weaving had come undone and flapped about in the wind.

I remember. *I ran back to tell him, Papie, you should run, they have left you! Papie, you must run! Catch them. They just forgot.*

It was time for everyone to go.

Everything had been picked. The sun was setting in the south sky now.

The wind ran across the topsoil and made it hard.

Our truck was packed. Daddy said get in. *We drove away to some other migrant camp and the old man in his red-and-black-checkered coat just smoked his cigarettes in his lawn chair as if he knew no one wanted him and he got smaller and smaller until finally looking back through the rear window of our truck he was like the specks of dirt that blew about.*

I could feel my plastic hero in my pockets.

〰〰〰

"They will never leave you. You are so afraid of it."

"What in the world do you mean, *they* will never leave me?"

"The people in your life, Nasdijj."

"You never know."

"So it was a terrible thing, and you saw it. The people who left their grandfather who was helpless. But it doesn't mean it will happen to you."

"But they were Hispanic and the image is . . ."

"The stereotype, you mean. Look at us. We are all supposed to be blood-hungry Apaches."

〰〰〰

Tso was outside rearranging things in the trunk of the car. We had more *stuff* (camping gear, comic books) now than I liked to have, but there it was. It took *arranging*.

Ronnie and I were still in the trailer.

We ended up squatting there for more than a week. I cannot even say why we loved that wreck of a place but we did. It was falling-down simple. Ronnie with her desert wildflowers picked and put in Pepsi cans. We even rode into town to do laundry at the Pronto Laundromat.

They had a mechanical game there where if you put fifty cents in the slot, you could try to get the steam shovel to pick your prize. Prizes at the Laundromat were cheap. Tso won a rather pathetic bear, which he gave to Ronnie.

We ate cans of beans we purchased at the Shell station groshermat. Ronnie said that the word *groshermat* sounded like the Latin name of a bug.

We took walks back into the hills and found potshards. An intact water vessel under a tree. It was painted black and white.

"Can we take it?" Ronnie asked.

"No," I said. "It's from another time. It was here long before we came along, and it will still be here when we're bones. Just leave it."

Ronnie nodded. But the notion of *not* taking something that was *there* and free was so foreign to her, she kept looking back at the potshard tree.

Our time playing house ended. We were leaving not because we wanted to leave—no, we could have stayed forever, playing house—but we were terrified that whoever owned this place, now, would show up, and bust us. We did not want to be busted.

~~~~~

Not knowing (it would take some years for the state of New Mexico to track us down) that we were the people who owned this place.

Daddy had paid the taxes on it every year. When he died, it would belong to us.

A wrecked trailer. A postage-stamp piece of scrub and sage.

With a view that would take your breath away.

14

~~~~~

The Cosmic Microwave Background (CMB)
Is a Perverse Radio Emission Appearing
to Have a Truly Diffuse Origin

The War Twins understood now that they would meet many strange beings on such a journey as the one they had undertaken. But they were convinced they could follow the journey to its end and not be destroyed.

It did not surprise them when they came upon an underground kiva—they had seen such before—where smoke was drifting from the smoke hole.

"Come inside my kiva," a voice beckoned to them and their curiosity.

The War Twins started to descend into the kiva on a ladder. But when they saw who had called to them they were overwhelmed with awe.

"Oh, Grandmother," Child Born for Water said. "Are you not Spider Woman?"

But at this the old woman who had spoken to them was silent.

The Cosmic Microwave Background (CMB) is a perverse radio emission appearing to have a truly diffuse origin.

Ronnie Spectacular would change her name. It was her idea.

She was a new person now. She would have a new name.

She thought about it all the way.

We would go to Chaco Canyon. Chaco is as good a place to become new again as anywhere.

I can always see them at Chaco. Walking into the desert. Long lines of them—the People—stretching out against the sunset. The coming and the going of the Anasazi.

They had lived in Chaco once. Now they only guarded it.

It was cold and we three huddled in blankets near our (new) tent at Chaco. She had never seen anything like it. We had seen it a thousand times. The three of us were cuddling under the blanket and Ronnie was explaining to us why she could be my girlfriend on Sundays, Tuesdays, and Fridays. She could be Tso's girlfriend on Mondays, Thursdays, and Saturdays. The middle of the week she needed off.

We adored her bullshit.

Suddenly, she leaps up, grabs a pine branch that has been burning in the fire, and runs around the old village, outlining the shadows of the windows and the doors. "I know what my new name is going to *beeeee*," she yells.

Yeah. Okay.

Her eyes are big as old, old sundials.

"Dancer. I will be Dancer now."

We shrugged and that is what we called her. She no longer answered to Ronnie Spectacular.

Now, she was (simply) Dancer.

She had small breasts that she allowed us to shine our flashlights on at night in our new sleeping bags.

Camping gear. Clothes.

Flashlights. Batteries.

Food.

It was night and pitch black in Chaco Canyon but I could see them everywhere. Little village kids playing games. They're running and they're running and there is no one who can catch them. But I want to. I want to *catch them softly in my hands like they were fireflies.*

It is all I have ever wanted.

〰〰〰

The Cosmic Microwave Background (CMB) is a perverse radio emission appearing to have a truly diffuse origin. Namely, a hot plasma that filled the universe when it was only four hundred thousand years old. Through the expansion of the universe, this radiation today is observed at a peak wavelength of about one millimeter, corresponding to a temperature of two-point-seven Kelvins. The study of the spectrum of stars and distribution of the CMB as seen at the rim off the volcano known to the Navajo as Ak'i Dah Nast'ani has provided compelling evidence for something known to scientists as the Big Bang.

To the Navajo, it is known as a "going up."

The People are always going up.

For there to even *be*, a going down is a great backward blasphemy.

At the beginning, there was a place called the Black World, where only Spirit People and Holy People lived. It had four corners over which appeared four cloud columns, which were white, blue, yellow, and black. The east cloud column was called Folding Dawn. The south column was called Folding Sky Blue. The west column was called Folding Twilight. The north column was called Folding Darkness. Coyote visited these cloud columns and changed his colors to match theirs. So he is called Child of the Dawn, of the Blue Sky, of the Twilight, and of the Darkness.

Great and glorious things had happened here. Guardian spirits had flown into the volcano to defeat monsters that had been ravaging the People. The volcano itself was a place of war, tragedy, birth, lust, hunger, and the laughter of nothing less than Coyote, the Trickster. Ak'i Dah Nast'ani was a landscape come alive. It could be seen powdered with snow or brilliantly lit up at sunset with the thunderbolts of blue, the bleeding of red, the buoyancy of orange, and covenants with yellows, relinquishing the light of day to the tenacious shadows of the night. It was a place of sheep camps where sheep hides hung in trees so the wild animals did not destroy what could be sold. It was a place of hogans and looms.

We came here between the migrant camps. We would stay with Sa and her family or we would stay with Nilch'i who was the wind.

Before I could talk, I would hide behind her skirts.

We loved her and were terrified of her. Nilch'i lived on the other side of the volcano's rim where in the spring the volcano appeared to be green. This was an optical illusion provided by the plethora of piñon pines. Nilch'i would send us out to pick the pine nuts. At other dry, less wet times of the year, that side of the volcano could appear to be golden brown evidenced by the longer angles of the sun, and the inability of the upper, drier stratospheres of air to keep the moisure down. The moisture dries and the dust kicks up, lending a lighter brown color to the volcano.

We would arrive at Nilch'i's hogan, and I would run into his arms.

He would swoop me up in one arm, Tso in the other. Everything he did was fun.

I do not know if Nilch'i was, in fact, our grandfather. Only that he was there for children and everyone called him Nilch'i, the wind, or Grandfather. I would immediately launch into an operatic rendition of *look what has been done to me.* Broken arms and fingers. Bandaged knees. Bruises.

He would always listen intently.

He would kiss my hurts. Here and here.

Nilch'i would touch my purple places with his finger and say some magic words to make the hurt go away and the hurt went away.

As a child, I had perpetual black eyes, and blue splotches like spider-arms that spread out on my forehead as if they were road maps to a violence only I could hear, and those scars on my forearms were from me, those strawberry teeth marks on my skin fit my jaws perfectly as if my life were a jigsaw puzzle of some fragmentation. I remember tasting my blood and thinking: *If only, if only, if only I could bite down into a vein that would be the end of it and me.*

But most of all that would be the end of them. The voices in my head pushing me into the eternal blackness of the down and down.

The black hole that was my life spread itself out before me like a yawning fracture in the universe where no light seeped through.

Just stars and pinpricks.

The down and down was a place. It was real. I was not in school yet. I was afraid.

There were strange and horrible voices in that hole, and some of them sounded as though the things were thunder.

Although the hole was deep, and seemed entirely dark at first, November's deepest dye, if you stood at the edges of its nocturnal sadness, and let your ebon, somber visions fly, a lividity like an electric glint would fleetingly reveal the blue of color's burnished steel, a schism ripped through flocks of silent melting crows, flowing rivers over water's rocks into the abstract woes of prose, and sailing through the lights of dawn our eyes can only pray that colors in the down and down are mainly gray today.

You could jump. You could think about jumping. I did not want to jump into the down and down. It smelled of animals. Dead animals and corpses.

I was always scratching my breasts off in my sleep. I did not know why.

I had no shoes. I ran outside the migrant shack and the screen door banged. I must have been on the back porch because I got splinters in my toes and I hated those green splinters. Someone had painted the back porch green. I was in my underpants and it was summer and hot. All the migrants were hot and many were sleeping outside and not inside those migrant shacks with the tin roofs.

Ovens. It was ovens.

Now they tell me it was fever from the tuberculosis. I had tuberculosis but we didn't know. How could we have known?

The migrant camps can be so very, very crowded, and we often slept on the floor or on cots in rooms with fifty other people. The floors are almost always cement, and always hard, and sleeping there was dreadful. The old men coughing. The young men fresh from Mexico burning up with fevers. People with diarrhea running for the outhouse and sometimes making it. Women nursing their babies in blankets. Toddlers running around with Kool-Aid in their baby bottles. Men chain-smoking as is their right. No one ever had the nerve back then to ask them not to. It never happened. You would have been punished for the insult. And then there were the radios. *Sleep* was not a remote possibility. We had to get up at four to make it to the fields by five. Often, the field you had been assigned could be thirty miles away.

That meant a bus ride with the migrant men again and the cigarette smoke.

We were often alone at the migrant camp in the migrant shack with the tin roof and all the sadness of that not-so-quiet place. We heard monsters outside the migrant shack one night when Daddy was staying over with the whores. We did not know what they were (they were the voices and we were whispering and afraid) but we shoved the kitchen table and the chairs against the front door so whoever or whatever it was could not come in and we would have shoved the bed against that door, too, but it was too heavy for us to drag or move. Do not let the voices in the house.

When the whores stayed over and the sun had crawled up the wall a bit— and Daddy was gone off into the fields—and the smell of morning lingered like someone's coffee grounds, sometimes the whore would have us boys crawl into the bigger bed. Their fingers were soft and they did not work in the fields. They were a mystery.

Under sheets with whores in your underpants. Tso was still small back then and sometimes the whore would put her soft breast in his mouth and he would suck like he could remember it. Watching me with that giggle on his face. The whore would stroke his dark long hair and call him her baby and maybe he was from the way he would look back at her with his eyes glazed wide open and her brown tit in his mouth. We could have stayed like that forever. Or at least until noon but the whore always had to go.

It had been raining and raining and the bullfrogs were up all night and performing musical operettas and the migrant boys had chased them down to plunder frogs with sticks and smash their skulls in so mamas could fry them frog's legs in flour. It had been so devil hot and I had been staring down at the edges of the hole into the down and down and now I was outside and sweating and the world was spinning with me and a whore was holding me by the hand and urging me to come back, please, come back into the house.

"Come here, boy."

Daddy picked me up and set me on his shirtless shoulders. Daddy was summer hot and nice and the sweat ran down his face and down his chest. I could put my hands around his forehead and I could smell his thick, dark hair, and the black, wet ringlets and the black grease in his hair, and I could touch it with my hand. Hot sweat. Hot grease. Daddy is laughing and Mama is saying: Don't you fall up there, Mister.

I was this Mister.

I was all alone. There was no one there. Just me shivering in my underpants. It was summer and I was cold. I had tuberculosis. I had scarlet fever. Both at the same time. I had no idea where I was or who I was.

The whore put me in her car and drove me to a doctor.

Who touched my breast and asked me who did this.

I did not know. My chest was the soft white immature chest of a little boy yet it was covered with scars and scabs and black-and-blue places now turning almost green.

That man in his white clothes held me for a long, long time on his lap. I went to sleep against him.

The down and down was a hole in the ground.

We were not supposed to go there. If I took my little brother, Tso, over to the down and down, Daddy would burn me with his cigarette. Daddy did hurting things to me so much.

You had to just stand still.

"Did I or did I not tell you *not* to take your brother over to those gravel pits? Answer me, boy."

"Yes, Daddy. Please, don't burn me, okay."

Daddy would pull my pants down and pinch the head of my penis when he burned me and the blood would come.

The blood. The blood. My penis was black.

You could not move when he burned you. If you jumped or moved he would burn you again and again. The white ones on my chest are the burning ones. The ones where Daddy did hurting me.

I have so many scars. I do not care about them.

I was standing at the edges of the down and down. Looking down there into the hole and the voices were going round and round like the Scrambler at the county fair and I was sitting on Daddy's lap on the Scrambler and Daddy had his arms around me and I did not have a shirt on.

Daddy was touching my breasts so softly with his hands and he had my small breasts between his fingers and his thumb just rubbing and rubbing.

The wind was touching my breasts and Daddy was smelling my hair that was blowing when the Scrambler went round and round and Daddy was telling me things about how he loved me and how he would do things to me.

The world went round and round on the Scrambler and the Scrambler was the whole goddamn fucked-up world.

It had been raining and I could hear the bullfrogs sing underneath my tree.

I ran away and ran up here to see the stars and ecstacy.

"Nasdijj, where arrrrrre youuuuuu?" my brother whispered.

"I'm at the down and down."

"What are you doing out here? If Daddy finds . . ."

"Look." I pointed down the black hole. You could smell the wet ground all around the down and down.

"What *is* it?"

I sighed. He did not know. But I did. I knew what was down there. I wanted to be dead.

"Can you hear them? I can."

Silence.

"I don't hear anything, Nasdijj. Come home. Come back. I'm scared."

"Daddy said I was beautiful."

My brother reached out and wiped some of the blood away that had been dripping down my chest and now I was smeared with it and so was he.

"What have you done to yourself. Why are you bleeding like this. *Nasdijj, what have you done!*"

I had no idea.

My brother took my hands and inspected my fingernails.

I would scratch my breasts off.

Stress leads to various antisocial, adaptive behaviors. It does not seem to matter if the stress comes in the form of sexual trauma, emotional warfare, or physical abuse. It does not seem to matter if the stress comes through starvation, or exposure to the horrors of the battlefield. Stress sculpts the child.

Stress sets off ripples in the waters of hormonal change that permanently wire a child's brain to cope with a malevolent world. Through this chain of connected events violence and abuse pass from generation to generation as well as from one culture to the next.

The middle of the cerebellum is called the cerebellar vermis. The vermis modulates the brain-stem nuclei that control the production and release of the neurotransmitters norepinephrine and dopamine. Like the hippocampus, this part of the brain develops gradually, and continues to create neurons after birth.

The brain builds itself.

In neurological studies abnormalities in the cerebellar vermis have been associated with various psychiatric disorders including varieties of manic depressive illness, schizophrenia, autism, and attention deficit/hyperactivity disorder. Dysregulation of the vermis-controlled neurotransmitters norepinephrine and dopamine can produce symptoms of depression, psychosis, and hyperactivity as well as impair attention. Activation of the dopamine system has been associated with a shift to a more left-hemisphere-biased (verbal) attentional state, whereas activation of the norepinephrine system shifts attention to a more right-hemisphere-biased (emotional) state.

I was standing at the edges of the down and down. I could hear them like claws and hooves going round and round so fast.

They were the voices and they would have me, too. Dervish voices from the past.

It was like drinking rain. You look up into the up and up. You open your mouth. The rain comes down. Filling you with rain.

But this was pain.

It was black like the hole. I was mad. Bats were pouring from my mouth.

Like that time your ears were ringing when he hit you. And he hit you again and again and the blood came from inside your ears and there was the ringing.

The voices came. I wanted them to go away. But the voices came from the down and down and I would hear them for a long, long, long time.

"When are you going to stop hearing and start listening?" Geronimo asked.

He was wearing one of those silly hats he loved. This one was a businessman's black derby, which seemed ridiculous with Geronimo's long Indian hair pulled back in a knot. He was carving a piece of wood with his jackknife.

"When did you arrive?" I asked.

"Yesterday," he said. "I arrived yesterday."

I was running in a panic on the railroad tracks, and the big train was chasing me like an animal in the night, and the night was the night of the voices, and the wild alarm was ringing in my head like music in a cavern, and I was running fast like an echo, and stumbling, and the train was coming, and the train was coming, throbbing and throbbing, and my pounding, rancorous lungs felt as if they would explode wet and red inside my screaming chest. I could pound the ground with my fists.

They are only voices. *Out! Out!*

I wanted Daddy's cock out of my mouth. Out! Out!

He would cum and I would throw up.

If I threw up on him he would smack me up against the wall.

"You see to it that Tso lives, Nasdijj."

Yes, Mama.

"You're the bigger brother. It's all on you now, boy. The whole weight of it."

Yes, Mama.

"You can't let anything *bad* happen to your brother. Do you *hear* me, Nasdijj? I need you."

I heard every word. Shaking my head.

Yes, Mama.

The sun is coming up and burns the fog and lifts the spell.

I knew that Daddy was fucking my brother in the next room with the door closed. The living and the dead of hell.

We never spoke of it.

I did not share this stuff with my brother and he did not share any of his with me *because we knew.*

We *already* knew.

The horror of it and our lives.

The voices were coming down like a cold rain from the black sky and I put my arm up to shove them away. What did shoving at the rain ever do?

I knew things.

I knew if I jumped into the water at the gravel pit I would drown.

It was so cold and black. You went down into the down and down.

Tso pulling me out by the hair. Sputtering. Angry. But he would not let me go. We could not discuss it much. I do not know why. Tso crying and begging me not to leave him alone.

The gravel pits were a place of timelessness. You had to jump in if you wanted to die. I wanted to be with the down and down. So cold in the gravel pit that nothing moves.

The voices were coming again.

Geronimo.

May he wander deserts. I have made a list.

15

We Took Dancer to the Gravel Pits

"Welcome to my house in the ground," Spider Woman said to the twins.

"Who are you?" they asked. They were smart to ask it.

"And where do you come from?" the old crone wanted to know. She seemed more smug than curious.

They gave no answer at first, as they had grown skittish. They lowered themselves down the ladder by yet another rung.

"We have nowhere to go," they said. "We are here because we do not know where else to go."

"You are welcome here, shivaazh," she said. "But you must tell me who you are, and where you are going following the Atiin diyinii, *trail of sunbeams, as you do."*

Deep within the liquid blackness of her eyes, Spider Woman was beautiful.

We took Dancer to the gravel pits. She would name herself. Like Apache warriors did.

The gravel pits were all still there. But we did not go in the water. It was far too cold. We three stood at the top of the bluffs and just looked down at the black still infinity of the water. There was snow on the mountains now. We fished Bluewater Lake and we caught fish, and we ate the fish we caught.

Tso and I could have lived like this forever. But Dancer was different. So far we had been camping out in old trailers, tents, and motels ready for the rat graveyard. Tonight we were staying in a place right by the train tracks outside Grants called the Franciscan. Dancer had charmed the desk clerk. We ate Lotaburgers that night. We were in bed. It was that middle place. Caught between the morbid and the mystical, the musical, and the misbehaved. Almost sleep.

"I know a record producer we should see in LaLaLand," she said. "He will offer me a record contract, but first we have to get there—*like in, you know, pleeeeeze?*"

Tso hugged her. "Hey, we've always been headed toward California."

"I know you want to see this volcano you're always talking about." She laughed. "We didn't come all this way not to go there."

It was as if we were strangers to the Navajo now. We were no longer those little sheep camp boys they had heard stories about. Sad Shima's sons. No longer holding Sa's hand and hiding behind those vast calico skirts. No longer hiding inside the darkness of our rugs. The stories belonged to another world. I did not know anyone who knew all of the stories. It seemed that they had been lost with Sa. Sa's hogan sat back by the rocks and the piñon pines. When a Navajo dies, the soul goes up through the smoke hole. The body, too, is brought out the smoke hole, and not the door, as the door is finished for this person. Then the hogan is nailed and shut up tight to prevent ghosts from moving in.

You see these tiny homes everywhere on the reservation. Small and secluded. All are ruins. Sitting silently from another time and looking back. No one goes there anymore.

Before she went, Sa had big bags of wool for us. It was only right that we give the wool away to relatives. There were two things Sa left to me that I wear even today. A silver bracelet and a silver ring. Sa had made both. I call the silver ring my ring of wings. Often, when I stayed with Sa, I did not speak. I had lost the ability. All I could do was hide behind her, and follow her around. She never pointed out my not talking. She never gave it attention.

Instead, she would show me how to pretend that we were birds. We were crows a lot, and we made crow sounds. We had our wings. Tso was too little then.

I was convinced that she could fly.

I would make my crow sounds and my mother would laugh, but my father did not think it very funny. A child who could not talk was going to be a problem. Maybe I was retarded. My dad would slap me across the face, sending me reeling, and demand that I talk. But I would not.

I was behind Sa when she chopped her wood.

I was behind her when she wove on her loom outside.

I was with her when she sheared her sheep.

I was on the ground with her when she watched the clouds so as to observe the weaving patterns for the loom.

I was behind her when she made her kneel-down bread in a hole in the ground. She did things the old way.

I was with her when she milked her goats.

I would sit in front of her and she would reach around with her old brown hands covered with silver bracelets and turquise rocks as big as a baby's fist and she would take my hands and show me how to grab the goat's teat and milk it.

Today, her hogan begins its journey blending back into the earth.

"I had many such wives."

"I know you did. Nine, I am told."

"Twelve, actually, but we were running from the soldiers. It was good in the beginning. We were camped on the Gila. Just below where the old ones made houses that are like caves."

"Yes. We call them the Mogollon."

"Tell me the story on this silver bracelet. You Navajo are always making stories. We were more the people of the wind."

"There are figures engraved into the silver. The silverwork is intricate; they'd be lucky to get work like this at Tiffany's."

"What is Tiffany's?"

"Never mind. There is the figure of the cow, the sheep, the Navajo with his wagon, the hogan, the cooking oven, the woodpile, and the horse. It's about what it doesn't say."

"There is no warrior. No symbol for violence or killing."

"Not even one. It is a place of utter peace. I am lucky to be able to wear it. When I need to remind myself that I am able to move to another place of being, all I have to do is look at my ring of wings. When I want to be reminded that peace is a place, *a place where the symbols of war are nowhere to be seen, all I have to do is look at my wrist and that story seems to move."*

Sa gone.

I would not be sad. I had promised. We shall not all sleep, but we shall be changed. Forever.

In THAT moment, in THAT twinkling, of THAT eye, at the last of the trumpets. But we SHALL be changed. And the dead shall be raised incorruptible, for the trumpeter will be known for THAT sound of trumpets, and we shall SEE, even the thorns in flesh, and SING.

Dancer's voice bouncing off the rocks. Like wine. The sweetness of eternity. The drums like time. And thence, we came forth again, to see the perfect star. To me a kingdom is that journey thrown so far.

The only way to Grandfather Nilch'i's hogan is to walk around the rim of the volcano. It was so empty without Sa. Dancer had never seen the world from the rim. From the rim of the volcano, the world, and the universe, is another place.

"This is where the People came up," I explained to Dancer.

"Is that what the Navajo believe?" she asked.

"No. That is what *some* of the Navajo believe. Other Navajo believe the emergence place was somewhere else. But try telling that to the Navajo who live around Ak'i Dah Nast'ani. The volcano is so dramatic, I don't know how you could fail to fit it into your creation story."

My brother is like a bird in this place, too. Dancer saw it. He sort of bounces along. His moccasins—his *makazinan*—make no sound.

I thought Grandfather's door was open so he could see the sky as it stretched itself before him for a good three hundred miles. Three hundred miles of sky and landscape broken not even once by the presence of a single human structure. Grandfather could not see the sky, but he could feel the wind when it came to sing with him. *The wind*, he used to say, *was ruthless.* The white snow on Mount Taylor in the distance seemed to waver softly as illumination in the desert is apt to do. "This does not feel like the desert," Dancer claimed. Yet the desert, too, is a complex living thing of many elevations, colors, spirits, beings, shadows, temperatures, and voices from the past. From the rim of the volcano, I could point out Chaco where we had camped only a few nights before.

The people in their stone cities. I am home in this place.

She kissed me. "I see a peacefulness in you that I have never seen before."

"He would live here if he could," Tso said. "Me, too. But there is hardly any way to make a living on the reservation. Still, this place is a part of us"—he pointed in the direction of Dinetah, the ancient hunting ground of the people who walk the surface of the earth—"and that is the sadness that killed our mother. Not alcohol. Not winter. Not suicide. But the sadness of not being able to live with her People in this landscape. Our dad can't keep a job on a good day when there are jobs that go begging. But Daddy keeping a steady job here?"

"It will never happen."

We both said it.

Nilch'i in Navajo means *the wind.*

Even as we stepped into the small hogan, a tiny gust greeted us. Dancer looked around for the front door but Nilch'i must have removed it. I rather liked the idea of no front door. The hogan is round with eight actual sides, and a small entryway like an igloo has. The Navajo and the Apache are Athabascan-speaking people who came down south along both sides of the Rocky Mountains. Some settled in the Pacific Northwest. Some settled in the arid Southwest. Anthropological linguists who follow the journeys of languages estimate that the Athabascan migration from the Arctic to the border with Mexico, and a bit beyond in the canyons and the gullies Geronimo knew and was so adept at hiding in, was not an overnight phenomenon but was, instead, a migration that lasted a good eight thousand years.

Grandfather was in bed under blankets only Sa could have made.

It took me a while to tell that he was blind.

"Tell me what the sky looks like today," he asked.

Dancer made a great performance of it and Nilch'i laughed. "But you have no door," Dancer said. "You can't see the sky. You are blind, Grandfather."

"What I have are people who can see there is no door. I am blind but I see more than most."

The people of the volcano came every day to tend to him. He still knew the stories of Spider Woman, and how she coaxed the War Twins into her home beneath the ground, and how they descended rung by rung on the ladder only to find that she was harmless, and the years had stolen only bones, only bones, and it was wisdom that broke like the sun breaks over Tsoodzil—or Mount Taylor in the east—like light upon the stones, only stones, and still the mothers and the fathers and the aunties and the uncles brought their children here. To hear the stories. While stands a voice with eyes. I stood among them. To touch the beauty of the seer.

My old grandfather. Nilch'i. His canoe was on the other shore. The wind. Was leaving.

That soft way the wind rolls on. All farewells but sounds like music in the trees. Moves the branches like the storms of thunder moves the eaves.

We all come here.

He holds my arm all the way to his outhouse. He could have the modern things. A white plastic commode beside his bed in his hogan.

The humiliation of it.

His visitors to see *that*? But no. His dignity like the mind, his moments to himself.

I leave him in his outhouse. But I do not go far away. He falters on the way back. Stumbles. And I realize how light he is. Maybe ninety old-man pounds. Not a gram over it dripping wet. We all come here. The women leave their warm casseroles wrapped in towels. While his quiet memory embraces them again as children. A forty-year-old woman's eyes sparkle when he reminds her of some childish memory. Some moment the two of them had shared in *tsintahgi*, a forest that was themselves. *Yeed`a`a niyi'de`e`.* A time in the past that now comes back from some inner place deep down inside of you. She holds his shaking hand. It is twisted with arthritis. Still, it is the good hand he picks piñon nuts with. He has been her rock. Now as he slips away from all of us, she has been baking and baking. That look between the two of them. I catch them as you might a warrant adolescent.

She has slipped some peyote in the corncake.

Which is why I cannot tell you his Anglo name.

Which is why I cannot tell you her Anglo name.

His privacy extends outside the confines of his outhouse.

His privacy is the chameleonlike mutability of the dead child and the veil. Till death like sleep steals over his shadows and his blankets. His privacy is dust in hues and half sunk down into him not unlike his black eyes swimming in onyx-liquid from the loftiest of stars unascended from his view that is, too, this vast sepulcher of heavens. His dignified autumnal privacy is like his bed pushed up against the far wall, now, all pictures vanished, and the door to the hogan utterly removed. Taken off the hinges the way some people are, too, and silently stares out into the vacancy of the desert like he does from his bed. Knowing that the desert he sees, and sinks into, is anything but empty.

He is too old to run, but not too old to eat corncakes. Or stare straight at the unforgiving high-desert mesa, Tsoodzil, or Mount Taylor in the distance, looming, and even at night when the red-tailed hawks are making swooping-noises-in-the-darkness-of-the-carnivores, and the bats scream infinite blood majestical-in-death, when a red-tailed hawk dives straight into his scream, the wind, the wind, loses himself to but a dream.

<hr />

Peyote. *Nilinidi.* Where it flows. *Na' iigeel nahaltin.* To dream where it is raining. To dream *it is* raining. To dream where it flows it is raining. To dream. *Niline`e.* The one who was. To dream. *Niliinii.* One who is. To dream. *Nasdijj.* To become again.

Grandfather.

Nishli nil. I am with you. *T'a`adoo haadzii'dah.* He said nothing.

Everything.
Yi'ash, yil. *He is walking with him.*

~~~~~~

She had wept and wept and wept over the death of her cat. Cats do not do well here. They are so domesticated, other creatures eat them. Nilch'i had taken the girl and the cat down into the pit of the volcano. Where the Navajo (it is said) once pulled themselves up and out and onto the spectacular place that was the earth. Small tasks die in great agony. *Wild Spirit, where art thou the breath of speed upon the din of dust?*

At that moment a great gust of sand blew up and, with it—Grandfather insists—*qqh mohookaad*, all the disappointments of a lifetime. Grandfather pulled me down so he could whisper in my ear. "Could you and your friends go to my cornfield and pick the corn?"

Nilch'i was giving us an extraordinary gift. There were people who had lived on the volcano all their lives who did not know where Nilch'i's corn was. His garden was not big. But it was magnificent. This would be the last one.

"All of this so you could be there to pick his corn."

"Yes. I think so."

"I think so, too."

"So many of the events that swirl around us are just the wind that brings us here."

"I had not seen him in a long time. This would be the last."

"Yes. So you picked the last of his Indian corn, and he told you stories about the corn and wind."

"Yes. The wind came and blew the seeds in turbulence everywhere, and the well-thought-out plans of the People had to be decided differently."

"Meaning that we have to learn to live even with chaos, as that, too, has its place. Coyote still throws pieces of the wind around."

We took bushel baskets. The corn was Indian corn of many colors. We ate some that night, and slept on the ground in the hogan of Nilch'i who was the wind.

The clouds parted at the volcano's rim as we headed west in the direction of Los Angeles. You could not even tell there were people and hogans up there.

~~~~~~

Whenever I am on the Navajo reservation, clouds of bats follow me overhead. If I go inside a house, and then come back outside that house again, the bats will all still be there. Waiting. They will be in trees. They will be upside down on telephone wires.

Whenever I am walking at night in Grants, New Mexico, the street-lights all go out as I pass them walking on the sidewalk. Blink. Blink. The electric company there wished I would go away and so I did.

Whenever I am at Kinnikinick Lake in Arizona, the mother bears all leave their cubs and will refuse to nurse them ever again. I no longer go there.

Whenever I am in Blue Canyon, it floods. And whenever it floods, an old man will come to me and say: *The water has never been this high.*

Whenever I climb to the top of Montezuma's Chair, a mountain in New Mexico, a herd of mule deer will come to that place and the deer will jump to their death onto the rocks below. I tried to stop them but the voices prevented me from doing it.

Whenever I am in Tuba City, the same old man crosses the road to get to the post office. But whenever I ask anyone in Tuba City who the old man is, they back away and say there is no old man who does that. No one.

Whenever I am at the Laundromat by Bashas grocery store in Crown-point, the same grandmother with the same white goats always arrives with the goats in the back of her pickup, and she always, always takes my sopping-wet laundry out of the washer, and throws it on the floor. Then she says *shiinilghal*, which means *you ate me up*. But I do not know her.

Whenever I am at the Chaco ruins at night, spirits come down from the mountains. I cannot tell you what it is they do or say, as they have sworn me to secrecy. The voices are afraid of them and they hide deep down inside my guts, where they shiver in the cold.

Whenever I am at the Zuni Pueblo for the carnival, the same dark man dressed in the same deerskin pants follows me around the carnival and when I ask him why he follows me he says: *Tsetahgo*, which means *because the place was rocky*.

Whenever I am in Canyon de Chelly, the same beautiful woman emerges from a small orchard of fruit trees and she asks me if I would like to try the fruit. I always eat the fruit but I never know what it is, and she will only softly laugh.

Whenever I am at Massacre Cave, I can always hear the screaming of the horses. I never hear the screaming of the Navajo or the voices from any of the American soldiers, but I always hear the horses scream there, and I no longer go to that place.

Whenever I am sleeping *anywhere*, I hear the horses of Canyon de Chelly pleading and pleading with me to save them. I try my best to never sleep.

I see Geronimo in bars. Playing pool.

My chest.

The smell of my brother's hair.

Why can't I always be like this: six, or seven, or eight, and racing with the trains, just breathing, not being compelled to be aware of much more than this, this bottom of the ditch, this dampness, and this holding my brother to my chest and smelling pine trees in his hair?

I was on my back and looking up. Hadn't our mother died like this? Was this particular configuration of stars a message of some kind from her? No. The moon was cold and packed tough as a snowball. Almost ice.

Nasdijj, are you alive?

Yes, I was racing with the train.

What shall you call this racing with the train, Nasdijj?

Hwiih—*inside him, satisfaction.*

"Hwiih," *I say to my little brother—my feather—whom I know (I do not know how I know, I just know) is flying to me.*

My squirmy little brother throws himself on top of me. Him breathing hard.

I'm here.

His dumb and silly ha ha.

~~~~~~

16

In 1963, the Desert Blacktop to Los Angeles Unfolded Like a Quivering, Silver Apparition

They had taken the path of the gods although they did not know that this was the path of those immortals as they were ignorant of this and many, many other things.

They had walked for many years but in that entire time they never once observed a single sign of life. Years, of course, being quite different to gods, who have given themselves many of the years the people would have enjoyed having, but the gods were selfish as we know.

They noted a wispy, thin pillar of smoke rising mysteriously from a spot where there was no flame—only horizon! Strange things!

The history of the earth was repeating itself.

"Grandmother, were we not in this place yesterday?"

Spider Woman dressed in her shawl was smoking her pipe before the fire. "Yesterday and yesterday and yesterday," she said. "You have been coming here for years and yet you refuse to come down another rung of my ladder you are standing on."

The boys lowered themselves another rung on Spider Woman's ladder. "We are uncertain as to who we are," they explained. "We only know that we are fleeing for our lives."

"You may rest safely here," she said. "I know who you are."

"We are the sons of Changing Woman whose sister is White Shell Woman, and we are fleeing the alien monsters who pursue us, as they have eaten most of the peo-

ple who walk the surface of the earth. Alas! We know we are yataashki—*born without the blessing of marriage. We were sired by the round cactus and the sitting cactus. And we are following the Holy Trail because we are fleeing in disgrace. The monsters who pursue us will destroy our people if they can."*

Spider Woman extended her arm in a gesture of welcome to the boys who had now moved to the bottom rung on her ladder in her underground kiva. "I will tell you who your father is."

The first brother sat himself down on a seat of pure obsidian. The second brother sat on a seat of pure turquoise.

"Your father is Johonaa'ei, *the sun, or some call him* Begochiddy. *He is a terrible god with lightning bolts and rage. And his dwelling is far above us all in the sky. The way to his house is long and dangerous. Many monsters will block your path and they will test the two of you. I cannot promise you that your father will be happy to see you. He may punish you for finding him. You must try to endure his rage or your people are surely doomed."*

I n 1963, the desert blacktop to Los Angeles unfolded like a quivering, silver apparition. Heaven was the road and the earth was the road and the past was the road and the lizards you ran over were the road and the arid scrub was the road and the now was the road and Howard Johnson's was the oasis-of-the-road where the nice orange roof suggested Disneyland was not-too-far-ahead. Nothing had arrived yet in 1963 but the suggestion that it would was everywhere. Big, big gas stations would go here. Half-finished shopping malls would go here. Big, big walls by golf courses would go here. Restaurant parking lots would go here. Housing sprawls would go here. The sprinklers that turn the desert air to mist would all go here. There had to be a plan. A Master Plan somewhere that dictated where everything would go.

In the middle of the desert off to the side of the road, almost in the ditch, were a family of Hopi Indians who had set up a dozen TV trays with trinkets that were for sale. Everyone wore cowboy hats and sat on lawn chairs as if they were at the powwow. No one went by and no one was purchasing trinkets. The air was still as stones and sixty times as hot. We pulled over to the side of the road, and I put the Corvette into reverse.

"This," my brother intoned, "is a test of the Emergency Broadcast System. This is only a test. And we are not really backing up. It is only a test."

I was all over the road.

"This has been a test."

It was his turn to drive. I handed him the keys. He backed us up perfectly to the Indian TV trays at the side of the road.

We bought Dancer some silver earrings. Los Angeles loomed.

～～～～

There aren't too many places in America Tso and I can say we have never been to. The Los Angeles we had seen before was the barrio where Daddy had purchased fake documents. He had left us in the truck and disappeared into buildings, and a bewildering number of men congregated all around a bewildering number of corners. Driving, stopping, backslapping, slipping pesos into hands. At the end of the day, Daddy had a glove compartment filled with fake documents, two boys who had wet their pants, and a woman named Carmella whom we liked very much.

We knew Carmella from the artichoke fields of Monterey.

She had been a migrant worker then. She had a family. Children.

It had all been taken from her by a drunk driver. Pieces of her children had been splattered all over the road, U.S. 1, near Big Sur where drunks roar around those turns. Carmella had been thrown without a scratch. When the CHP and the ambulance arrived, Carmella was attempting to reconstruct the pieces of her children, but she could not tell what belonged to who. It was news among the migrants for a long time. Everyone spoke of it, and Carmella. The Cowboy was one of the few people who really knew her. She could not work in the fields anymore. It would have driven her insane. There was enough of *that* going around.

Carmella found herself a nice three-bedroom apartment in the center of the city. The place had been built in the early twenties, and it wasn't fancy, but it was clean. She had geraniums in every fucking window. Carmella made more money, now, than she ever did as a migrant, selling fake documents to other migrants. She was the only person my dad knew who could deal in passports. They were good friends, and she was not afraid of him. "Or his mouth," she claimed.

We were maybe four and five when Carmella moved to Los Angeles. I did not know until I was older that Carmella was something of an artist, and many of the forgeries she sold were done by her very own hand, which was said to be flawless. Carmella called Daddy's papers junk. Daddy would laugh and say Carmella was far too expensive for the likes of him. After Mama died, Daddy would breeze into Los Angeles, and we would spend the week with Carmella.

By the second day, and never any longer than the third, she was over his nonsense, and she always kicked him out. Usually by throwing his stuff out the fifth-floor kitchen window. He could *go* wherever he wanted, but we were hers forever.

Carmella had hundreds of pictures of her own children in an altar on a fireplace mantel. She prayed to her children every day. There was not a suggestion of a husband anywhere in this mix. It was said she blamed him.

I was her *el cometa*.

Tso was her *la estrella*.

Daddy was her *el agujero negro*.

Just a big black hole "goot for notheen."

Carmella wore earrings that dangled and high heels with holes for the toes.

When we were children, she'd stick us in her big *la banera*, and we were to soak and wash every molecule of the migrant grime off with *el jabon*.

She would dry us off with huge towels, and we would drench the floor of her bathroom as Carmella ran back and forth trying to spray us with her very large perfume sprayer with the old-fashioned bubble. It was a mistake to have shown it to my brother.

Everything in Carmella's apartment would now smell infinitely like Citrus El Peacho.

A week or so would pass and Daddy would come to scoop us up.

I never really knew why. He could have rid his life of us so many times. But he never did.

Dancer had pending recording contracts in Los Angeles, but nowhere *to stay*.

Tso called Carmella from a Ralph's Groceries.

The door swung open and we were seven years old again.

Let Carmella lookatchoo! Turn around.

She cried. We knew she would.

Dancer got the eye.

I got her room all ready for her it's nice room with some nice dresses in case you dontagot none.

There would be no hanky-panky at Carmella's.

Carmella had her daughter's old dresses. They were a little small. They were a little old. They were a little heavy with the ribbon.

Dancer was fine and didn't need clothes.

Okey.

There was a long, long, long moment of awkward silence as Carmella's clock ticked. Her cats walked around. Carmella said nothing. Her fingernails tapped, tapped, tapped. We three looked at the walls.

"So!" Carmella said. "Whoze iz gonna be the one to tell me about one: zdealing that car you got parked out there likea cherry tomato, and two:

running away from your papa, may some saint bless him, and tree: who zaid you old enough to have no girlfriend, El Cometa, you still in *orbit*, boy, ha? Don'tcho know some policeman or some *la pistola* will throw your weenies in *la carcel*—pop. Done. I donno them. They died in gas room. Nice boys. I knew their mama. She would *weep* on her *knees* if she could see it, the disgace. What, you, La Estrella, you the big macho man now, ezz that it? I donno. I donno."

Carmella wore an ankle bracelet that went up and down as the right foot protested the state of things far more fluently than a finger waved ever could.

"Younh leedy. You gotta record contract, eh? Well, lemme hear it. Stand up, girl. Zing."

"Zing? Here? Now?"

"See. She no zing. No Johnny Carson. No record contract. Pop! I donno. *La verguenza!* The shame has come to my house."

"I thought you said she sold forged documents . . ."

"Aut! Aut! Aut! We are talking about *shame*! Not me. Me, I takea the bus. You—that car is a cherry tomato. You boys are in beeeeg troubles. Now, you two, go get in that *la banera*. You, Miss. We unpack yous."

The next day, we three criminals were sitting on the fire escape. Tso and I were dressed in our (now cleaned and ironed) jeans. Miss *La Verguenza* (with new beehive) was dressed in a ridiculous crisp, white, Catholic version of something (heavy on the pink ribbon) you would have worn to a wedding in 1947. Black patent leather shoes. White socks.

"I feel like I'm going to do it with every guy in the rectory," Dancer said. "I look like a slut from some girls' school applying for a room at the nunnery. No wonder those girls are *bad*. Have you *seen* my underwear?"

"Not today," my brother said.

Tso had been fed and he was happy.

Until the Cowboy walked into the lobby of the building. Two hundred and ten feet below us.

I almost jumped.

"What is it?" Dancer asked.

"Our dad just walked into the building," Tso said. "Shit."

17

In the Beginning It Was Not at All What I Expected

When their mothers awoke, they saw that the twins had taken flight.

The sisters went outside to look for them and examined the ground for fresh tracks. But they found only four footprints for each of the two boys, and these pointed toward Dzil na'oodilii, *the Traveler's Circle Mountain.*

It seemed that they had taken Atiin diyinii, *the Holy Trail, so that they would not be followed. But by taking such a path they could easily arouse the anger of* Haashch'eeh dinee, *the Holy People.*

In any case, to try to search for them would be useless. So Changing Woman and White Shell Woman returned to their dwelling, where they would wait in fear and apprehension as was their way.

As was their way, the boys were filled with many questions.

"You will have to cross many dangerous places," Spider Woman told them. "You will have to walk past the rocks that cut people to pieces. You will have to walk past the rocks that crush all travelers. You will have to cross among the reeds that cut people to pieces. You will have to cross between the cane cactuses that tear boys to shreds. And you will have to cross the boiling sands that burn all passersby to ashes."

It was not at all what I expected. I expected hysterics. But there was none of that.

This was a negotiation.

Daddy sat on one side of the room. We three sat on the other side of the room.

Carmella sat in her chair.

I was very calm. On the outside. On the inside, I had just vomited in the bathroom. But Tso had held me up, and I needed that.

He handed me a cup of water. "Here. Everything will be okay."

The only way to do it was to look Daddy right in the eye. He couldn't handle it. Daddy just stared at his cowboy boots.

"I did not know about the sex," Carmella said. "I knew my friend, Shima, had killed herself, and it made no sense. She had children. But I did not know about this hurting boys. This . . ."

She had to breathe heavily for a while.

Her eyes closed. She was seeing it now for the first time from our point of view. "I did not know you had hurt them. My babies. And you are hurting them. God will not forgive you, Patron. You will have to make your own peace with him. La Estrella, come sit by me, honey."

Tso went to sit by her. She lifted his shirt up. She put it down. She was calm.

"*La verguenza*. In my world, my brothers would kill you, Patron. My brothers might still kill you. I want to."

It was coming out.

My father was very tired.

"I'm not here to get the six thousand back, Tso," he said. "It's been taken care of. It's been set right. There were people who owed me money, too. I collected. I paid off the six thousand. I need you to let me have the car. Or I will be a dead man by tomorrow. And that might be fine with you. I understand that."

"You *should*," Carmella said.

"But you would be next. These people don't care—all they want is their money."

"El Cometa, you *will* give him this car tonight. You will, boy. I no have you shot dead in my parking lot. Okay. No car. No moneys. Everything is taken care of except for my shameful one with beehive."

"I'm not going back."

"No one said you going back," Carmella said. No one said anything else for a long while as the noise of Los Angeles came in the window.

As children, we would go to Indian ceremonies where I would hold my brother's hand and all we knew and all we saw was that it was about the light. The light around us. We were the light.

The light was coming out of our chests. We could touch it and taste it and put it in our mouths like candy.

Where Christianity has the Garden of Eden, what the Athabascan have is a cycle. A cycle that opens with a highly patterned description of two rivers crossing at a central point. It is at this point that social conflict occurs. The original inhabitants of the region where the rivers meet—squabbling among themselves—find themselves, too, being expelled by the gods who find them annoying.

The moral being: *Think and be quick about it before your family disappears down the river.*

When I was eight, and Tso was seven, we built a raft. No, neither one of us had read Samuel Clemens. We knew nothing about Tom or Huck. We were two migrant boys who built a raft. We called it *our ship.*

Nails. Wood. Rope.

Some ship.

This was West Texas and the White Salt Fork of the Brazos River. I do not know why we were there or why we were in half the places we were. We were there mainly to pick.

Whatever.

I did not really *care* what we were there to pick.

We whined and complained.

We would run down to *our ship.*

Which we pulled into the river. To see if it would float.

It did. But in the place where the water started to move a bit more quickly, *our ship* fell completely apart.

In the West, there is such a thing as a flash flood when it has been raining upstream. The water is coming and you do not know it.

There was rope where there should have been nails, and there were nails where there should have been rope. We were a thousand pieces.

I could swim.

Tso could almost swim.

The next thing I knew was that Daddy had dived into the White Salt Fork of the Brazos River. The three of us were sitting on the bank of the river. *Our ship* completely gone. I knew I was going to get it. I *was afraid. I was very afraid.*

But Daddy just held us to him and his wet dripping clothes, sitting in the mud.

It had been decided.

I was not unhappy to see the strange car go. We had never really bonded. I do not bond with cars. I am the kind of man who bonds with trucks. The only reason we never had an accident in the Corvette was because I rarely ever drove it over forty-five.

Dancer was staying in Los Angeles with Carmella. We called her Carmella, Queen of the Desert, because so many of her memories started there, as did almost all of her stories, which never seemed to end. Dancer was changing her name again.

Rhonda was a nice name. They tell me true nobility is exempt from fear.

I was afraid. For us. For her. We kissed Rhonda in the dark. The name would never stick. Everyone's face was wet.

We dared not make a single sound. Her tears were like salt and I licked them. She just stood there like a shivering statue with her eyes closed. Good-bye.

The way out of Los Angeles by streetlights. Two young boys on the highways of Los Angeles.

To pick our pumpkins.

Thumbs out. We saw the ocean. And pumpkins for as far as eyes could stretch themselves.

We two stayed with the other pumpkin migrants in a trailer. Hefting pumpkins onto trucks. We sold pumpkins, too, in a little shed they had out by the side of the road. At night we could hear the train that ran from Los Angeles to San Francisco like a faraway echo.

We ran into the surf and gave our clothes to a young woman who would wash them at the Laundromat.

The freezing water just went over and over us.

18

We Rode Sticks and
Brooms for Horses

So it was that Mo'ii, the Coyote, could look down from the constellations and see everything.

He had turned living things into players like the playing pieces of a game. Not knowing they did this and that to amuse the Trickster. If Coyote were to have his way, he would steal the stars. But first there would be the sun to consider, and he did not move easily.

Ordered to do so, the two youths entered the sweat lodge.

Hot boulders were placed inside, and the opening of the lodge was sealed with four sky coverings.

Outside stood Johonaa'ei, the sun.

"Is it hot in there?" he called.

"Yes!" replied the boys.

It was so hot that planets too close to the sun melted along with all the beings on those worlds.

Only a few of the People on the earth knew or understood the significance of things.

The boys crept into the hiding place Nilch'i, the wind, had made for them in secret. There they were sheltered against the roasting heat that was capable of killing them.

They heard the sun climb to the top of the sweat lodge where he poured a great deal of water through the top onto the red-hot stones inside. When it landed on the hot boulders there was a hissing and boiling. In time, the steam cooled, and the War Twins crept out from their hiding place.

The sun bid the boys come out.

Truly, the sun said only to himself, they must be mine for they are made with a great fury and an even greater strength. *The Navajo called it patience. The sun knew then that they had endured terrible hardships.*

From his even higher perch, Coyote began to worry that these two surprising boys would in time find him and take the stars back.

We rode sticks and brooms for horses.

I do not remember when we put those away but I remember that we did.

It was not like the other times.

This time our mother had died, and Daddy did not seem to know what to do.

Our truck was gone.

Our things were gone.

Daddy did not want to answer our questions and told us to shut the fuck up.

But I knew.

I did not know how quite to explain it to Tso. I had to search for my words while he waited.

I would explain things and he would shake his head. That is how it worked then.

I knew these things because I listened to the men at night. I was always listening. It helped to listen so you might know what was coming next, but there were no guarantees you would know.

The men playing cards were laughing but Daddy's voice was not one of the laughing ones.

It's the kind of game where you have cards, and you bet that the cards will come out the way you think they will but if you are wrong then you lose things.

As kids who did not have much to lose, this made sense to us but only to a point.

What is hard to explain is how anyone can lose everything. And to the people who supposedly were your buddies and why didn't they just give it back because if they were nice they would do that, just give it back. Like today.

These were men who had always been nice to us. Joking with us. Ruffling hair. Asking us questions like what had we done in school.

And now they were taking everything.

Tso just sat there with his hands folded and his eyes to the ground.

In no time at all, it was gone. All! All! All!

We left the migrant camp that afternoon, carrying a bag each. We walked and walked. We slept that night under a bridge.

I remember waking up the next day, and my body ached like someone had kicked it.

Thinking: We will go somewhere else today, but we never did.

All Daddy could do was stare at the highway bridge above us. The cars and the trucks would rumble across it and the world would shake.

It rained in horizontal rushes as the big interstate rigs screamed a bitter agony in the terror of the grinding night. In that night, our eyes shone yellow like the deer. Truckers would honk.

I was very scared.

All his failures on a ledge and his flesh impermeable as a vagrant's eyes. "I got to get you boys out of here," he said.

In the blinking of an eye, we had lost everything.

It was not impossible for our childish brains to fathom this.

What terrified us was the possibility our father would not be able to rectify it, and we knew what that meant, too.

We had seen it in the migrant camps many times.

It is always the same. Even the people involved all seem to look alike.

Sometimes we wondered aloud and to each other that the people *who did it* (that is what we called them) were the same exact people (this made sense to us), *and that the people who did it in Ohio were the same people who did it in Georgia and that the people who did it in Georgia were the exact same people who did it in Minnesota.*

It always unfolds in the same way.

1. It appears to be a normal day like any other day. There is never anything out of the ordinary on the day *the people who did it* arrive.

2. The sun will be going down. Dinner will just be beginning to be over for almost everyone else in their migrant shacks up and down the migrant lane of migrant shacks with the cars and the trucks and the dogs and the bikes and the plastic Hot Wheels. The sun will be going down and, still, they will not have eaten dinner yet at one house.

   Everyone on the migrant block knows the house.

3. Three cars arrive. Two of the cars will be plain. Each one of them will contain two women.

4. The third car to arrive is a cop car. There are two officers in the cop car. No one bolts, although sometimes, rarely, but sometimes, someone, usually a man, climbs out the window in the back, and heads into the woods. They let him go. At the moment, there is no time for this guy. His crimes are irrelevant.

5. The four women are holding many papers.

6. There is crying.
7. The children are split up and taken away. On the way to where the children are going, they stop to eat.
8. The children wonder if they will ever see their brothers and sisters again.
   We had seen parts of this from bikes, from behind the shades of our own migrant shack next door, from our perch in trees. The migrant camp will buzz for days.

Now us. It can all go. I do not know where it can all go when you lose everything. I only know it can.

We sat outside on our suitcases while Daddy was inside giving blood. We wanted to see him give blood but no. We were to sit here, not move, and be quiet for once in our lives, and that is what we did. We figured it was like a gas station, and there'd be big machines pumping blood.

After several hours, Daddy came out of the building with a man, obviously another migrant, this one named Miguel.

Miguel knew where there was work, and he would drive us there, since that was where he was going, anyway.

Did we like artichokes?

This question is always put to you—*artichokes, cherries, apricots, nectarines, plums, avocados*—in terms of whatever your parents will be picking (and maybe you, too).

Locos y ninos dicen la verdad.

You nod your head: yes. Because if you don't your dad will cuff the back of it with his hand. *Did we like artichokes?*

You had to be kidding.

But it would be better than Daddy selling us to go to cars with other men. That would be next. We were sure of it. We had held off the arrival of the unraveling, and with any luck, and with a lot of hard work and sacrifice, we would get back up on our feet again.

Enough anyway, for our father to buy us an old school bus to live in. We thought it was fun when he drove it into the desert and parked it there.

We called it "the De-Ja-Vu" because that was what the sign said at the side of the brick building. The tiny apartment was on the second floor. I stood at the top of those stairs and wondered if I would even let Daddy in.

I did not know that I would.

If I let him in, he might want to stay. And I could not allow that. There was no hope for it. No, he could not stay. Not under any circumstances.

He could visit briefly. Then he had to leave.

Downstairs, there was a convenience store that sold beer, and a small hardware store. Across the street, there was a lumberyard. Daddy put the money down on the place. It was the least he could do. I did not feel one iota of guilt over him paying and paying. It was not that bad. I liked it. And we didn't have to see him. He promised that.

There was a little table with two chairs in the kitchen. A huge couch about the size of a Cadillac. A bed in the bedroom. It would more than *do*. He was a little amazed at how thin we looked. Ragged. Hitchhiked *out*.

He was nervous around us. It was as if he hadn't really looked at us in years. And maybe he hadn't.

He knew his goddamn sins. We regarded him like we might a snake.

I wanted to push him up against the wall but I didn't. Our voyage across the country had given me some testicles I did not have when we left New Jersey like surly dogs. He had gotten most of his six thousand dollars back. Here we were thinking we had spent like big spenders high-on-the-hog, and we'd spent about five hundred bucks. Even we were shocked. The Corvette had been returned without a wrinkle to the people who had stolen it in the first place. He owed us. I shrug.

Now that at least a few people knew, the man was scared. He promised to pay the rent, but by then the promises were rolling too thick and too fast for me to believe that Daddy could could keep up with them.

Daddy would pay the rent.

Right.

I did not mind making rent day. Really, I didn't.

Not if it kept Tso in school. He liked school. It wasn't easy.

I could get up in the morning, and know I wasn't in a migrant camp.

Every now and then when I needed it, I could drive to the volcano. I could fish Bluewater Lake and be happy about it.

We shoved the bed (there was a real bed, yes!) so the foot end reached the window.

At night, we could put our hands behind our heads, and see the stars.

Around midnight, the neon signs downstairs got turned off.

I had three jobs. I was a pool hall sweeper. It was okay. Guys were always bashing into me and pretending they didn't mean it, and they'd ask me to play some pool.

Word got around the cowboys.

I did not lose at pool. I do not know why. But I have never lost a game of pool, and finally, for the sheer novelty of the thing (hey, I was sixteen), I turned to bumper pool, and even got Cranky who owned the place to buy one table of bumper pool.

I owned the pay phone in the back. People would call and I would deliver six-packs to your house. I got a real deal and kickbacks from the De-Ja-Vu. Cowboys love their beer. Ten bucks a six-pack. The cowboys would groan like Houston and Dallas had both dried themselves of oil. What! Ten bucks for a six-pack. Are you *nuts*!

Hey, Petunia. You called me.

That is the price. Or get your ass back in the saddle and buy your lazy ass self your own six-pack.

All of this was about as illegal as it comes. But no one gave a fuck mainly because I was busting my chops for *dinero* and not attending school, which I was no longer obliged to attend anyway—not that I did much attending when I was obliged to attend.

I tried.

School was not worth the paper it was printed on.

My third job was every now and then showing up at a ranch to help out with whatever they needed me to help out with.

Branding cows.

Fixing tractors.

Cleaning out the fucking barn.

The rancher had a son who liked me. I was not all that sure I liked him, though. He wasn't all that arrogant or obnoxious like rich boys can be if they want to really kick Daddy for turning out a *brat*. No. He could even have been a nice guy (he would need lessons). But stay out of my way while I am working, and if I am shoveling horseshit into a wheelbarrow for your mother's garden, do not just stand there in your cowboy boots, talking to me, or trying to, okay, *go-get-a-pitchfork-and-PITCH-in!*

I walked into the barn one time and this boy was having sex with one of the other ranch hands.

They were embarrassed, and so was I.

I thought the best way to go was to ignore it.

My phone at the pool hall rang. It was Jimmy. The boy at the ranch whose daddy could have bought that boy Mars had he wanted it. He did not want Mars.

He wanted me.

We were playing Geronimo before we could even walk.

Geronimo always seemed somehow to be our third and silent brother.

Both the hero and the villain. Great generosity and great audacity. We knew this: Life was rarely if ever all good or all bad. Life was complicated.

As a man who lives in the contemporary world, a world that is most definitely run, maintained, and managed by an upper class of white males, I am often asked questions about "Native American mythology." Whatever that is. It always shakes me a little. In my world, the stories are real. I am from a world where those stories imbued our lives with extraordinary vividness. The vividness was reality.

We live in a culture that refuses to accept the universe as a complex place. Complexity requires too much work. It's easy to see a universe where all the laws of physics are simple. Not twenty shades of gray. It's easier to manage things with a more simplistic understanding of how things work.

The imagination cannot be real.

We would pretend that we were Geronimo, too, and we would wrestle in our underpants and jump down from the big mountain that was really the pile of Navajo rugs we slept under. Our world was that bed of rugs and blankets on the floor. We loved living in it. We always slept safely tucked away in all that woven warmth, and removed from the trials and travails of the worn and worried world.

Geronimo conquered the known universe and he ate all the babies. He was a ferocious warrior and the stories about him scared us shitless.

As Geronimo left the villages he plundered, he raised his dripping-red sword high above his head, displaying for all gods and devils his naked, plump, and skewered victims. All impaled down to the wet hand that held the babies high.

We stood in awe of this.

Geronimo would gallop away taking his dead babies to his lair, where he would eat them like the dragon he was.

19

I Should Have Known

The sun spread the four sky blankets on the ground. Upon the blanket of red dawn he placed the robe of blue sky. Upon the robe of blue sky he placed the counterpane of yellow evening. And over the counterpane of evening he spread the black shroud of darkness. Then he bid the young men to sit on these layers one behind the other, each facing east.

"My daughters," the sun commanded. "Dress these two strangers as my other sons are dressed."

Whereupon the two young women of the household approached the twins, undid the knots in their hair so that it hung loose like the hair of their two brothers, molded their faces and forms in the manner of the aknowledged sons of Johonaa'ei, and fashioned their clothing to suit the taste of their father.

The twins accepted war gifts from their father. Streaks of lightning and fire reflected from their very limbs once they were dressed for battle.

Indeed, they looked like warriors.

I should have known. I did know.

How many ranchers *pay you* to go hunting with them?

Yet I was willing to do just about anything, work any job, perform any humiliating task so I could feed us, and so my brother did not have to work, and could tend to his time in school.

At least this is what I told myself maybe to imbue myself with some romantic and noble notion.

I was willing to do just about anything, work any job, prostitute myself, and sell my soul to the devil for twenty bucks if it would keep the nightmare of being hungry away from us. I kept telling myself that it was all for Tso and a lot of it was. But it was for me, too, and the demons I kept in my belly to keep the hunger away. We ate spoiled food all the time because I was too cheap to throw it away. Throw food away? It would never happen. Not when you've felt your intestines move around like you've eaten some evil rat whole, and it's clawing its way out of you. I was and am terrified of being hungry like that ever again. I vowed to never have to sit in some migrant shack on the floor and there is no food and the only money you have is the spare change that buys a soft drink from a machine that gulps your money down in great gulps and makes the inner sounds you make when you try to sleep hungry on the floor. I would not do it again.

I wondered how much his touching me like that might be worth.

We were so far back no one could see us. His hands had no right. No permission from me to be where they were.

Touching me.

I hadn't been abused, now, for some time. But it all came back like a flood.

Like the memory of hunger, too, where some vast emptiness is swallowing you, and the message of flight-or-fight hits you harder than adrenaline ever did.

There was no one in that town who didn't know how poor we were. All they had to do was call the pay phone at the pool hall to jerk my chain.

I came running.

To me, *it's a job*. That is all it is.

This boy is not getting the response from me he thought he would get.

We were simply going through a hole in the fence when his gun went off. An accident.

Bang. Damn. A heavy, heavy warmness spreads from my belly up.

I do not know *why* but after hearing the gun go off, and after being aware of the fact I had been shot, I remember feeling waves of enormous regret I had never made things *better* between my father and myself. And now, I thought, it was too late.

I do not know much about the history of my father. Although my dad always saw himself as a cowboy, he was a drifter if there ever was one. The Wild West was not really big enough to contain him, and somewhere out there I have to believe *he lost his fucking mind*.

I have tried to put a scientific spin on it that never works. I have read all the books on mental illness and none of them describes my father. I do not know if mental illnesses like schizophrenia, depression, and personality disorders are matters of biology and are best treated by professionals pharmacologically; or are these diseases-of-the-mind the product of psychosocial factors such as family dynamics and the kind of traumatic early-childhood experiences my brother and I had? I suspect it isn't *either–or*. Any more than *happiness* is something anyone can really seek. That was the fundamental difference between Tso and I. Tso just wanted to be happy, and that is exactly what he said about a hundred thousand times. I did not buy it—*happiness*. I wanted to be *effective*, and if happiness is a by-product of that, then fine. I saw happiness as the exception, not the rule.

Every time I attempt to put a scientific spin on the behavior of my father, I can hear him off in the corner sucking on his warm bottle of tequila, and daring me to eat the worm.

There are no worms in tequila.

But I didn't know that, and whenever he threatened to make me eat the worm I'd run somewhere fast, and not come home until maybe the next day when he'd be too hungover to know I had escaped his grasp again. He always *worked hard*, but it never got him anywhere. My dad worked cows and horses like any other cowboy. Before he married my mother (there is no record of a marriage) my dad worked fishing boats up in Alaska. There were a couple of very tight, cash-strapped times, too, when we had virtually no money whatsoever, and Daddy disappeared only to reappear again with wads of cash he had earned working fishing boats, and crabs.

It was hard to be too exasperated with him when he did come back, and with more money than all four of us could have earned picking cucumbers.

My dad picked his share of cucumbers. He knew what hunger was.

My father's hands were like bloody cabbages. You did not want them to touch you. They were like balls of meat pushed down into the ground.

When push came to shove, and push does come to shove in the Wild West, even today, my dad had more options than most other cowboys who were limited to one more cow-dirtball town somewhere in the West. Daddy could go anywhere. It amazes me to know that most Americans have *no fucking idea* that there is work for migrants in virtually *every single state*. I know places in New Jersey where in the nineteen fifties you could stand up and take a break from picking tomatoes and look right over at Manhattan.

Daddy drifted. Today they would say that his instability was a part of whatever condition was used to describe him. I have my own word for what he was.

Hopeless.

My father was hopeless. It is worse than being hungry.

I do not know where he finally lost the last fragments of hope he ever had. I do not think it was while butchering horses. It came long before that. The butchering of the horses is where I *lost* it—hope. That was my final separation from the idea things would improve. Not his. His came somewhere I do not know about and I am glad to not know what it was. What pulled the hope from his empty intestines and up through his throat like wire? I do not know. I do not care to know. I look at my brother and hope he is not a hopeless man. A man who fishes like my brother does has an awful lot of hope still in him.

I do not know exactly what high crimes and misdemeanors my father committed during his time on the planet. I suspect there were a few. Thing is, I do *not* want to know. What would *knowing* do? Make it better? I do know he smuggled more than a few Mexican folks across the border. As a cowboy, he had driven lots of cattle through Texas. Driving migrants literally still soaked to the skin across the border to the migrant camps paid a whole hell of a lot better than driving cows through the same sun-beaten territory. Daddy did not like to talk about his crimes. I know at one point he had a chop shop business going. He stole American trucks, smuggled them to Mexico, did whatever it was they did to the vehicles in Mexico, and then smuggled them back into the States.

Asked about it, he froze, got quite formidable. He'd light a cigarette, and his hands would shake.

We lived for a while in an old school bus Daddy bought from a church that was closing down. The evangelical churches especially come and go. Daddy drove the bus into the middle of the desert.

Mama had died.

At first, I thought this was so much craziness. I was just a kid, and what did I know about craziness anyway? But Daddy spent an awful lot of time just in the school bus; he might not leave it for days on end, always staring off into the distance with his shotgun on his lap, as if he had seen a whole army of jackrabbits go by. Day after day of nothing but staring out the window. I would see him and know, even then, I would die in pain.

Tso and I were off playing on some rocks when we heard the sound of Daddy's shotgun. We were sure he had killed himself and ran back to the bus. But Daddy was a survivor, and he had only shot the tires of the bus.

We never knew why. When we left that place, we walked, and carried everything we owned, which was very little.

The driver of a desert school bus going nowhere. Waiting for someone to show up who never did.

Sometimes Daddy owed money to something called gambling debts. We did not know what gambling debts were but whatever they were, our daddy had more of them than your daddy and when we bragged about how big our daddy's gambling debts were, other children would laugh and run away.

One day, men in cars came to the migrant camp looking for men who had gambling debts. They had baseball bats.

Daddy threw us into the truck and we floored it out of there, leaving everything we owned (junk mainly).

This included a picture I had of our mother who was dead. Now I had nothing of her to remember her with. I was afraid I was losing even the sound of her Navajo voice and that accent she had. A cloud of smoke, a mighty hi, ho, Silver, and a-w-a-y-y-y.

I wished I could have picked her voice up and smelled it.

My mother still lives inside of us. Inside of both Tso and I there are warm places of the heart that speak to her and with her always.

"Where did you meet Daddy, anyway?" we asked her.

She thought about how to put it. "He was passed out under the pool table at the Bucking Bronco Bar and Grill in Gallup and I couldn't take my shot cuz his carcass was in the way. I had to pound him some with the pool cue to get him up."

She would laugh but even her laugh couldn't hide her sense of frustration with herself. After all, she had gone off with him.

"At first I thought he was dead," she explained.

Migrant men had stayed over. Dead drunk. Falling into bed with us boys late at night. The dark and the hands.

Always the hands finding their way to our penis.

Pushing them away. *Get off me!* Their finger in you.

Migrants were never steady people. They fell over a lot.

People were always reeling over face-first into the creek where they had been doing the laundry on the stones. I thought doing laundry in the creek on the stones was fun because I got to crawl around naked and splash. My mother did not think doing laundry in the creek was as thrilling as I did. The creek was also where we washed our dishes, filled our water buckets, took our baths, and peed. Our mom told us that if we did not stand still in the creek so she could wash our butts then Geronimo was going to come get us and eat us.

He had teeth.

Big teeth?

Big big teeth and he liked to eat the bones of naughty boys. So stand still. Tso could not stand at all. He was too small to stand independently. But I could do it. For about a minute or so.

We did not know who or what this mysterious Geronimo was but we would make it our divine quest to figure him out.

Sometimes Geronimo was the horse.

We were playing Geronimo in the creek and peeing and falling over naked into the water and making huge splashes and not holding still for our mother with her soap and her washcloth when Mrs. Vargas from the migrant shack next door, who was doing her dishes in the creek, fell over dead straight into the creek.

Real dead.

Not pretend dead or Geronimo dead. Stroke dead.

The kind of dead where they had to drag the body of Mrs. Vargas back to her migrant shack but they couldn't get her body (it was too big) up the wooden steps so they had to load it into a wagon pulled by a tractor and take it to church.

We thought they took Mrs. Vargas to church because that was where we saw her next.

Church dead.

~~~~~~

We did not know it at the time but our very own mother would go church dead herself not all that long after Mrs. Vargas. We liked Mrs. Vargas. She gave us tequila—her brother used to arrive from Mexico with cases of it in his trunk, which made Mrs. Vargas very popular in the migrant camp—to shut us up when she took care of us.

Mrs. Vargas took care of us at the time when I was learning how to walk. Mrs. Vargas would put tequila in my baby bottle and I would weave and wobble more than walk. When you walk you sort of have to do it in a straight line.

People cried at the church. People wore church clothes. They sang songs. We played under the pews and my brother wet his pants. People danced outside and barbecued a goat. *Dead* was okay. Everyone drank Mrs. Vargas's cardboard cases filled with tequila. Death was like the guy next door. You knew him but you didn't want to know him too well.

All the migrant men stood around their trucks in the gravel parking lot by the church (most of my world was a gravel parking lot with cowboy boots and trucks) and shared religious stories about Mrs. Vargas, whom they all seemed to know rather intimately. They were going to miss her and her tequila very much.

When they were finished with the tequila that night someone broke out the bottle with the worm in it.

It wasn't tequila. It was mescal. The worm (a butterfly caterpillar) sort of tasted like a small dill pickle.

That was the first time (it would not be the last) I had ever eaten a worm. I usually ran from the invitation. I remember my mother had a screaming fit about it.

But the men laughed. I remember that a warm feeling of belonging washed over me and seeped, too, straight into my bones like a moonglow rush when my father picked me up so he might pop the worm into my open mouth, as if we were playing my version of a game called *bird*.

All the men in the parking lot laughed, and clapped, and applauded. I would do anything for that kind of attention. My dad even set me high up on his shoulders with my baby bottle of tequila.

20

~~~~~~

We Had Always Known
Our Father Was a Coyote

Life went on as it always had while the War Twins were being put to many tests by the sun who was their father. They were not cared for. They were trained. In time, the War Twins would come to know that many of his ministrations were not worth the effort and neither was he. But they were only boys, now, and did not know. They would, however, grow up. Finally. But not before their father would put them through many stupid and dangerous tests.

It is also said that with more room in the Fifth World, the People began to travel.

First, they traveled east. After one day's walk they reached Ni'hahoogai *or White-Spot-on-the-Earth as* bilagaana, *the white man, would call it.*

There they camped, and sang, and played drums, and wore masks.

And during that night, a young woman gave birth.

She was a beautiful maiden who, during the separation of the men from the women in the world below—another of Coyote's pastimes, laughing as he does at the silliness of the People—had reached the age where she longed for the company of a man.

So early one morning, she had torn off the antelope horn, which was fuzzy at the time as growing antelope horns usually are. After warming it all day long in the light, she had inserted it into herself as darkness fell. She spent the whole night trying to make her vagina shout.

Now she was giving birth to an offspring who had no head.

*Coyote from his hiding place way up high in the constellations jumped from star
to star just to keep his balance.*

*Here was a set of trials and tribulations worthy of a magician, which is what
he was, even if he was a dog. Changing as he was, the world, the universe, he could
not change that. A council was held and it was decided that the People would abandon the headless creature.*

The sun was not amused.

First, two War Twins. Now, this. Thing. This problem.

The People threw it into an arroyo and hoped it would die.

It did not die.

Deelgeed, *the horned monster, would swoop down from the skies and carry off
so many creatures to devour them, even Coyote was frozen in his piss.*

We had always known our father was Coyote. A myth made as real as
the dreams that troubled us.

The man terrified us. When he came for us. To touch us.

We had heard his devil songs and his provoked music maneuvering the
shadows of the moon. The driven screaming of the dogs. As if they had had
their guts cut open and thrown steaming into the snow. Outside our little
houses of pain and rage. The dogs in argument. The singing and the biting
and the growling done to keep the children up.

The howling. The communication with other creatures of his kind. The
coyote is one of eight species of the genus *Canis*. Four of these are jackals
of Europe, Africa, and Asia. Other members of this family tree of dogs in-
clude the gray wolf *(Canis lupus)*, the red wolf *(C. rufus)*, and all the breeds
(including the wild dingoes of Australia) of the domestic dog *(C. familiaris)*.

Every god on every mountain from Canada to Mexico knew the Trickster for the dog he was. The Athabascan creation stories all begin with his
infinite curiosity and his playful meddling. Always meddling. Always shift-
ing shapes. Always in a quest to have his way.

Always impregnating someone. The Trickster never really cared too
much about whom he stuck it into. The reports of his shenanigans are numerous. He almost seems to have invented sex. Maidens. Wives. Brothers.
Warriors. Monsters. Princesses. Children. Himself.

Fucking the gods was nothing. He was one.

His image is a warning.

As little boys, we were not sure what of. But his image was a warning
nevertheless, and one that stuck with us like the mud we played in.

Our father was the man who made our truck and our stuff go places. Our mother was the person who gave it all a color and a context. He drove the truck to the mountain. She stopped the truck so she might get out to touch and smell the wildflowers growing there. He gave it solidity. She made it dance. She made dead things like history come alive. She knew how to take things most people would throw away, like wooden shavings from a carving, and turn what was on the floor to be swept up into an adventure that would make our eyes go as wide as deep-dish hubcaps.

Our mother was a Navajo who lived conceptually and linguistically in a universe in motion.

"Mother, we saw Hak'az asdzaa, the old woman of harsh winters," we told our mother. "We saw shamans, demons, the wind, water monsters, To neinili, the rain god, the furies, Big Giant, White Shell Woman, Leeyaa Neeyani, Ye'iitsoh, Johonaa'ei, and Sa."

Every small Navajo boy sees Sa.

She is the Goddess of Age and we would kill her.

Were her stories real?

It was better to assume they were real rather than to be caught dumb and unaware.

So many of her stories felt like warnings.

"Yaaa. They're real. Don't be afraid cuz I will hold you."

She scared the hell out of us, but every night we waited in electric anticipation.

Late at night when chores had been put into the cupboards of our migrant shack, and our young nomadic father burned red and bronzed by the migrant sun he worked in had slipped into his liquid world of numbness, head tilted back and snoring softly in his kitchen table chair, our soft and plump and brown Navajo mother with her own green Mason jar filled, too, with what to her was comfort, would come and sit by us on our collection of Navajo rugs and blankets on the floor. To relate to us the stories of our lives, the witcheries, and more.

Much, much more.

"Can we have a taste?" we would ask.

Of whatever it was she was drinking.

We got one taste.

Under the rugs we pretended that we were drunk.

"Will you rub our backs, Mama, please?"

She would hum and rub our backs.

In 1954, Davy Crockett was all the rage. Every boy (but us) had a coon-skin hat. *Born on a mountaintop in Tennessee . . .*

We had been there. Picking cotton. String beans. Corn. Tennessee was catfish. Our daddy hitchhiked through Cherokee into the Great Smoky Mountains—our truck broke down, it did that—where he was arrested for hitchhiking, and we did not go through there again.

There was the outside world (there were things in it that would eat you), and there was our world under our rugs.

In our world, our mythologies were alive. They were not dead and buried in any way.

Soon after Altse hastiin and Altse asdzqq, First Man and First Woman, and all their children had gone to the eastern mountain and returned, it was ob-served that sometimes they wore masks like the masks worn by Talking God and House God.

Even our house had gods in all the rooms.

Whenever these masks were worn, those who wore them prayed for the good things (like food) and the necessary things like clothes to wear when winter comes. They prayed for such things as the desert rain, and healthy crops. They especially prayed for much corn.

But during their visit to the eastern mountain the people learned terrible se-crets, too. For witches also possess masks like these, and they, too, marry their close relatives.

This would bring much shame into the house.

The marrying of close relatives.

Tso and I contemplated this strange warning night after night. Finally, we asked our mother what we should do if confronted with the possibility of shame.

I remember she looked over at our father that night with her sad brown eyes. Our father had not brought shame to our house.

Or any shame we knew of.

Yet.

"Do you know what Coyote teaches?" our mother asked us.

No. We did not know what Coyote teaches.

"He teaches forgiveness," Shima explained.

Forgiveness. We did not understand.

She pulled the heavy rug up to our chins.

"Do you know what a secret is?" she asked.

We shook our heads no. She rubbed noses with us.

"The secrets are the things we do not tell. We keep the secrets in the house."

We essentially told anything and everything. If we had seen a dog pee we told everyone all about it.

It was time to know about the keeping of the secrets in the house.

Outside as always—coyotes howling. We didn't even really hear it anymore. Hands, hands, hands over our ears, ears, ears.

"What happens when the coyotes come too close to the shacks?" she asked us.

We knew. We were eager to tell her we knew. We were great and learned men.

"They shoot 'em," my brother said. "*Pow!* With *big* guns!"

POW! We fell all over our rugs dead and dead again. Now we were jumping up and down in our underpants.

"Yes. They shoot the coyotes because if they get too close they will eat the chickens and the cats."

"And the cats?" We did not know about the eating of the cats although we were suspicious that one night we had had a particularly gamey meat.

We did not want our father, a coyote, to be shot. We resolved to keep the secret.

I remember being asleep one night under our rugs when Daddy came home (he had mysteriously been gone all day) with a whole other family, and not a word of English among them. I did not speak Spanish but I would learn. Learn. Unlearn. Little kids. Women. Men who drank. An elderly woman with long white braids. There had to be at least fourteen people in those two rooms. They were covered in dust and hungry. Their leather shoes had holes in the soles. A baby cried. Shima made tortillas. The smell of the fresh tortillas filled the two rooms with warmth and life. It was a simple smell and we were happy to get warm pieces of corn tortillas to chew on.

Coyote.

To speak of trucks, long rides, and rivers.

They also called him the Trickster, is what she said.

There was always more spending money around after he arrived at night with his mysterious Mexican *familias*. They would disappear and we would not know where they went. Then the white men would come in shiny cars. We drove trucks. No one in the migrant camp wanted to speak to the white men in the shiny cars.

She would laugh and sparkle when he kissed her. He would buy her a red box of chocolate candies. Inside the chocolate was a sweet red cherry. Tso and I shared one candy. The red cherry was like God. Our lips dripped with sin.

"*Niy'dee.*" From inside of you.

"*Ya dilhil.*" The blue sky.

"*'Anashdloh.*" I am laughing.

I would lick the chocolate from his lips.

He would lick the chocolate from my chin. We would play airplanes under the table. It was always the same table.

The same candles. The same sky always breaking.

The same tortillas in the night.

Some nights he came home with Mexicans we would be up the entire night with. *Dahootaal.* They sang songs.

We were beginning to put the pieces of the puzzle together. *'Eehodoo-ziil, shil.*

I shall know many things.

⌇⌇⌇⌇⌇

Tso and I were at that puppy age where we were attracted to odd, ordinary things. Like trucks.

And tires. We liked tires.

We liked going over to Sam's migrant shack because Sam had an entire yard filled with tires. Sam lived in a dark, incredible world of worn rubber with a pack of hungry dogs. Sammy was not too unlike his dogs.

Tires got you places. They made things go. We were obsessed with hiding under cars and trucks because adults did not go there. We were small and hiding in those greaseblack places was our refuge (one of many). We could spend hours and hours at the Gallup Big O where they put tires on trucks and had machines that made great and horrendous noises as the Big O *whirrrred* and *rrraaaaaammmmmmed* the old tire off and jammed the new tire on and we wanted to be Big O Tire Men with Big O blue coveralls and black grease ground into our skin that would not come off no matter how hard some woman might scrub us with a brush.

⌇⌇⌇⌇⌇

The far recess of my summers sit upon my sleeping lips. It was dark. I was in my motel bed. I could smell my brother's soft hair like you smell warm popcorn at the carnival.

I had blue pajamas. No monsters could get me in my blue pajamas. My brother did not have blue pajamas. He was naked and I could see his penis. I do not know exactly where we were. Everything was warm. A motel. I think outside Las Vegas. I remember a powwow. Or dancing. I definitely remember drums. I remember crawling to the window. "You better not go out there," Tso warned.

They had powwows in Las Vegas then. The white tourists would come and take photographs. The ladies wore hats and the men wore white shoes. Some white people always looked like they had just left church. There are places where white culture and Indian culture don't so much bump up against each other as they grind away at the edges like continental drift and you've got one tectonic plate moving and one that is immovable and the result is an earthquake deep within the bowels of the planet. Something gives and something moves. Sometimes something snaps. Something deep within the earth. My parents were attracted to the cheap electric glitter and the neon glow of Las Vegas (and those powwows) like moths flit and dance their death dance against the arc of a single desert light. There were warriors with their spectacular feathers. I saw Geronimo everywhere. There were drums. There was square dancing and cowboys dressed in boots and hats and women dressed in skirts that showed their slips and legs. There were men selling hot dogs and tires crunching motel gravel.

There were Indian girls from Winnemucca and Sparks and Pyramid Lake and Tonopah walking around in buckskin with bells eating hot dogs, and the bells tinkled when they walked like the sea had parted. And I always wanted a hot dog, walking around my whole childhood wanting one, and there were hookers and juxtaposed against the dancing, singing of the Indians, there were lights and cotton candy, too.

People screamed at the Ferris wheel.

Even now, I hear those bones against the drums. Vegas was a thunder. I'm running around the powwow in my blue pajamas. I am barefoot. I do not know where my mother and my father were that night. Drinking.

Poker cowboys spilling out of silver, aluminum Airstream trailers into bales of hay. Whores slurping pink snow cones and shooting rifles at plastic ducks for teddy bears and when they won a teddy bear, it was like being fucked, screaming and jumping up and down.

I was lost in crowds. I wanted Little Debbie cakes. And hookers would come and swoop down like vast birds in bright makeup and pick you up and ask you what you were doing there at the powwow in your blue pajamas, little boy, and you would play twisting the jewelry they wore on their necks like princesses and they would take you home to motels behind gas stations *it's only until we can find his parent, they would say and the hookers would protect you from their boyfriends and their pimps and they would put you in the motel tub and wash your hair.*

Lice.

Everyone could see your peenie in the tub (it floated) and all you had to play with was a bar of soap.

But the hookers had Little Debbie cakes and you'd be eating one, stuffing your rat-cheeks, satisfied as the King of Shazaams when the boyfriend would go off in his cowboy boots to find your mom and chances were good she was staying in the same motel right there or close by (close enough) and there she was. Walking in the door like Where Were You?

"We gave him a bath," the hooker said. "He needed one. And he ain't got no shoes walking around the powwow barefoot in them blue pajamas. Frankie, here, saw him playing under some truck, and I thought, well, shit, that baby is gonna get run over like a dead dog . . ."

My mother would go Old Stoneface. Like the Navajo just go cold. Eyes like river water. Takes my hand. We would go. Thank you for the Little Debbie cake.

"I told you not to walk away like that!"

"I wanna hot dog."

"You get back in that bed is what you gonna get, Mister, walk around the Powwow, some monster will come and bite you, boy."

My little brother would be hiding under his motel pillow. "I told you she would find you," he said. "Whatcho get?"

He could smell Little Debbie on my Indian breath.

Nothing! And we would scream and roll and giggle and fall off the bed and go hold hands and walk around the powwow and pee behind cars until our feet got cut.

We would hide under trucks and smell the tires.

The tires ripe from the Vegas blacktop would be hot and we were from *Big O!*

This time our dad would find us and it was not good. That Odyssey of fury. Shadows and the singe of fire. He would burn me with his cigarettes and he put holes in my blue pajamas.

My memories are filled with the images of adult men walking around and falling down and throwing their guts up in parking lots.

I remember my father shoving my mother against the motel walls. She would crumple like a moth. He would never miss the opportunity to kick her (or anyone) once they were down and his boots would go into her like the breaking of her bones.

Sometimes she couldn't take another day of it. She was always leaving him. But no one could ever leave him. He was always showing up. Begging forgiveness. Her bones had that, too, forgiveness, not that he deserved it.

She would scoop us up in blankets. Throw us into trucks. Oceans of coffee and Little Debbie cakes.

Announcing pregnancies to us and to her mother, Sa.

I sat with Sa and with the sheep and Sa cried.

Tso and I blamed her for not leaving him for good.

For not finding some beautiful home somewhere with a swing set where we could swing. A home in the suburbs with a white picket fence. A home with dogs and bikes.

Our mom wore cowboy boots and moccasins.

She was a flea market mom and a rodeo mom who sold trinkets at a card table at the county fair.

Before she drank herself to death and froze in her goddamn ditch, my mother took my brother and I up to the top of Ak'i Dah Nast'ani on horseback. Just the three of us.

This was where she found the clay she made her pots with. She would dig into the earth with her hands. She found the pigments she used here. The reds. The yellows. The pigment is uranuim ore. Her bowls always had wings on them but they never took us anywhere. We blamed her.

We blamed her for years and years.

She wanted us to see the borders of the reservation. She pointed to various mountaintops and distant deserts. We saw the world together from a volcano's rim.

Finally, she pointed to the ground.

Another boundary.

"All of this was soaked in blood," she said. "It will speak to you."

She looked at me. She knew.

It already spoke to me, and had been speaking to me for some time. She smiled.

We walked back to the sheep camp where Sa lived.

I am the crow. Wings gone electric.

Geronimo.

21

That Night You and Daddy
Buried That Dead Baby
in the Sugarcane

The War Twins had had enough.

Test after test.

To see if they were his sons.

They were his sons. The question was—did they want this sun for a father?

Their attention was briefly interrupted by the laughing of an old woman.

Below.

Spider Woman was smoking her pipe. And the smoke went up through the smoke hole in her kiva and mingled with the constellations.

The War Twins followed this strange smoke up and up and it lifted them on this part of their strenuous journey.

Holding hands, they went up and up.

Coyote could see them coming from his hiding place. But he had run out of tricks.

"That night you and Daddy buried that dead baby in the sugarcane. That dead baby Mama had."

Yes. We did. Mama aborted late in yet another pregnancy. The baby in a tomato bucket. My brother not quite but almost accusing us. Of what I do not know, nor does he.

Our play was always war. Always blood. Always horses.

We came to time with our nakedness, and our innocent curiosity.

And our warpaint.

Visions. We had visions.

"What do you see?" Tso would ask me. There were no words. I would open my mouth but nothing would escape from there.

There he was—*our father*—that great ballistic monster. A man who had given us virtually nothing.

Nothing but perhaps a mouthful of his fear and another mouthful of his penis.

Watch the teeth, boy.

It was important. If you bit down even slightly with him in your mouth the back of his hand would find your face and he would smack it.

It is so hard for people who have not been there to imagine. Nothing. We were naked. He had given us nothing. We were furious with him for that. Not seeing, not understanding that it was the very closeness we possessed that other people never had. We had something utterly invaluable. It was a closeness where you can smell the sweetness of your brother's breath and when he's fast asleep beside you with his back turned to you you taste him with your tongue. Our closeness was an intimacy we would spend our entire adult lives attempting to outrun. A reconstruction of the wills. As children we slept together in migrant camps, sheep camps, hogans, tepees, pickup trucks, Quonset huts.

Under heavy Navajo blankets.

Under buffalo robes.

Under the stars and naked.

"I see all our dreams," I said.

He thought about it. "My dreams, too?" he asked.

"Everything."

Our loyalties were divided. Sheep camps. Migrant camps. Yet it was all the same to us. We never saw people as Indian, Hispanic, African American (we did not know where Africa was), or even Anglo. You were a cowboy or you weren't.

We lived with the real cowboys.

We didn't even know the television cowboys because we didn't own a television.

Even today you can't get television signals in the places we grew up in Navajoland. Unless you have a satellite dish.

We had something far more visceral than Hollywood. We had minds.

It was kill or be killed. It was play. The blood ran thick upon the ground. We slaughtered. And we slaughtered. And we slaughtered. It was a flood of death and bones and smoke drifting and rain in your face and war.

And horses.

It was the beginning of everything. We came to time with our silent, steadfast toughness.

And our warpaint. Red.

For as long as we could remember white people had always called it *Indian time*. We did not understand that behind the smiles and the chuckles was something less than humorous. We were unsure how Indian time was different. But it was different. Very different. And so were we.

From them. From everyone.

What mattered as children was who you played with. We played with brown and black children because that is migrant America. We were with them because we were them. There were white migrant children, too. A few.

But only Indians or those of us who lived with Indians were on *Indian time*.

Indian time meant you were lazy. It meant you were drunk or hungover or slovenly and it meant you smelled like urine. *Indian time. Indian whiskey. Indian piss.* You showed up for work when you wanted to. Whenever it might please you. The same could be said for school. Indian children who were late for school were on *Indian time*. Everyone said so.

When should I be there?

Indian time. Anytime you want.

Long before the sun was up, we were up, and depending on where we were there were usually chores. The day spread itself silently before us not unlike the running of the river. We knew where the river was. The San Juan. The Rio Grande. The Pecos. The Rio Puerco. It was all the same river to us. We had strict instructions not to go down there.

Shit. We had paid for hell and for the privilege of coming back again. Hell to pay? Shit. What could the man who was our father do to us that he had not done to us twenty times six already? Even then, I knew I would die in pain. Our daddy was psychotic.

I had these visions.

"Did she come to you tonight?" my brother asked.

He meant our mother. She came to me in visions. I see every fucking thing.

"Go to sleep," I'd say. "Daddy says we have to work tomorrow."

We knew he would murder us if given half a chance.

He usually tried to kill us directly after he had ejaculated inside us. We knew what ejaculation was. We had swallowed it a thousand times. He threatened to knock our teeth out, too.

Our hands tied behind our backs.

Give me your hands, boy.

On our knees. It was not unlike praying.

The man loved us and hated us. That it was a deep disconnect worthy of the devil was another thing we fathomed with our very souls.

Psychotic: mad, insane, psychopathic, deranged, demented, lunatic, unbalanced, disturbed. Our daddy was all of this and more. He punished us to hell and back again.

"If I catch either one of you boys down at that river I will . . ."

Which meant we were swimming down there whenever possible. We would defy him and all the things that ate at him like snakes. The river was a cool mystery. Time was the river and the current and the rocks up high and the feeling of the air against your naked skin as you literally dived from the high rocks straight into the glittering, moving river. The river could wash him from you and make you clean again. We were beautiful and we knew it and arrogant (we were not aware of our arrogance) and we would not allow him to see us here or even know us if we could control the unfolding of events. When we were with the Navajo in the Navajo sheep camps we were not aware they were Navajo sheep camps. To us, they were simply sheep camps. We did not think of Dan Yazzie or Curly Tso or Fred Descheene or Hosteen Whitewater or Frank Goldtooth or Mose Denejolie as Navajo. They were simply our friends and cousins.

~~~~~~

It was a time of conformity and abundance but we did not know that. We had seen starvation, and the starving of the Mexicans. Starvation usually arrives with anemia, then wasting, then disease, then ironically loss of appetite. The diarrhea is what kills you. You are not hydrated. Among our many, many secrets was that when things were truly down to nothing—not even crumbs—we had eaten horsemeat. An even bigger secret than that was the one where we were eating dog. Someone's dog. If we thought about it, which we did not, we would get all-quiet, tight-lipped, and sullen. Eating someone's dog was a bad thing. It was the lowest thing a human being could do and we had done it. Our father had made us watch when he shot that migrant dog. He was a mean son-of-a-bitch.

He was always hell-bent to teach us something. "I will make you men," he said. We doubted it.

No man who had clubbed horses with a baseball bat to kill them and turn them into dog food was going to turn us into men.

The night of the horses was the first night I remember sleeping naked in the bed with my brother. I assume we had done this many times before but I was not aware that we were naked. Not until that night. We had taken a bath and we were clean. Not covered in all that blood. The feeling of him next to me was one of softness and serenity. I wanted to be with him like that forever.

"Do you think we will dream about it," Tso asked me.

"You mean, dream about the horses?"

Tso was silent. Even in the dark I knew he was biting that lower lip. I could smell him then like milk. I wanted to kiss him. I think I did.

"We might. I hope not though."

"I hope not, too, cuz I might throw up."

Throwing up was bad. You should always tell your brother if you were at all close to throwing up. No one wants to be thrown up on.

It was the middle of the night. "I'm gonna throw up," he said.

I had to hold his hand as we stumbled barefoot in the dark to the outhouse.

My job was to make sure Tso did not fall in. A fate worse than death.

He had fallen in the hole of the outhouse once. He has a tiny, tiny butt. I had had to fish him out, and I did not want to do it again. We always called that night the Night of the Horses.

Then there was the Night of the Migrant Dog. There is nothing more pathetic than a migrant dog. This one screamed when Daddy shot him.

"You're gonna eat that dog," Daddy said to Tso at the table in our migrant shack.

Tso could only fold his arms and shake his head. No. He would not eat that dog.

Tso threw up on the dinner table.

That did it for me. I could feel it coming up myself. Daddy said we were ungrateful sons-of-bitches. When he aimed his gun at my dog it made me vomit up the dog I had been eating.

The dinner table was covered in dead dog and vomit.

We were crying.

Again. Daddy aimed his gun at us. Cool as the wind on snow. We stopped crying. Now we had to eat our vomit *and* the dead dog.

Ever since that fateful reckoning, I have always associated the taste of dog with the taste of vomit.

Like any other children, we would run joyously into the world of play.

Into the darker world of barns.

Into the shadows dry and the sweetness of the hay.

Sometimes I was the army (they wore blue and they were always white men and they had guns).

Sometimes my brother was the army. You pretended.

We did not own a single toy. We did not know a single child who did.

Sometimes the migrant girls had dolls. Raggedy things they fussed over, and took care of. We would grab their dolls and throw them in the pigmud. The girl always cried. The boys never cared. What made them think they could have toys? There was a mean streak that ran down the back of every boy we knew. We were tough, quick-eyed, liddle sums-of-bitches who lived by their wits. We had very little adult supervision. Almost none. Being abused is not supervision. Daddy was with the men. At night, he was likely to take off for the bars. He was always bringing whores home. We were often required to perform for and with the whores. When the whores realized the man was serious (about bringing us into his bed) we could see the plotting begin for her escape behind her disingenuous smiles.

It was not unusual for the other migrants to see some half-naked whore hightailing it for the road early in the morning.

For all their supposed sophistication, I can only remember one who understood that this was Daddy's way of wiggling out of paying them.

She made him pay her. She had a knife.

When she turned around to walk outside, Daddy kicked her clean through the screens. I was yelling at her inside my head: *Don't turn around, don't turn around,* but she could not hear me. Most people had no goddamn idea the extent to which Daddy could tear the walls down with his bare hands. I had seen him do it. Tearing the walls down with his bare hands was how he usually came for me.

Daddy would pick me up and throw me through the window. The trick was to get up quick and run for the trees. Do not mind the blood. Do not slow down to feel where you were cut. Just go. Quick. Climb up into the tree. Do not look back. I kept rags in the tree that I could tie around me for bandages. Every new migrant camp, I would find me a new tree and new rags for bandages.

We were filthy, blood-encrusted little snots.

Being filthy, blood-encrusted little snots meant the adults were less apt to grab you and put you to work at something, and when we left the river we made sure to roll in the dust before we got back home. Like dogs. Mongrels, Mama said.

There were mothers, migrant women—usually the mothers of girls—females with aprons and brooms who were convinced we boys were not all that elevated from the status of an animal. In fact, we were animals, and we knew the names of every stray dog in every migrant camp. We itched like dogs. We had lice like dogs. We pissed like dogs. We ate like a growling pack of drooling-at-the-mouth junkyard dogs. We ran with creatures of our kind. We regarded all adults dubiously and we would sneer. Adults would grab you, and hurt you. If an adult made a move toward us, we flinched. We backed away. We ran from there as fast as our bare legs could take us to the fields.

We lived in fields of weeds. We went to them with our arms opened wide.

We would shoot everyone with walking sticks, and then die long and agonizing deaths ourselves. Falling to the ground and rolling in the scrub, and in the burrs, and in the prickerpatches. To get back up and repeat the entire violent representational process again and again, changing roles and taking turns. Play came with the dynamics of dominance, submission, torture, and bondage.

How many times did we tie some poor wretched new boy up to a post in the barn, pull his pants down, and leave him there.

Go tell some girl that so-and-so wanted to see her in the barn. Girl takes her doll and goes.

We'd run. By the time we reached the trees the screams of outrage were too far away to affect us.

It was what we knew. There was only one rule: No one survived.

You were obliged to die. So someone else could take your place. It was the migrant land of blood and woe.

Riding the ponies of Geronimo.

We would build our tree forts high up in the tender branches of ancient oak trees. At night we were so far up and so close to the stars, we thought we might taste them with our tongues.

Looking back, I understand, now, that those trees were about a seeing beyond the boundaries, the limitations of our lives.

Being that far up in a tree was a dangerous thing for a small child. We took risks because taking risks was about seeing beyond the boundaries, too. There might be other universes out there you could lose yourself in.

Bear stars. Coyote stars. Changing Woman stars. Stars with stories and mythologies and histories and connections. "Look up there," I said, pointing to a new collection of blue-electric stars we had never noticed before.

"What are they?" Tso asked.

"They're Geronimo stars," I claimed. "They're running from the bigger stars."

I know things now, too.

My little brother needed me to know things. Our mother (who had known some things) had died by the time I was seven. Tso was very sad not to have a mother so I attempted to take her place for him (by knowing things) as best I could.

I knew how people really died (they froze solid in ditches). I knew it was impossible to pick all the lice from some boy's infested head. I knew how to run away. I knew how to make a dog like you (feed it). I knew the names of all the planets and the stars. I had seen a book once with the stars listed in it.

If we weren't pretending to kill ourselves, we were killing ourselves.

We were hanging from our long arms from the branches of the old oak tree we liked the best. "I'm going to jump," I said. "I bet I can fly, I can."

"Cannot."

"Can, too."

"You will fall and break into a hundred pieces. Don't."

"Why?"

"Why what?"

"Why shouldn't I let go of this tree branch right here right now? Give me one good reason I got to live for. Name me one."

I meant it, and he knew I meant it, too.

Sometimes he cried when I tortured him like this.

The tears dripped frequently.

"What about me, huh? If you jump, what about me. I will be alone."

The thought of it terrified my brother something considerable.

This struggle defined us. I had no burning reason to live really. And my brother was terrified to be alone.

I would threaten him with the possibility just to hear him say the words.

"I love you and I don't want to be alone."

"To have to fend off Daddy by yourself, you mean."

"You jump, I'm jumping, too." My brother took in a deep, deep breath.

Tso looked down at the ground. It was getting dark, and the ground appeared to be a whole hell of a lot farther away than it really was. Monsters lived down there inside the spider blackness.

"You jump, I'm jumping, too." The weeds below us had eyes that seemed to pop and move about the night.

My brother's threats never worked for me. Not then. Not now. I have always labored under the suspicion we would die together if we died at all.

Things have always looked hopeless.

I gave him my hand. He took it bravely. His hand was wet. He wiped his tears and his snot with his other hand.

"It's gonna hurt," he said.

"Dying always does," I said.

We jumped.

My brother screamed. It was a bloodcurdling death scream. Mothers for a hundred miles felt the hair on their necks stick up like needle-cats.

What they say about your life flashing before you is true. I saw my whole ridiculous life flash like flames on the way to the ground.

Thud.

We didn't get so much as a scratch. Tso was breathless. He gasped a few times.

Then we did it again.

And again and again. Defying death was what we did. We did it relentlessly.

Death is highly overrated.

We slept in trees and no one missed us.

We often wondered if the man who claimed to be our dad was, indeed, our dad. There has always been at least some hope for the proposition that he was not, in fact, our dad at all. Unfortunately I look just like him.

Even we knew he didn't act like a dad.

No dad we knew of. No dad we knew of was as solidly hateful as the Cowboy.

We found an awful lot of hope in the possibility that he was just some migrant mongrel we had hitched our wagon to.

"I'm going out tonight," he'd say.

We would have to suck it and lick its balls to get rid of it. He would cum on our faces and you had to be quick not to get it in your eye. It made Tso's left eye go blind for about a month once. We were not supposed to look up at him while we were busy doing this bad thing. But I looked up at him once and he was silently crying. The tears were running out of his eyes anyway. Then he came and we tried to make it look like it didn't make us sick but it did. We did not know him then.

A stranger. Please, God, do not let him be like us. We were with him—that much was true—but we were not him.

We knew he hated us. He said so all the time. Every time he said it, every time he told us he hated us, we seemed to slump and grow a little smaller. We hated him, too, but we still wanted him to love us. "Do you think he wonders where we are?" Tso asked me once when we were sleeping outside in the trees.

I consulted my stars. My Geronimo stars blinked brighter for about half a second.

"The stars say no."

"I wonder if he wonders." Tso was beginning to drift. I could not see my brother's eyes. But I could feel the warmness of his flesh as we were always twisted around each other like a tree of twisted roots.

You learned not to move when you slept in the big branches of the oak trees.

They were the arms that enfolded us.

All we had were those stories.

Monster Slayer.

Child Born for Water.

The War Twins.

Changing Woman.

Crow.

Coyote.

The Sun God.

First Man.

First Woman.

The Beings on Sis Naajini.

They were our friends.

This was *the one big thing* that separated us from children. Everywhere.

We had, indeed, been chased by violence, and we knew it for what it was. If we were going to be chased, and we were, if given a choice—and we were never given anything like a choice—we would pick violence over indifference. Indifference is far, far more powerful than violence because it has one thing violence does not possess.

Indifference has the ability to endure.

Violence does not.

We had seen the children of indifference. Their eyes were clouded and vacant. They did not play. They worked. We avoided them. They were the walking dead. They were not loud at sunset. They could pick and pick and pick.

They terrified us.

They moved like the snow fell slowly. You could have held a thousand of them in your hand and not even know they were there.

We would make a dash to our forts in trees. Daddy never liked to climb them—especially if he was drunk.

If Tso successfully managed to avoid him, my brother would join me at the fort in the ancient oak.

He would climb up. We would cry until the darkness and the wind that came with it had turned the day into the night and the warm into the cold.

I was not there when Daddy died. But I have been to see his grave. Buried with the paupers beside a field of corn and wheat. Buried with the poor. The dead thrown in.

I saw him die, too.

I saw him drop dead in a tomato field. Just like that. It was a dream.

I am shaking. Do not let go. How many trees have I fallen from. A few. Breaking bones. At one time or another, every bone I have has been broken. From falling.

From being pushed. Daddy would crack my arm as easily as he could crack a stick for kindling.

I do not sleep. I try not to. I know what waits for me in that dark place. Now that I am as old as he was then.

From the eternal weight of him on top of me. Breaking my ribs. They tape you around and around when you break ribs. It's awful when they rip the tape away and some of your skin, too, with it. I have broken every rib I have. My arms around his neck like love. Hoping and praying that at least some representation of tenderness from me would help him to be tender with me, too. But no. He was a lousy lover with his tongue in my mouth. The same tongue that had just been inside my bowels. I had made the incorrect assumption that this was sex. That his massive cock ripping my anus apart was sex. That the river of blood running down my buttocks was sex. That the lake of blood saturating my back and my bed was sex. I knew what sex was. It had been around me all my mongrel migrant life. The fucking and the sucking and the screaming and the disgusting smells and the men taking what they wanted—some visceral form of punishment—all of it, sex.

I was compelled to know what sex was. He had made it crystal clear. There was no room for misinterpretation. "I will kill you, boy," he said.

After he was done.

I knew this: He meant it. I would beg him to stop.

I would cry. Nothing.

Once, I just did what I was told. No comment from me. No reaction.

"What's wrong with you," he asked.

With me?

His penis inside my hole was killing me in increments. His fingers inside my guts with my hairless legs spread for him was killing me with the violent wet invasiveness of the thing.

Breathe through your nose. Try not to panic.

Go somewhere else. To some other place where no one was breaking you into pieces. Squeeze your eyes shut tight. Geronimo will find you.

I have hated my father my entire life. I wanted him to pay. For what he had done to us.

In the end, he paid and paid. In the end, what you are forced to look at is the face of time.

<hr>

I see my father an old, old migrant worker. A migrant worker is old by sixty. The lines on his face are deep as canyon rivers. I do not know how anyone can do this work, this bending, draconian presbytery, this flaying of the flesh inside the temple, after the age of sixty. By then, your flesh would simply peel off from your bones like a fish filleted and skinned, and your guts hang out.

I see him bending now as he falls into the dirt. A slow-motion falling in the house of prayer. I see him dying in my arms invisible and I am trying, trying not to care.

Daddy, I cared. I tried. You pushed me away and you pushed me away and you hurt me, Daddy, badly. Daddy, I stand naked in front of mirrors as if my body were a collection of stories and this scar was the story of this, and that scar was the time when . . .

Daddy, I cared. I was afraid. I looked into the down and down. The voices wanted me to jump. I would have jumped, too. But I scratched and scratched and

*scratched at my breasts and made them bleed to remind myself that I am more
than seed.*

Your sperm's basilica.

And the rest is only silence.

*Nilch'i is the wind. I can hear the wind, Daddy. He was my daddy when you
were somewhere else and unavailable and angry.*

There was something you gave to us, Daddy. You gave us whores.

*They touched us. They allowed us to touch them. We were starved for touch.
They taught us the value of gentleness. They showed us the power in tenderness.
They showed us fearlessness. They were fearless to touch us like they did.*

Men who know how to be tender to the women in their lives. That is us.

*My small, small brother with some whore's soft breast in his brown mouth, and
his small penis hard against her belly.*

And so now you die. Falling into the dirt.

They would bury him among the other paupers.

I could hear him weeping.

Some boy far, far away.

You want a *timeline*? It's ridiculous. It's absurd. The night Mama died, he
was raping me. I was seven and he was raping me. I was eight and he was
raping me. I was nine and he was raping me. I was ten and he was raping
me. I was eleven and he was raping me. I was twelve and he was raping me.
I was thirteen and he was raping me.

By the time I was fourteen, I had to be very careful not to go to the bathroom in my pants. I hated school because it was always a possibility. He had
raped me so often and to such an extent that he had just about ruined my
bowel muscles. Not that he gave a fuck. He would have made jokes about
me shitting my pants. But he didn't because he didn't know. Okay, rape me,
and get it over with. I would squat and shit him out of me, and get on with
my life. Him raping me took maybe fifteen minutes. It was just something
I had to endure until the day came when I no longer had to.

I was fifteen and working in the migrant fields and suddenly I would
have to run to the bathroom.

Migrant women know. They know the prying of the eyes when you have
to run and squat. Sometimes I have to wonder if there is any dignity to life
whatsofuckingever. I honestly do not think there is. I was fifteen and there
wasn't exactly any toilet paper in a migrant field. I had been raped for so
many years that my body didn't retain food for very long. It just drained
out of me and in front of everyone. I was nothing more than a hole for my

dad to fuck. I was nothing more than a hole for my dad to sell and the other men with their deep masculinity could fuck me, too. All the fission in the universe is draining from you in waves while you squat in a pickle field and weep. The men would laugh. The women and the girls would glance at me and my humiliation and then look away.

My eyes told him what he needed to know. I would kill him now. The sky was irrevocably broken.

The abuser understands the power of intermittent reinforcement. You are the one who tortures them yet they love you because occasionally there are good times. You never know when the good times might come. From the age of six when it all began, to the age of fourteen when I was at long last able to physically represent something of a threat. To fifteen when I could raise my fist to him. If he had not stopped when he did, I would have killed him. I wanted to kill him.

I wanted it bad.

Him dead.

I prayed for God to kill him. I would make any kind of deal God wanted. Just kill him.

It never happened. The three of us would be driving in the truck. Daddy would be drunk and all over the road. No one saying anything (God forbid). He was a menace to some other family. Safe in their car coming the other way. I would close my eyes and pray that God would kill him and we could crash somewhere off the road. That was how we got to migrant camps.

Instead, I would attempt to kill me. It was easier. And I deserved it.

How many times did he tell me that? A hundred? A hundred thousand? So many times that as a preadolescent I truly believed it. I am sure I still do. How could it not be true if he said it so many times? I *was* my daddy's shitty little whore.

Here, boy, dance for me.

He took it all away. Anything clean and decent and fun. Baseball. Grass. Girls. Friends. I tell myself that I have forgiven him. I even write the words down and look at them to see if there is something in them that I do not understand. But there is a part of me that cannot forgive him. Not because I haven't tried. Oh, how I have tried and tried. But I cannot forgive him beyond saying it and writing down the words. Inside, I cannot forgive him. That part of me is ice and it's dead.

You idiot. Why can't you just love us. The way we wanted to love you.

I have been told that my use of poetry is, in fact, a wall that keeps me from feeling the impact of the events of my life.

I agree.

Without that wall to protect me, I would be crushed.

I am now entering a long, long sabbatical where I will be *doing* forgetting!

It wasn't me he did those things to. That was some other boy I could see and then I had to turn away and not look at it.

Tso was there. He had gone through what I had gone through. He had seen everything I had seen. And more.

He was pretty.

I was never that.

But he was, and destroying him was easy.

I rang the buzzer. Thick green ivy climbed up the brick wall obscuring the otherwise institutional look of the building, and you might think the place was an old apartment house, or even a college fraternity.

A wooden sign on the brick announced that this was Mill Cottage.

There were other cottages.

You had to be let in.

By a very big man dressed in nurse white and wearing nurse white shoes. He smiled when he saw me. We knew each other now. He was a nice guy. I liked him. He was strong and steady.

He needed to be.

But what really distinguished him were the keys. He carried an enormous set of keys. Your status in this place was determined by how many keys you carried. There were people here, part-time people mainly, who had no more than two keys. The very large man who let me in had an enormous assortment of keys, and he was intimidating even to me—those keys, all that metal, could hurt you. It could let you in or lock you out.

"He's up in his room waiting for you," I was told. I smiled. I knew he would be.

Waiting. I loved him.

He loved me, too. And he made that so crystal clear every time I saw him in this place.

I would often find him rocking just a little bit although we had ended the rocking or so I hoped.

No one really knew what was wrong with Tso.

Except for me, of course. I knew. I did not attend their psychiatric conferences where they discussed what was wrong inside my brother's head.

I had been invited to do so. But I saw it for what it was: It was a ruse. It would establish a paper trail that would imply my involvement with treatment modalities I did not, in fact, agree with at all. I did not attend these conferences, which reduced them to the effectiveness of spinning wheels, which was fine with me.

I owed him.

I held the keys here. I had been given power of attorney by my brother. They did not dare implement treatment modalities without my consent. My consent was never routinely given. I know psychiatry. I know pharmacology, too, right down to the molecular level, and that is usually a bit deeper than most psychiatrists understand it.

There were a few of them who wanted to do bad, bad things.

Like surgery.

Not no how. Not no way. Over my dead, cold body.

There were a few of them who went straight to their magic bag of drugs. Sleep helped. When you could get him to sleep.

He had been in Mill Cottage for six weeks, now.

My brother had been found by a kind elderly woman. He was hiding under her car in her garage. He would not come out.

The lady needed to go to the grocery store and she could not move her car because if she did, Tso would have been run over.

Most people would have called the police.

There are exceptions. "I'm bored, you know," she told me later. "There was a nice young man hiding under my car in my garage and I wondered why. Nothing like that had ever happened to me before. I'm glad I could help."

Her name was Myra. Her husband had been a physician. He had retired and they were about to embark on a cruise to Alaska when the old gentleman keeled over with a stroke. Everything changed in that blink of fortune's eye.

Instead of calling the police, Myra sat down on the steps that led into her house from the garage, and she proceeded to speak to my brother, who had lost fragments of himself. People bend. People break. Myra was able to get my brother to come sit by her in her garage. There was a refrigerator in the garage and it was filled with Dr Pepper because Myra had grandchildren who never came to see her.

"That's the problem with people nowdaze," she told me. "Nobody comes to see you."

By the time she got Tso his Dr Pepper, my brother had lost his ability to articulate anything.

Who he was. Where he was from.

"He just didn't know," Myra said. "He was terrified. Who wouldn't be?"

I was able to get my brother into a psychiatric ICU, and then, later, into Mill Cottage. Tso did well in both settings. He responded to the treatment, but it wasn't without its struggles. I have worked with children in acute psychiatric treatment settings supervised by university-based neuropsychiatric teams of broadly based treatment specialists, and I knew what to do. We were lucky. We could and did get "the system" to offer us a treatment environment where my brother could put the pieces back together.

I took Myra to Mill Cottage with me once. She was a tiny lady with a big purse and a heart about the size of the city and county of Los Angeles.

There was a delivery once a week to Mill Cottage, too. Flowers. "People like flowers," Myra said. A bouquet of flowers arrived on Mondays.

"Mondays is group," Tso said. Mill Cottage was run by the state. It was not a prison. It struggled to keep up with patching the cracks that spread here and there and back to the center again not unlike a spider *and* her web, but Mill Cottage was *not* a prison.

My name had been in my brother's wallet.

"Your brother is hiding under my car," Myra explained on the phone. "I live in Pacific Heights. He's come out once. For a Dr Pepper, and long enough to give me his wallet. I don't want to call the police. He's harmless."

I came to get Tso.

~~~~~

He came with me compliantly like a puppy with a broken leg.

I wonder, too, at numbers, at the power of numbers. Why is the age of ten any more or less valued than the age of twenty-nine?

We want to *save them while they're young*—why—*is it because the young are easier to reach thus they have more value to society?* I was not so stupid as to assume my brother would spring back and be his old gregarious self.

No.

How many times has my brother saved my worthless life? Far, far too many times to count.

Reaching into gravel pits.

I took him home from Myra's. "Do you want to talk about it?" I asked. My apartment then looked out over the rooftops of a vast city, and it was a moving scene Tso could watch forever. I had a big picture window and the panorama was one of green hills, cable cars, ships out in the bay, and always, and always, the steam that rises from the tops of modern buildings, and a few roofs with those old and rusting water tanks.

"No," he said. "Not really. I don't understand what happened. You say you found me *where*?"

I would explain it again and again.

Nothing. Just numbness. No recognition that he was coming apart.

Tso spent days writing in his journals. All of it Athabascan poetry, and all of it a deeply painful collective description of battles lost by warriors: *pour the sweet milk of concord into hell, uproar the universal peace, confound all unity on earth.*

There were little things. He always wore three pairs of underpants. Three T-shirts. Three socks in shoes far too big for him. Sweatshirts. Sweaters. Anything he could layer. Layer after layer. Fingernails bitten down almost to the cuticles. I was getting worried.

Not worried enough, however.

Tso had walked out on a life. There were people who depended on him. A marriage that was not unlike my brother's fingernails. Gnawed down to the nubs.

"You just don't know," his wife told me. I liked her a lot. We were friends. We had a history. To this very day I still call her Dancer.

But how does any man *know* the context and the flesh and the bones of *any* other man's marriage? She was right. I did not know. There was a long and painful silence on the phone.

My brother's wife was crying. I could barely hear her. "It started just before his birthday. I'd find him in the tub all curled up like a fetus and incoherent. I pleaded with him to get some help but he wouldn't do it. We'd be making love and Tso would start crying out that he was sorry, sorry Daddy—he was speaking to his father like the man was in the room— and he couldn't have an orgasm, and then he started screaming that he couldn't cum in his Daddy's mouth ever, ever again, and he was so sorry and he started asking, begging, pleading with his father to beat him up. I was *mortified*."

You could hear the bells at the Columbus Square Cathedral as clear as the afternoon was warm. My brother's wife's voice seemed to emanate from some planet far far away.

I knew now.

That afternoon, I got on the phone and I ordered some things I needed anyway.

Like rugs.

Three rugs. Three big rugs. Three rugs big enough to sleep in.

Rolled up like a cocoon.

He never questioned it. Or my undressing him and then dressing him in pajamas.

We slept on the floor in the rugs that night.

Just like we had slept in rugs as little boys. He told me everything. Two brothers in their rugs (I could not afford Navajo rugs but these would do), staring up at the smoke hole of the hogan. Their spirit dreams drift away into the night where the dragons live among the stars.

Daddy had hurt him. Daddy had done things to him. Daddy had humiliated him. Daddy had torn him into a thousand million pieces and he no longer knew the numbers on the pieces so as to put the jigsaw puzzle back together. It had all flown apart when the wind came in.

"Tell me about this wind," I said.

My wind was Grandfather Nilch'i. My wind was that thing that moved the fog and spoke to me in songs and moved me to a safer place than this in whispers with the pines.

I knew the power of that wind.

His wind was the kind of wind that wore black robes not unlike the robes of Sa. Old age with her negotiations. Monster Slayer had lost the ability to slay anything—let alone dragons—years ago. He could not do it. The universe was crashing in on him. The gravity of suns was sitting on his sucking chest. I held him while he ate his fingernails and rocked and rocked and rocked.

"Do you remember the Mexicans," he asked me as we both sat on his bed in Mill Cottage.

The Mexicans?

Our lives had been filled with Mexicans. Half the people I knew were from Mexico.

"That time we helped them get across the river."

Oh, that.

Yeah, I remembered.

He meant the Mexicans who drowned.

I wished my father could have been in the room that day at Mill Cottage as Tso attempted to turn the story of his life into something orderly.

Oh, those Mexicans.

What pisses me off about the assumption that my life, and the life of my brother, can be explained in linear ways, is, too, an assumption that my father was destroyed in degrees, and that the destruction itself—the very explosion we refer to as the Big Bang—can be explained one-step-at-a-time. In fact, our father was destroyed in a thousand ways, a trillion ways, ways far beyond our limited ability to understand even as it was happening in front of our eyes. Even as it was happening to him, it was happening to us. To us in our beds. To us in our heads. To us in our dark basements of endurance.

Oh, *those* Mexicans. The Mexicans who picked beside us with their buckets, bent and sweating in the sun. The same Mexicans who made tortillas with us because that was all there was. Corn flour, lard, salt, water. The same Mexicans who picked us boys up and bathed us with their own little sons, because our mother and our father were still out there working in the dark and they didn't mind sharing and they were kind. Oh, those Mexicans. In fact, I knew them well. I had slept with them, eaten with them, bathed with them, gone to church with them, and I had loved many of them with that thing that is the running fluidity of my soul. Had my father been with us that day in that room at Mill Cottage, I would have tied him to a chair and beat him myself. Just one of the meaner tricks he liked to pull on us. Our rage with him came and went, and came and went.

My brother, having arrived at some artificial if momentous age and milestone, and having no fingernails, was no different than the child who had once been me, in my scratching frenzy to remove the part of me that my father found so arousing—ripping my breast into a scab.

I would not have remembered the Mexicans but for my teeth. That night both the river and my teeth were black.

Every single tooth in my head had turned black. I did not know why. My teeth simply rotted in my head because my parents did not know about brushing teeth. I had abscessed teeth and my head was so swollen, my mother had to tie it up tight with my father's handkerchiefs so as to keep the swelling down. My head was tied up tight. I was in dire agony. This is why I remember the Mexicans.

We were waiting and waiting that entire night on the riverbank. The river had gone black. I saw them swimming through my fever. Soon, I would be toothless.

"Like an old coyote," my dad would say. Running his fingers through my hair. Laughing as was merciful, as was his way.

We knew, too, he was not too unlike that dog he had become.

Smuggling more and more and more and more of them across that dark and shining river that divided us from the Mexicans.

Coyote and his trickeries.

Our mother had called him *Mo'ii*.

~~~~~~

As was his routine, Coyote went exploring each of the four directions. Everywhere he saw sorrow and suffering. The Beings pleaded to leave. First Man smoked and blew the smoke in the four directions. In this way he removed the power of evil from the people of the First World, who were the Insect Beings. Next, First Man and the others prepared to leave the Second World. First, he laid a streak of Zigzag Lightning toward the east, and then next a streak of Straight Lightning, and then Rainbow, and finally Sun Ray. None of these moved, and so he shifted them to the south, to the west, and finally to the north. Each time he changed the shape of the lightning bolts, there was a small reaction, but not enough of one to move into the next world. Finally, the people began to notice that Coyote was hiding something. They searched him and found that he was holding Water Monster's baby. What is absurd is the confrontation between what time is like, the spilling of the light, and any culture's need for clarity, which resounds only in our understanding of the past.

~~~~~~

The Mexicans came just as the sun was coming up over the Texas mountains. The desert night had been cold. We had slept on again, off again.

Now we sat on the north side of the river and wondered what the Mexicans would do next.

We both looked up at our father but his impassive face was impossible to read.

The Mexicans went to the river in halting steps.

There were fast words in Spanish. We could not make them out as they were on the other side of the river.

Daddy chewed on his silent toothpick.

A man was explaining to the women that they should remove their clothes.

One of the men strips down to his underpants that are two sizes too big for him—he has actually lost that much weight on the trek across the desert—and the underpants are brown with dirt. Mercifully, he does not remove them so as to preserve the dignity of the women.

Now the women are arguing among themselves.

The Cowboy scans the horizon. There is no time for this.

You would come. Or you would not come. It would be dangerous. There were no guarantees.

The Mexicans went into the river.

Not quickly but slowly.

The way you would sit in a cantina. It is late afternoon and the sun out-side glares with the kind of harshness only a lizard could survive. You are knocking back tequila shots. Not slowly. But quickly. It is your *being there* that is accomplished slowly. Your feet are slow. Your bones are slow. Your arms are slow. Your head is slow. Your eyes are slow as turtles.

The women in their floating dresses were like angels. They struggle with the current and the cold water for a little while. The river pushes them downstream like some silent brown vomit. We were drowning with them, Tso and I. Our father looked away.

They were floating in their cotton dresses.

Our father forced you—you, too—to do things you did not want to do. You were proud but not that proud.

Like jumping into rivers when you could not swim. Oblivious to the consequences.

Your cousin slips under the water.

First, he slowly hauled off his boots. The man wore no socks. His feet were dirt-filthy and looked like claws. Next, the hat and shirt. You are a kid and the sight of your naked father makes you look away.

Tso grabbed the back of my pants by my belt.

You will both remember this. Seeing that horrible penis. That mad dead thing. That thing that spit and touched you in the dark. He folds his clothes. He is in no hurry. He dives into the water.

Dragging a Mexican to the shore.

Not one Mexican could swim.

The Mexicans are starting to drift down the river like singular sailboats.

Terrified faces going under.

Our naked father dragging them to safety. They were only Mexicans and no different than cattle to the man who was the Cowboy.

The bedraggled, soaked group stood around in their wet cowboy hats. Our father naked and his belly breathing hard. He stands there dripping and regards them with contempt.

The long ride home—back to the migrant camp we had come from—a rushing of the early-morning headlights and the night caves in, surrender-ing. The yellow eyes of jackrabbits caught upright in the ditch. The man beside me the maker and the breaker of the dead.

I was among the dead.

Sometimes we would smuggle Mexicans near the Time Zone Boundaries where time was the Rio Grande and magic and my dad, stripped naked, would drag the Mexicans violently from the river by their hair.

"Do you remember the Mexicans?" My brother was asking me if I could remember far, far more than the Mexicans.

We were sitting on his bed at Mill Cottage. It was not a bad place. It was safe. At least my brother wasn't hiding under the cars of elderly ladies.

There were even fresh flowers in his room.

"Do you think Daddy was being kind? Kind to the Mexicans by saving them from the river?"

All I had was a brother and I wanted him back. I pushed the hair away from his dark Navajo eyes.

"Yes. It was kindness. Daddy was being kind to the Mexicans. He did not want them to drown in the river."

"He wasn't *all* bad then? There was something that was good about him? Something?"

"No, he wasn't *all* bad. He had his moments."

Not many. That fuck.

Tomorrow and tomorrow and tomorrow. Tso was in time ready to leave Mill Cottage with his bag and his pills. He was okay and did not spend too much time back there in the past. I bear a charmed life and do not think of it.

Much.

I went back to that spot where time was a fading infinity and the river goes by slowly to dissolve in sunlight even as the dust there is a total mystery. Daddy smuggled Mexicans across the border into Texas to be not much more than slaves. To imaginary lives in the land of milk and honey with real jobs with real paychecks. Minimum wage and glad to get it. He sold green cards, too, or whatever kind of cards it was he passed to them. The Mexicans with their black eyes, eyes as luminous as the river they crossed, standing around dusty parking lots in their cowboy boots. Their trucks baking in the heat. Their cowboy hats pulled down to cover the resignation in their eyes. Only God knew. Only God was aware of some proud man's surrendering. God and the man who was my father. Shaking their heads in capitulation.

I went back and sat on that sandy Texas riverbank. Going back is what I do. It is all still there.

But a fence runs through there now. There was no one climbing it that I could see, and the place is hot as Venus. The earth to liquid. *That* hot.

The only thing crossing the river there were snakes. The only thing that saves me from it, from remembering the *all* of it, every detail, is the writing of the story down. My journals overflow like some untamed river that does not know where it should and shouldn't go and must be contained by thousands of sandbags.

~~~~~

22

Geronimo's Moon Lit the Desert

They were back to Spider Woman's kiva and did not know how they had arrived there. Their many visions overwhelmed them. They knew who and what their father was.

The moon had grown very large and was whiter than anything that they had ever seen.

Spider Woman handed each of them a hoop.

"There is a song that you may sing," she told the War Twins. "It might help your father understand that you only wish to love him. He will need help. But he will understand in time."

Rub your feet with pollen and rest them.
Rub your hands with pollen and rest them.
Rub your mind with pollen and put your mind to rest.
Then truly your feet become pollen.
Your body becomes pollen.
Your head becomes pollen.
Your spirit then becomes pollen.
Your voice will then become pollen.
And what pollen is, that is what peace is.
The trail ahead is a beautiful trail, and your father and all his fathers will
*   listen to you.*
There will be no blows. Long life is ahead and the moon shall light your way.

Geronimo's moon lit the desert.

We had left Dancer in Los Angeles. My brother tried not to pout about it, but he pouted about it. He missed her. We had hitchhiked to Half-Moon Bay and we were okay with picking and selling pumpkins.

Nothing lasts forever or very long for that matter.

The moon disappeared and the sun came up and lit my brother's face in a dreamcrossed twilight. Somewhere between the sun and the moon and the shadows of my brother's still-unbroken wings, the ground beneath us purred like hot asphalt in the desert is supposed to purr. We were in the back of our father's pickup. We had been there all night. Asleep.

Daddy had come to Half-Moon Bay. We *almost* jumped up to see him, but the past jumps, too, up, and out and pouring from our eyes in memory. The past is like a prairie dog and it can whip itself down one hole, come out another, and chatter at you like a pissed-off bird. When prairie dogs leave their holes, rattlesnakes move in, and sometimes before the prairie dog wants to vacate.

Daddy had left Los Angeles. No one there wanted to see him, either. Imagine. You have alienated *all* of Los Angeles. No one could do it. But Daddy did.

He knew where he could find us in Half-Moon Bay, and it had to be with pumpkins. We asked about Dancer and she was fine. We missed her. And everything about her. Her laugh. Her pale white skin and breasts.

We kicked some stones, too, at the side of the road. "Why are you here, Daddy?" I asked. I was suspicious. Daddy was the demon in all my night-mares and the reason my brother sometimes took refuge in the darkness under beds. At thirteen.

Tso had said nothing.

We were standing at the pumpkin stand as if we were pumpkins, too. My brother had been happy here for the three weeks we had stayed. Tso was always able to just leave a thing, and it seemed as if he did not remem-ber it, and maybe he did not remember it, but sooner or later it usually came back to him to haunt his days.

Now, silently, my brother has wet his pants.

A dark stain of urine spread around his jeans. I was sorry for him. His pee just poured and poured down his leg like a faucet had been turned on at the sight of his father. Still, he said not a word. What was there to say? You make me wet my pants?

Daddy just looked at his youngest son and sighed. Then he looked at me.

"He has *wet his pants*," Daddy said.

Like this was my fault, too.

"The sight of you in the flesh has a tendency to do that," I explained. "At thirteen, he is afraid of you."

So was I.

I did not wet my pants or go catatonic. I did not hide under beds. I did not embrace the darkness. But I *was* afraid of him.

"I thought you might be on your way back to the reservation," Daddy said.

In fact, we were. It wasn't that he could read our minds (although my brother thought so). He was simply cognizant of our habits, and as the whispers of winter approached in this beginning or suggestion of the fall, it would be safe to assume we might be headed back to the reservation. And we were. We had always been safe there.

From him. Daddy would never stay there long, and without our mother not at all.

"I have a job working construction on the Glen Canyon Dam in Page," he said. "We are pouring concrete. Me and Johnny Knocks Them Down got jobs about a week ago. You remember Johnny Knocks Them Down and his son, Henry?"

I did, indeed, remember Johnny and Henry Knocks Them Down. They were Navajo from outside Kayenta. They were friends. It did not surprise me that the Cowboy would team up with Johnny Knocks Them Down, and that they would both work construction at the dam.

In 1963, the Glen Canyon Dam was being finished, and Lake Powell was just beginning to rise from what had once been the wild running of the Colorado River.

Henry Knocks Them Down was camping on the river. On the weekends both Johnny and my dad would find Henry and the three of them would fish what was the end of the Colorado River there, and the beginning of an enormous lake. The life of the river was over.

Daddy would take us there if we wanted to go. Seeing as how we were headed in that direction anyway, it was a free ride.

We were also getting very tired of hitchhiking. Sometimes you could stand there with your thumb out for half a day in the soaking rain before anyone would pick you up, and they were only going one mile your way. You enjoyed whatever time you had out of the rain even if it was only a minute or two.

Tso always used to say that we were lucky in that the folks who picked us up were almost always nice, and it was true.

We had slept all night in the back of Daddy's pickup just like we used to do, and when the morning sun illuminated the desert all around us, we knew we could not be far from Page, Arizona. Now the passing signs said so.

There was a coffee shop in Page. Page itself boomed with the trucks and the construction from the enormous dam just outside the city limits. The Cowboy was red-eyed and bone-weary, as he had driven all night straight through to get here. I realized this was Monday morning. Daddy kept looking at his old watch on his hairy arm. He was not going to make it to work today. Not and get us out to the remote campsite (down into a canyon) and get back into Page again in time for work.

Henry Knocks Them Down was my age, and he was camped about twenty-some miles north of Page on the slowly rising river that was soon going to be one of the largest wonders of the man-made world. Daddy drank his coffee in silence and stared out the window at the trucks and the men who looked just like him.

"I will have to drive over to the construction site and explain to my boss I can't make it in today with getting my boys upstream."

His boys.

It irked me more than a little he would even think that.

I was independent and belonged to no one but myself.

Daddy was sitting in the booth just across from us. I secretly squeezed my brother's hand so he would not pee himself sitting here actually having a conversation with the man who had raped him how many times? Tso would rock softly, imperceptibly, back and forth searching for some internal, neurological comfort.

If Daddy was looking for forgiveness, he was going to have to find it on some other moon.

"Did you see my moon last night, Nasdijj? I have some pretty amazing colors," Geronimo said.

"I didn't notice the moon," I lied.

"The shadows of my moon are like the colors of your brother's hair. I noticed how it blew and fell all around in the wind last night."

"It used to fly around like that when he was a kid, too, and we were traveling from migrant camp to migrant camp."

"But you're not migrating anymore."

It was not a question.

"No. I think we're doing this to have a nice time on the river before the cold comes, and I think we are doing this to see if Daddy has changed at all."

"And you doubt it."

"And I doubt it."

"The moon changes colors easily. A cat like this one, I do not know."

That was the first time I had ever seen the Glen Canyon Dam close up. It took my breath away.

It was going to fill an awful lot of spaces in. Water everywhere.

Just being with Daddy made my wings feel heavier than they had ever felt before. Soon he would leave us with Henry and Henry was a good old fishing friend. Fishing with Henry would be like old times.

We stopped, too, at the beaten trailer Daddy was sharing with Johnny Knocks Them Down (Johnny was at work so we did not get to see him), and Daddy filled a cardboard box with food. The trailer itself was littered with dead cigarettes, overflowing ashtrays, pizza boxes, empty cans of cheap beer, and bottles of Johnny Walker Red. Apparently there had been a sale at the ABC in Page.

It was supposed to be enough food to last us a week but we knew better.

Because we knew the Cowboy.

A couple of boxes of macaroni and cheese were not going to be enough. I had Daddy stop at a Safeway, and Tso and I bought our own groceries with our own money. Daddy and Johnny would be back in a week and they could drive us to the store again, or if we wanted, Daddy would drive us to the highway, and we could hitch back to the reservation. Daddy offered to drive us the whole way, but Daddy had done enough so I said no. Daddy in his giving moods could not be trusted any farther than you could throw him.

Henry Knocks Them Down was ecstatic to see us.

Who wouldn't be? Out here in the desert alone. It could drive other, more hollow, men crazy, and it had.

Death had undone warriors here. Moons and stones towered over you. That was the desert.

The landscape Geronimo had flourished in.

In some ways, I was in my naked element again. Where most people see nothing, I see life flourishing all around. Big sagebrush, blackbrush, shadscale, Mormon tea, greasewood, juniper, piñon, bighorn, cougars, sidewinders, desert slender salamanders, pocketed freetail bats, western mastiff bats deep inside the caverns and the caves. Granite night lizards. When I tell people there were bighorn there, they scoff. But I saw them. Scampering up and down those precarious red rocks. At night, they would come out to stare up at the moon. You cannot even be sure you saw it. Geronimo's moon. It crept up on you not unlike a cougar might, and left you wondering.

Like a woman. Like Dancer had left me wondering so many times. And

I would berate myself because I was not the one she wanted. The one she wanted was far more vulnerable than I could ever afford to be.

He needed me to hold his hand.

When Daddy left in that trail of dust that followed him like an epilogue, Tso had haltingly hugged the man. The toothpick and the zombie. Daddy did not know what to do. Tso did not know what to do. I knew what to do and turned away.

"There are cougars out there," Henry said. Our fire crackled brightly. Henry's camping spot was just a few yards from the slowly rising water. We would sleep safely in the rough-hewn confines of an old hogan. Tso laughed and said that Henry was only trying to scare him.

Henry did not laugh.

They did not come. To pick us up.

Perhaps they had forgotten us.

It would have been a *long, long, long* walk out and we were afraid of it.

It wasn't like you could walk downstream toward Page. The towering canyons and the rising water prevented it.

I cursed him. Every night I cursed him. Night after night after night after night I cursed and hated him.

Neither Henry nor Tso seemed the least surprised. "They will show up when they show up," they both said. I cursed him anyway.

We could see our breath now.

The sidewinders were getting as scarce as hen's teeth so we speared one with a lance carved sharp from a juniper. We roasted and ate that snake. Rattlesnake always tastes like old pork to me, and I do not care for it, but we had run out of macaroni and cheese weeks ago. Even the battery on the transister radio was going out and crackled like a far-off glimpse of voices traveling wires and spitting static.

We tried spearing fish and did spear a few browns of good size, but most of our jabs into the water were just that. Jabs into the water. Sitting around the fire and the aloneness of it was caving in and the three of us with arms held around ourselves.

Not even really listening and then sitting up.

Nineteen sixty-three had been a nothing year when nothing moved.

Nothing too spectacular. It had been another year of glittering promises.

You held on to that.

There had been an assasination. A death far away hovered over us in the static of the transistor radio that usually played sports scores and rock and roll and Elvis and see the USA in your Chevrolet and America's the greatest land of all.

We were stunned. With our loneliness and with this new death we could make no sense of. It was sad and we went to bed in our tiny hogan in the safety and the warmness of our sleeping bags.

Only we were cold.

Just yesterday, Henry had made the perilous climb to the gorge's rim. He did not make it down to us until it was almost dark. *He said the sky was breaking.*

He pulled me aside. "What is it?" I asked. I did not think it could be good news.

"I didn't know if I should tell Tso or not," Henry explained. Henry was kind and straightforward. "But when I finally reached the top of the gorge it looked like there had been a frost."

I knew what this meant. Frost can turn to snow down here. We were not prepared for that.

We did what we could. We insulated the hogan with mud and sticks. We made sure we had firewood from piñon. There was always fish, and the three of us were excellent fishermen. I was not afraid of starving. Henry had a .22, and while it's a small gun, it was still good for bringing jackrabbits down, but the problem with eating jacks was that they were always so filled with parasites. We knew that just from looking at coyote scat on the many trails around our canyon home.

Autumn, 1963. The sunsets were as dazzling as they were cold and the blues seemed the color of steel on the horizon. Autumn, 1963. I was a thousand years and counting.

We did not really have the foot gear for it, but we started thinking about walking out. I was so stupid to have not brought a map. We had no idea as to exactly where we were. Once again, we had fallen asleep on the way out here, and I kept kicking myself until both Henry and my brother demanded that I stop.

"Our dads are like that," Henry said. It just was.

Geronimo's moon came to us in reds and yellows most every night, and surrounded by a deeper black, the thing glowed in the illumination of another universe. Nothing that beautiful could exist in ours.

Finally, we had to zip sleeping bags together so as to share our body heat.

There were cats out there. The cats were not hibernating felines. They were only hungry and usually settled for deer. But they would settle for a human if they had a mind to or a taste for one. I did not especially like the cougars. They walked through our campsite at night. Sometimes they knocked a pot down from a rock where we kept the pots and pans. We did not keep anything inside the hogan that might attract an animal. I knew I could handle a bear. But cats are not predictable in any way.

Henry played his flute at night down by the rising water. In time, there would be no hogan.

The rocks and the caverns would vanish as the water ate them up.

"Who do you love?" my brother asked me one night. I was drifting off with hunger howling in my dogbelly and nipping at my innards.

I could only squeeze his hand, which was the temperature of an ice cube. It was the end of desert canyons.

"They told us to be farmers. 'Here, farm this,' they said. We tried. I tried. But the desert could not be farmed. Now they think they will make an ocean of it. Don't they understand it is the desert? She always wins. She always comes back and takes what you think you have wrought from her. 'We will now make the red desert into an ocean.' "

Lake Powell is a hundred and eighty-seven miles long with ninety-six major side canyons and a coastline longer than the coastline from Seattle to San Diego. Lake Powell contains some eight and a half trillion gallons of the Colorado River. The lake did not entirely fill until 1980. In 1995, the planet started to warm. By 2003, Lake Powell had lost fully half of its water, and people were wondering.

What if it dried up and the ghosts of the Anasazi finally returned?

What if the rain did not come?

By summer 2003, the rain had not arrived.

I do not know because I do not *care* to know what day, or week, or month it was when our fathers arrived to get us.

Out of there.

"If you fight with them," both my brother *and* Henry advised me, "it will only make it worse. Let us just *go* without a fight."

Our dads were dead drunk. Falling all over each other. Laughing. Spilling Colt .45 malt liquor. A woman we did not know dressed in shorts and sandals. I ignored her.

Not far behind our dads was a small truck with one national park ranger who sat in the truck watching us. Not unlike a nocturnal cougar.

We were not supposed to be there. I knew that. The Cowboy suddenly got it into his head to practice hitting beer cans with the .22.

I do not remember *how* we got him out of there, or *why* we were not arrested. But there was an unspoken agreement between law enforcement all around Page, and the construction companies that drew construction workers, mostly male, mostly alone, into that company town so they could finish building the Glen Canyon Dam.

Daddy drove us drunk as a skunk at Christmas all the way back to New Mexico, which is where we were from and where we wanted to be.

We would have our own place there.

Just a place above a bar and a hardware store. The De-Ja-Vu.

Nothing fancy to it except at night you could see far off and beyond the city limits to where the desert breathed easily.

If you listen to the wind through the memory of stone you will hear the haunting sound of a Navajo flute. Like a pouring of the bats black as blood into the coming of the night and a hanging on to princes. In time, the desert turns again to sea. It would all become something else in the flooding that is time and so eventually would we.

The lake now gleams in the dry blueness of a glow. The evolution of Geronimo.

23

I Had Been Shot

Coyote limped and looked behind him everywhere he walked as if his past might pass him by like the light did. As if some hunter behind him had wounded the animal.

And so it came to pass that the War Twins gathered their lightning bolts and did battle with every giant on the spinning planet. The dragons came after them with much snapping of the teeth and hissing blood. The dying softly and the great great flood came to drench the planet in the blood and dead bodies of the dragons.

Came to turn the deserts into the sea.

The last giant was decapitated just as he was about to devour Child Born for Water, and Changing Woman said: "Oh, let these two be my sons, for their father does not need them. Let them return to the bosom of their mother."

The sun growled. But he was a fraud as benevolent, and he burned things that came too close.

The boys had wisdom beyond all molecular life and never came close to the sun again.

Nor did they seek him and thus condemned him to the position of being there.

There was a beautiful volcano, still rumbling as was its way, and steaming some, but prosaic mainly. And this was where the boys would live.

Walking home, Child Born for Water snapped his fingers—click—and Monster Slayer simply smiled. His power was his smile.

Coyote struggled to keep up with them and let them know he was painfully aware of who he belonged to.

I had been shot.

I do not remember running the three miles back to where my truck was parked but I am told I ran almost that whole way. The *miracle* was that my brother was looking for me. I am told he threw me into the truck. He left the boy who had shot me standing with his mouth open, and flew like a madman to the closest emergency room. I am told my brother ran into the ER, grabbed a stretcher, and, screaming at the stunned ER personnel that he had a patient shot with a 12-gauge shotgun through the abdomen, threw me onto the stretcher, pushed the stretcher into the ER, ripped my shirt off with his bare hands, took one look down at me, and fainted.

I do not remember the next three months of coma. But I do remember him reaching me.

There was a chair in the corner of the room. The chair was blue. My brother was the man sitting in the chair. Day and night. Holding my hand. Speaking to me as if we were both underwater.

That all your spook is, honey?

—P-A-I-N—

And the coming of the cold. Hold me.

"As a warrior, your brother would have known that the day would come when you would leave to follow your own path and he to his."

"Yes. We both knew that."

"Alope and I left our safe place with the people on the river, and, taking our children with us, we joined the Chiricahua going south. We would find what we would find."

"You found death."

"Yes. The soldiers killed my wife, and my babies. But I also found a fire in my belly I did not know was there. I did not know then what I was capable of. I see you leaving the house of your brother."

"Yes. In time. I was well. My brother had to learn to live his life without me. I had to learn, too. It was hard as hell. Neither one of us was twenty yet."

Come. Children.

Gather round.

Push my bed over by the window so I might see the animals in the woods, please.

Go get me the picture book.

My children turn the pages. They, too, will have, and have had, pages of their own.

"That is me on my motorcycle. The boy standing at the screen door is Tso. He is waving good-bye to me.

"This one is me in Latin America. I traveled all around there. In this one, I am teaching Mescalero Apache children.

"In this one I am building a community center for the Chippewa."

Today my brother's struggle is to just stay well and sane.

He fixes trucks. He fishes (with his dancer wife and his dogs) the remote lakes of Canada where there are no cars, no people, and no phones. In the winter, they go down to Mexico. People drive him crazy. He needs them to respect his privacy. He needs them to respect his hanging on to his sanity—hard—as he does. I rarely see him. Yet he knows I am there.

I pull out the next to the last of the family pictures.

In this one, Tso is standing in a migrant field with his hoe. He isn't weeding, and he isn't picking. He is dreaming. Dreaming in that swirling dust. He who can only wait and wonder. Half dazed by the torrents of thought that lie just beyond the limits of his understanding.

In the last picture in the book, we are exploring the red rocks of Glen Canyon, knowing that in a matter of days the sand we were standing on would be submerged. In the First World, there is darkness, and the beings there are insects. In the next world, there is light, and there is a going up on reeds. We were explorers and all explorers seek *something that they lost*. It is rare that they find what they have lost, and rarer still that the attainment of what they have lost brings them greater happiness than their quest.

My children have set my bed over by the window and the animals of the woods walk by in tender apprehension mixed, too, with curiosity.

My Kree crawls into bed with me laughing and wearing the most outrageous black leather jacket I have ever seen with the word HOG printed on the back.

"And where did you get that jacket from, my dear?"

"Do you disapprove, Dad? I like it. In fact, I love it."

My memory is spotty. Plaque on the brain where bacteria proliferate.

"I found the jacket in your stuff."

"What stuff?"

"The stuff I'm supposed to inherit when you die, but since you *always bounce back, Daddy, dontcha think I could wear it now?*"

"Only if you treat me to breakfast at a pancake house."

"A pancake house?"

"It's a long story and some of the loose ends will drive you crazy. But you know what?"

"What?"

"All lives and all memories have them. Loose ends. If you don't have loose ends, you never had a life. No life is tidy. All we are left with sometimes is the loose ends. Mine are everywhere."

"Like where, you nut?"

My loose ends and my untidiness form a long line of entangled kites that fly from one desert to another. The woods soothe me, but the desert saves me. I have emerged from the volcano, and have done battle with dragons. "Wanna steal a car and drive to California?"

"Ohh, Daaaaad."

Of all my children, Kree was the one who wanted (and got) the most hugs. She was always hugging my leg. The black leather jacket she was wearing with the word HOG printed on the back had once belonged to a boy from Puerto Rico named Angel. Then it was given to a girl (now, Kree's aunt) whose name was Ronnie, then Dancer. Then it was passed down to my brother, who gave it to me the day I left him standing there at the door shirtless drinking the image of me in as I was leaving on my motorcycle for exotic places south.

"Awee would have loved this jacket," she said, fingering the leather.

Yaaa. He did. The HOG had been added a long time ago in Oakland.

Don't ask.

It has taken some time, but my children are learning how to *see.*

With their wisdom. With their dancing. With their singing. With their lives.

"They have never left you, Nasdijj."

"Did they ever leave you? You of the pounding horses."

"My children all rode with me," Geronimo said. Geronimo's eyes were black as cold desert nights in the dead of winter. Geronimo is the past.

"Even the dead ones, they rode with you?"

"Even the dead ones."

As do mine.

All lives are messy things with loose endings, contradictions, dirty underwear, and socks thrown around the room like *what a mess!*

Ride with me through these deserts and the journeys and the dreamtimes, too. Through seas of blood and the sky turned blue. *On the first part of the sleepwalk, I was looking at all the skies. There were trees and plains and rocks and pains, and the desert was almost dry.*

And the world and the world and the world is yours upon thy climbing vine, and the world and the world and the world is mine through pain and love and time. The sky is breaking.

See?

NASDIJJ was born in the American Southwest in 1950. He grew up partly on the reservation—his mother was Navajo—and partly in migrant camps around the country. He has been writing for decades, making ends meet by reporting for small-town papers, teaching, and migrant labor. He is the author of the critically acclaimed memoirs *The Boy and the Dog Are Sleeping* and *The Blood Runs Like a River Through My Dreams*, which was a *New York Times* Notable Book, a finalist for the PEN/Martha Albrand Award, and winner of the Salon Book Award. "Nasdijj" is Athabaskan for "to become again." He lives in Chapel Hill, North Carolina.